"Given that David Tracy is, without question [...] theologians in the contemporary period, one wonders why there are not more accessible introductions to this 'theologian's theologian.' Stephen Okey's work wonderfully fills that urgent need! He covers all the major themes of Tracy's work thus far, pitching them perfectly for the reader to want to plunge into a more careful study of Tracy's work itself. This is no small feat and an incredible service for all the 'publics' of theology. Kudos!"

> — Dr. Julius-Kei Kato, SSL, PhD
> King's College, Western University
> London, Ontario, Canada

"The breadth and depth of David Tracy's theological scholarship and understanding is breathtaking for those who want to grasp the complexity of contemporary culture and its religious dimensions. Stephen Okey's *A Theology of Conversation* provides a clear and solidly researched guide through the many developments in Tracy's work. By focusing both on the prominent themes in Tracy's theology, as well as the chronological development of those themes throughout the entire corpus of Tracy's writings, Okey has admirably given all of us a guide to David Tracy's thinking and introduced his work to the next generation of those who want to understand what theology is all about."

> — John McCarthy
> Loyola University Chicago

"With his deft introduction to David Tracy's wide-ranging work, Stephen Okey has chosen just the right point of entry. For Tracy is a theological and cultural conversationalist *par excellence*, willing to dialogue with all who share his 'obsession' with the hidden, impossible, and loving God. Okey's insightful analysis of Tracy's focal concerns provides a clear map to the contributions of one of the most interesting and important theologians of our time."

> — Anthony J. Godzieba
> Professor of Theology and Religious Studies
> Villanova University

A Theology of Conversation

An Introduction to David Tracy

Stephen Okey

Foreword by
David Tracy

LITURGICAL PRESS
ACADEMIC

Collegeville, Minnesota
www.litpress.org

Excerpts from documents of the Second Vatican Council are from *Vatican Council II: The Conciliar and Postconciliar Documents*, edited by Austin Flannery, OP, © 1996. Used with permission of Liturgical Press, Collegeville, Minnesota.

1   2   3   4   5   6   7   8   9

Library of Congress Cataloging-in-Publication Data

Names: Okey, Stephen, author.
Title: A theology of conversation : an introduction to David Tracy / Stephen Okey.
Description: Collegeville, Minnesota : Liturgical Press, 2018. | Includes bibliographical references.
Identifiers: LCCN 2018022814 (print) | LCCN 2018034325 (ebook) | ISBN 9780814684429 (ebook) | ISBN 9780814684184
Subjects: LCSH: Tracy, David. | Catholic Church—Doctrines.
Classification: LCC BX4705.T73545 (ebook) | LCC BX4705.T73545 O34 2018 (print) | DDC 230/.2092—dc23
LC record available at https://lccn.loc.gov/2018022814

For Paige

Contents

Foreword

It is an honor to introduce this fine, thoughtful, critical book by Professor Stephen Okey. Professor Okey not only writes excellently about the nature of a pluralistic theology grounded in conversation or dialogue; he practices his theory.

Since Plato, dialogue or conversation has proved one of the major forms of thinking in Western culture. Conversation includes argument, not the reverse.

It is a misfortune that we lack the dialogues of Plato's most famous student, Aristotle. Both Cicero and Quintilian praised Aristotle's dialogues. We possess only fragments of a few of them. Happily we do possess the arguments in treatise form of Aristotle: some from student notes (as with a good deal of what we have from Hegel). Some of the texts of Aristotle that we do possess were probably edited by his own hand as their more conceptually defined and stylistically refined form shows (for example, Aristotle's splendid *Nicomachean Ethics*).

But Plato with his incomparable dialogues—Cicero and Hume are the only real competitors to Plato—always included arguments and close analysis when clarity or evidence demanded them. Aristotle, famously called by Dante "the master of those who know," is indeed the master of logical analyses and of evidential scientific reasoning. He was, after all, a marine biologist far less interested in the role of mathematics for philosophy than was Plato but far more given to careful analytical definitions (i.e., propositions that apply to all cases of X—e.g., justice—and only cases of X) than earlier philosophers, including Plato.

My own intellectual instincts, as Professor Okey makes clear and persuasive, have always been more with Plato and with Hans-Georg Gadamer on conversation as the primary intellectual mode. However, I have always tried to be completely open, as Professor Okey consistently argues, to the need for arguments when necessary (as they so often are). At the same time I have learned from mentors like Bernard Lonergan with his love of modern scientific reasoning and cognitional theory and from Paul Ricoeur with his brilliant corrective of Gadamer by adding explanatory theories to the model of conversation. This brief excursus on conversation and argument may serve, I hope, as praise for Professor Okey's expertise in both.

Besides a theory of conversation, which Professor Okey persuasively finds in my work, he also possesses strong interpretive skills as well as conversational and argumentative skills that he employs to both hermeneutical and conversational-argumentative effect through his calm, considered work of interpretation, analysis, and critique.

Professor Okey employs his considerable hermeneutical skills in his very selection of categories and themes in my work that he chooses as central:

> conversation itself;
>
> theology as public;
>
> pluralism (not only plurality);
>
> a lifelong concern (thanks to early study with Bernard Lonergan) with the issue of theological method;
>
> the relationship of the categories, a "classic" and a "fragment," whose intrinsic relationship and difference Professor Okey brilliantly interprets;
>
> a Christology related principally to an "interpretation" of New Testament Christologies and of some contemporary christological controversies (e.g., on the christological role, or lack thereof, in the endless debates on the quest for the "historical Jesus");
>
> above all, on the question of God—as Duns Scotus saw so clearly—the category of the "Infinite" is the first name for God both metaphysically and theologically (i.e., from God as metaphysically Infinite to the trinitarian understanding of God as Infinite Love).

In sum, I remain deeply thankful for all the careful research of Professor Okey on my work as that study has blossomed into this very readable, artful, and valuable book—a book that, on its own, contributes substantially to contemporary theology. As I near the end of my own theological journey, I salute Professor Okey at this welcome beginning of his theological journey.

David Tracy
September 2, 2018

Acknowledgments

Writing is weird, and I am deeply grateful that it is part of my job. At times the experience of writing this book was isolating and my idiosyncrasies were fully on display. At others it was collaborative and lively. Sustaining the project through these alternating phases depended entirely on a wonderful community of family, friends, and scholars, and here I wish to thank them.

I must first of all thank David Tracy himself. I first met him when I was a student at the University of Chicago Divinity School and my roommate Andy asked if we could give Prof. Tracy a ride to his apartment. As he stepped into the used car I had recently bought, I asked if he would bless it, which he obligingly did. I, like so many others, have continued to benefit from his generosity, especially as I was researching and writing this book.

I would also like to thank all the scholars whose conversation has helped bring this book into existence. The research for the book grew out of my doctoral dissertation on Tracy's theological anthropology, and I remain indebted to my director, Mary Ann Hinsdale, and two readers, Roberto Goizueta and Frederick Lawrence, for their guidance, insights, and conversation. Kevin Ahern, Andrew Staron, Julius-Kei Kato, Paul Schutz, Anthony Godzieba, Mark Yenson, and Carolyn Chau all gave feedback on various sections of the book, which helped to strengthen the argument. My understanding of Tracy has been greatly enriched over the years thanks to conversations with William Myatt, Andreas Telser, Barnabas Palfrey, Nichole Flores, Daryn Henry, Daniel Rober, and Timothy Hanchin.

It is a great and increasingly rare gift to have a permanent academic home, and I am doubly blessed to have found a brilliant and charitable group of colleagues at Saint Leo's Department of Philosophy, Theology, and Religion. Moreover, the monastic community of Saint

Leo Abbey has been hospitable to me since I moved here, and has more than once welcomed me into their guest house as I sought a distraction-free refuge in which to write.

The editors and contributors at Daily Theology have helped me to hone my writing over the last eight years, and this book is better because of their work.

The people at Liturgical Press have been stellar, supportive, and above all patient as I worked out the kinks of my first book. Special thanks to Hans Christoffersen, Tara Durheim, and Stephanie Lancour for all their work in bringing this book to press.

Finally, my thanks to my family. My older brother John was the first writer in the family, and I probably got some of it from him. My parents, Mike and Susan, at first seemed confused when I decided to study theology, but they've ceaselessly encouraged me ever since. My wife Paige, to whom this book is dedicated, has been integral to my success in this project. She is my best conversation partner, and I look forward to many more years of conversation.

Abbreviations

ABL David Tracy. *The Achievement of Bernard Lonergan*. New York: Herder and Herder, 1970.

AI David Tracy. *The Analogical Imagination: Christian Theology and the Culture of Pluralism*. New York: Crossroad, 1981.

BRO David Tracy. *Blessed Rage for Order: The New Pluralism in Theology*. Chicago: University of Chicago Press, 1996.

DWO David Tracy. *Dialogue with the Other: The Inter-Religious Dialogue*. Louvain Theological & Pastoral Monographs 1. Grand Rapids, MI: Eerdmans, 1990.

MT Bernard Lonergan. *Method in Theology*. 2nd ed. Toronto: University of Toronto Press, 1990.

ONP David Tracy. *On Naming the Present: Reflections on God, Hermeneutics, and Church*. Maryknoll, NY: Orbis Books, 1994.

ND George Lindbeck. *The Nature of Doctrine: Religion and Theology in a Postliberal Age*. 25th ann. ed. Introduction by Bruce D. Marshall. Louisville, KY: Westminster John Knox, 2009.

PA David Tracy. *Plurality and Ambiguity: Hermeneutics, Religion, Hope*. Chicago: University of Chicago Press, 1994.

Introduction

As a dialogical theologian, Tracy's thinking has evolved and is evolving through continuing conversations.

—Timoteo Gener[1]

Conversation is risky. At its best, conversation brings partners together who are committed to deepening their understanding. It might be their knowledge of the world around them, of traditions received from the past, of the person on the other side of the table, or even of the self. It is true that conversation is stronger when the participants are knowledgeable about what they speak, and it is even better when one's conversation partner has something distinct to offer. Herein lies the risk, though: entering into conversation puts one's understanding at risk of disillusionment, of ecstatic wonder, of frustration, of joy. Conversation risks *change* that, even when it is for the better, can be frightening. Although the ideal conversation among committed, intelligent, and charitable interlocutors may not be the norm, it remains something to aspire to.

Such conversation is at the heart of David Tracy's theology. To start, simply reading Tracy's work is to enter into conversation with him, to participate in the back-and-forth between the reader and the text. Yet by entering into that conversation, one recognizes the much wider conversation taking place. Throughout his work, one finds Tracy in conversation with theologians, philosophers, sociologists, psychologists, artists, and more. Even a simple perusal through the endnotes of *Blessed Rage for Order* and *The Analogical Imagination* reveals the wide breadth of Tracy's conversation. This approach has not gone unnoticed; Tracy's colleague Matthew Lamb wrote in the

---

[1] Timoteo D. Gener, "With/Beyond Tracy: Re-Visioning Public Theology," *Evangelical Review of Theology* 33, no. 2 (April 2009): 118–38.

early 1980s that "few express as fully as [Tracy] the character of a wide-ranging conversation."[2] Tracy is the "theologian as host," who brings an ever-growing party of divergent voices together in conversation oriented toward discerning the truth of the Christian tradition in the contemporary world.[3]

This pursuit reveals a further sense in which conversation is central for Tracy. Not only does his work seek to bring together a wide range of views and insights, but he understands the essential method of theology as being conversation itself. From the beginning stages of his career, he has used what he calls a "correlation" approach that seeks to connect the depths of the Christian tradition to whatever cultural or social context it finds itself in. The specific terms of the correlation have changed (Christian fact became the classics of the tradition while common human experience became the contemporary situation), but the core emphasis on theology as the back-and-forth between a religious tradition and its wider context has remained constant. This conversation too is risky, as Tracy posits that it is possible not only for the religious tradition to offer some insight or answer to questions raised by secular and cultural concerns but also for the secular and cultural to have insights for the religious.

This book aims to be a guide, perhaps an interpreter, for entering into conversation with Tracy. Despite widespread recognition of Tracy's contributions to theology, he is also considered by many to be a challenging and idiosyncratic thinker whose depths are difficult to explore. That, coupled with his extensive publications, can make him a daunting figure to engage. Many who do engage him tend to focus on narrow topics or particular texts, thus missing the richer sense of the whole of his work and of his conversation. This book takes this more expansive view, seeking to chart the overall develop-

---

[2] Matthew L. Lamb, "David Tracy," in *A Handbook of Christian Theologians*, ed. Dean G. Peerman and Martin E. Marty (Nashville: Abingdon Press, 1984), 677. See also John P. McCarthy, "David Tracy," in *A New Handbook of Christian Theologians*, ed. Donald W. Musser and Joseph L. Price (Nashville: Abingdon Press, 1996), 468.

[3] Nathan Crawford has made an intriguing case for comparing Tracy's conversational approach to theology to the improvisation in music, especially jazz. See Nathan Crawford, "Theology as Improvisation: Seeking the Unstructured Form of Theology with David Tracy," *Irish Theological Quarterly* 75, no. 3 (August 2010): 300–312, especially 308n41.

ment of his theology throughout his career. As a first step toward doing so, it may be helpful to find out who David Tracy is.

A Brief Biography of David Tracy

David William Tracy was born in Yonkers, New York, on January 6, 1939, the middle son of John Charles Tracy, a union organizer, and Eileen Marie Tracy (née Rossell). He had an older brother, John Charles Jr., and a younger, Arthur.[4] He describes the strong focus on education in his upbringing, leading him to a deep and early intellectual interest in literature, history, and criticism: "Our home was filled with literary stimulation. My father . . . read to us, writers like Dickens and Henry Adams. My parents were always bringing us to visit places like the Adams home near Boston."[5]

Less than two weeks after Tracy's thirteenth birthday, his father died at the age of forty-six.[6] That same year, he felt "a very intense call" to the priesthood and entered the Cathedral College, the minor or high school seminary for the Archdiocese of New York.[7] Initially, he felt called more to the ministry of the parish priest than to the academic life. On finishing at the minor seminary, he went on to study at St. Joseph's Seminary (1958–1960), colloquially known as Dunwoodie.[8]

Recognizing his intellectual promise, Tracy's superiors sent him to the Gregorian University in Rome to begin his theological studies in 1960. The Second Vatican Council had been announced already in

---

[4] He dedicated *Blessed Rage for Order* to his mother and *Plurality and Ambiguity* to his father and older brother *in memoriam*.

[5] Eugene C. Kennedy, "A Dissenting Voice: Catholic Theologian David Tracy," *New York Times Magazine* 136 (November 9, 1986): 25.

[6] Obituary of John C. Tracy, *The Herald Statesman*, January 18, 1952.

[7] Todd Breyfogle and Thomas Levergood, "Conversation with David Tracy," *Cross Currents* 44, no. 3 (Fall 1994): 305–6; Wendy Doniger, Franklin I. Gamwell, and Bernard McGinn, "Tributes to David Tracy," *Criterion* 46, no. 1 (Winter 2008): 7.

[8] Dunwoodie was widely considered to be one of the best Roman Catholic seminaries in North America. Founded in 1896, when the seminary for the Archdiocese of New York was moved to Yonkers, it was home of the well-regarded *Dunwoodie Review* in the 1960s and 1970s. In addition to Tracy, notable alumni include Joseph Komonchak, John P. Meier, and Bernard McGinn. For more on the history of Dunwoodie, see Thomas Shelley, *Dunwoodie: The History of St. Joseph's Seminary, Yonkers, New York* (Westminster, MD: Christian Classics, 1993).

1959, and its first session opened as his third year of studies began. Of course, as a young seminarian he had no formal role during the 1962 and 1963 sessions that he was present for, but he attended lectures given by some of the major theologians who had been brought to the council as *periti* (theological advisers to the bishops). Recounting his time as a student during Vatican II, Tracy quoted William Wordsworth:

> *Bliss was it in that dawn to be alive,*
> *But to be young was very heaven!*[9]

In 1963, Tracy was ordained to the priesthood in Rome, and in 1964 he completed his licentiate in sacred theology (STL) at the Gregorian University. Pursuing his desire to serve in a parish, he went to work at Saint Mary of Stamford Parish in the Diocese of Bridgeport, Connecticut. Although only there for one year, he made an impression on his parishioners. For example, in the midst of liturgical changes coming out of Vatican II, Tracy convinced his parishioner William F. Buckley Jr. to volunteer as a lay lector at the Mass.[10]

One result of his year of parish work was discerning his vocation to the life of academic theology. Tracy returned to the Gregorian for the doctorate of sacred theology (STD) and studied under Canadian Jesuit theologian Bernard Lonergan. The period from Tracy's return in 1965 to his successful defense of his dissertation in 1969 corresponded with some of Lonergan's work on theological method, later published in 1974 as *Method in Theology*.[11] Tracy's dissertation, *The Development of the Notion of Theological Methodology in the Works of*

---

[9] Michael Fishbane, Kevin Madigan, and David Tracy, "Tributes to Bernard McGinn," *Criterion* 42, no. 3 (Autumn 2003): 42. The poem is "The French Revolution as It Appeared to Enthusiasts at Its Commencement" by William Wordsworth.

[10] Buckley, most famous for founding the conservative magazine *National Review* and hosting the TV show *Firing Line*, notes in his spiritual autobiography that despite his initial hope that liturgical reforms might have a positive impact (he "hung on as a lector/commentator doggedly for three years), he eventually grew disillusioned. He noted that this was after Tracy had left the parish and returned to his academic studies. William F. Buckley Jr., *Nearer, My God: An Autobiography of Faith* (New York: Doubleday, 1997), 95–97.

[11] Bernard Lonergan, *Method in Theology*, 2nd ed. (Toronto: University of Toronto Press, 1990).

Bernard J. Lonergan, S.J., would pick up on this work and would later form the basis for Tracy's first book, *The Achievement of Bernard Lonergan*.[12]

He began his teaching career in 1967 as an instructor at The Catholic University of America (CUA) in Washington, DC. Soon after, in 1968, Pope Paul VI issued the encyclical *Humanae Vitae*, which reaffirmed traditional Catholic teaching against artificial birth control. Tracy's CUA colleague, Fr. Charles Curran, authored a public response arguing that Catholics could, in good conscience, dissent from the encyclical's teaching without calling into question their Catholic faith.[13] Twenty-one other CUA faculty members, including Tracy and Bernard McGinn, signed on to the statement, as did more than six hundred theologians from other universities.[14] Because of CUA's status as a pontifical university, the dissent by so many of its theological faculty was especially striking. All twenty-two faculty were brought to trial by the CUA faculty senate and ultimately fired. Represented by the American Civil Liberties Union, the dismissed faculty brought suit against the university and were ultimately reinstated.[15]

As this controversy went on, both Tracy and McGinn were invited by Jerald Brauer, dean of the Divinity School of the University of Chicago, to lecture and give a seminar. Although Brauer was confident they would be successful in the lawsuit and get their jobs back, he hoped that he might be able to poach them for the Divinity School. Brauer was motivated in part by the Second Vatican Council, as he saw many Catholic students coming to the formerly Baptist divinity school and hoped to expand the Catholic presence on the faculty. Tracy and McGinn both formally joined the faculty in 1969, and each remained until their respective retirements.[16] Tracy's arrival at

---

[12] David Tracy, "The Development of the Notion of Theological Methodology in the Works of Bernard J. Lonergan, S.J.," (STD diss., Pontificia Universitas Gregoriana, 1969); David Tracy, *The Achievement of Bernard Lonergan* (New York: Herder and Herder, 1970).

[13] Robert G. Hoyt, ed., *The Birth Control Debate* (Kansas City, MO: National Catholic Reporter, 1968), 179–81.

[14] Including Richard McBrien, Bernard Häring, and Roland Murphy.

[15] David Gibson, "God-Obsessed: David Tracy's Theological Quest," *Commonweal* 137, no. 2 (January 29, 2010): 16.

[16] McGinn retired in 2003 and Tracy in 2006.

Chicago "was widely greeted as evidence of the optimistic new ecumenical and intellectual spirit infusing postconciliar Catholicism."[17] As part of this spirit, Tracy became involved with the international journal *Concilium* in the early 1970s, later serving as an editor and regular contributor.[18]

Tracy wrote or cowrote nine books and over two hundred articles and reviews during and after his tenure at the University of Chicago.[19] Following the release of his dissertation revision, *The Achievement of Bernard Lonergan*, he published his first constructive work of theology, *Blessed Rage for Order: The New Pluralism in Theology*, in 1975.[20] Initially intended to be the first book in a trilogy, it attempted to develop a fundamental theology in light of the situation of increased pluralism in theology. *Blessed Rage for Order* was greeted with acclaim and critique from the scholarly theological community, while the Congregation for the Doctrine of the Faith (CDF), who was concerned about the process theology–inspired notion of God in the book, requested some "clarifications."[21] Tracy responded to the CDF's request, but he never heard back.[22] Following the publication of this

---

[17] Gibson, "God-Obsessed," 12.

[18] *Concilium* is a journal of Catholic theology that was founded after the Second Vatican Council by Johann Baptist Metz, Anton van den Boogaard, Paul Brand, Yves Congar, Hans Küng, Karl Rahner, and Edward Schillebeeckx. Its mission is to "reflect on Christian tradition (supported by solid scholarship) in the light of cultural and religious experiences and socio-political developments" ("About Concilium," accessed April 21, 2018, http://www.concilium.in/about). It was later joined by the rival journal *Communio*, founded in 1972 by Hans Urs von Balthasar, Louis Bouyer, Walter Kasper, Henri de Lubac, Marc Ouellet, and Joseph Ratzinger. Typically, *Concilium* is considered the more "progressive" journal and *Communio* the more "traditional" one. In 1994, Orbis published a volume collecting many of Tracy's contributions to *Concilium* under the title *On Naming the Present: Reflections on God, Hermeneutics, and Church* (Maryknoll, NY: Orbis Books, 1994).

[19] For the full bibliography, see the first appendix at the end of this volume.

[20] David Tracy, *Blessed Rage for Order: The New Pluralism in Theology* (Chicago: University of Chicago Press, 1996); first published in 1975 in New York by Seabury Press.

[21] Typically, the CDF begins investigations into a theologian's work when there is some concern about the orthodoxy of some text or texts. The theologian in question is usually asked to clarify certain points to clear up any ambiguities. This process may continue until there is a resolution, but if none is reached the theologian may receive a "notification" that the book is problematic. In some cases, such as Roger Haight, the consequences may extend to the suspension of one's teaching faculties.

[22] Gibson, "God-Obsessed," 16.

text, Tracy was elected president of the Catholic Theological Society of America (1976–1977) and later received that organization's highest honor, the John Courtney Murray Award, in 1980.

Tracy followed *Blessed Rage for Order* with the 1981 publication of *The Analogical Imagination: Christian Theology and the Culture of Pluralism.*[23] This text, which more clearly outlined Tracy's claim for the three theological subdisciplines of fundamental, systematic, and practical theologies, was designed to be the second entry in his trilogy.[24] Widely regarded as his most influential work, this text develops several of the concepts with which he would become most closely associated: the method of mutually critical correlation, the public role of theology, theology as a hermeneutic discipline, the classic, and the analogical and dialectical imaginations.

The success of *The Analogical Imagination* was a watershed moment in Tracy's career. In 1982, he was elected to the American Academy of Arts and Sciences, which at the time was a rare honor for a theologian. He received his first honorary doctorate from the University of the South (Sewanee, Tennessee) in 1982.[25] The University of Chicago named him a Distinguished Service Professor in 1985, and two years later he was appointed the inaugural Andrew Thomas Greeley and Grace McNichols Greeley Chair in Catholic Studies.[26] In

---

[23] David Tracy, *The Analogical Imagination: Christian Theology and the Culture of Pluralism* (New York: Crossroad, 1981).

[24] Tracy never completed the expected third volume on practical theology. He did offer a brief outline of what this work would have looked like in his article "The Foundations of Practical Theology," in *Practical Theology*, ed. Don Browning (San Francisco: Harper and Row, 1983), 61–82. He followed this article with an examination of practical theology in global context in "Practical Theology in the Situation of Global Pluralism," in *Formation and Reflection: The Promise of Practical Theology*, ed. Lewis S. Mudge and James N. Poling (Philadelphia: Fortress Press, 1987), 139–54. He later reconsidered his view of practical theology, calling for more emphasis on a "correlational practical theology" in David Tracy, "A Correlational Model of Practical Theology Revisited," in *Religion, Diversity, and Conflict*, ed. Edward Foley (Berlin: Lit, 2011), 49–61.

[25] Over the next thirty years, numerous institutions followed suit, including Fairfield University (Fairfield, CT), Catholic Theological Union (Chicago, IL), Georgetown University (Washington, DC), Williams College (Williamstown, MA), Loyola University Chicago (Chicago, IL), and Wabash College (Crawfordsville, IN).

[26] The chair was endowed in 1984 by sociologist Fr. Andrew Greeley in honor of his parents. The endowment for this chair was made possible by Greeley's successful side career as a novelist. Following Tracy's retirement from the Divinity School in 2006, Jean-Luc Marion was appointed to the Greeley Chair in 2010.

1986, he achieved national recognition when he was the subject of a *New York Times Magazine* cover story.[27]

His theological focus turned in the 1980s more and more to the idea of conversation as a model for hermeneutics and for theology. In 1987 he published *Plurality and Ambiguity: Hermeneutics, Religion, Hope*,[28] which affirmed that theology must always be open to the risks of genuine conversation amid the challenges presented by the diversity of and ambiguity within spiritual and intellectual traditions. His 1988 Dondeyne Lectures, published in 1990 as *Dialogue with the Other: The Inter-Religious Dialogue*,[29] focused on interreligious dialogue between Catholicism and Buddhism, thus signaling his interests beyond strictly Catholic and Christian debates.

Tracy's place among the most influential religious thinkers of the late twentieth century was cemented when he was invited to give the prestigious Gifford Lectures at the University of Edinburgh in 1999 and 2000. Widely considered one of the highest honors in theology and philosophy, the lectures are typically given over the course of an academic year at one of four Scottish universities: University of St. Andrews, University of Glasgow, University of Aberdeen, or University of Edinburgh. The lectures are typically revised and published within a few years of being given, and some of these texts have become seminal academic texts.[30] Tracy had initially planned to publish his lectures, focused on the question of God and how the Christian tradition has sought to "name" God throughout its history, in 2003 under the title *This Side of God*. Moreover, it was meant to be the first volume in a new trilogy, which would focus on God, Christ, and the Holy Spirit, while engaging with questions of theological anthropology and interreligious dialogue.[31] Publication of this volume or

----

[27] Kennedy, "A Dissenting Voice: Catholic Theologian David Tracy," 20–28.

[28] David Tracy, *Plurality and Ambiguity: Hermeneutics, Religion, Hope* (Chicago: University of Chicago Press, 1994); first published in 1987 in San Francisco by Harper and Row.

[29] David Tracy, *Dialogue with the Other: The Inter-Religious Dialogue* (Grand Rapids, MI: Eerdmans, 1990).

[30] For example, William James's *Varieties of Religious Experience*, Alfred North Whitehead's *Process and Reality*, Reinhold Niebuhr's *Nature and Destiny of Man*, and Charles Taylor's *A Secular Age*.

[31] David Tracy, "Form and Fragment: The Recovery of the Hidden and Incomprehensible God," in *The Concept of God in Global Dialogue*, ed. Werner Jeanrond and

the others in the trilogy, however, have been continually deferred in the nearly twenty years since he first delivered the lectures.[32] He has nonetheless persisted in his work on "naming God" since his retirement from the University of Chicago in 2006, and scholarly interest in the "God book" has not abated, as evidenced by the number of invited lectures Tracy has given and conferences held in his honor.

Outline of the Argument of This Text

This book investigates the theological work of David Tracy in light of his commitment to theology as conversation. It considers several key themes of this thought, including those he is best known for (public theology, theological method, the classic) and those that are sometimes overlooked (Christology, God, and the varieties of pluralism). As each chapter takes up a particular theme, it looks at the chronological development of the idea throughout Tracy's career. It seeks to account for how the genesis and evolution of those ideas are tied to the major figures, texts, and events that he has been in conversation with. These conversations have led to shifts in his thought, both sizable and subtle, revealing the seriousness with which he takes the "risk" of conversation.

Chapter 1 offers a look at the meaning and significance of public theology for Tracy. At heart, public theology is rooted in Tracy's conviction that fundamental questions about reality are universal and that the divine reality these questions ultimately point to is God. As such, theology has to be intelligible beyond narrow religious silos.

Aasulv Lande (Maryknoll, NY: Orbis Books, 2005), 98; Lois Malcolm, "The Impossible God: An Interview with David Tracy," *Christian Century* 119, no. 4 (February 13, 2002): 30.

[32] One possible personal factor in this delay was the death of his mother Eileen in 2004. She moved with David Tracy to Chicago in 1969 and for decades assisted him by reviewing and typing up many of his handwritten manuscripts. Amid the encomia given at Tracy's retirement in 2006, Bernard McGinn added praise for Tracy's mother, saying she "enlivened and enriched this community with her love, her care, her wit, and her down-to-earth good sense that did more to puncture the balloons of academic self-importance than a thousand negative reviews ever could. As we salute David for all he has meant to the life of the Divinity School, let us not forget how much Eileen was also a part of our lives during those years." Doniger et al., "Tributes to David Tracy," 9; Gibson, "God-Obsessed," 10.

The idea of the public, particularly the publics of society, academy, and the church, becomes the organizing principle around which his entire approach to theology is structured. This builds on his early commitment to a "revisionist" theology, which allows for the mutual asking and answering of significant questions from both secular and sacred sources.

Chapter 2 takes these revisionist and public structures for theology and considers how Tracy's approach to theological method developed from his doctoral work through to his retirement. Conversation serves as the central metaphor for his method, as it draws on the back-and-forth that characterizes theology's engagement with both a religious tradition and the situations that traditions find themselves in. Moreover, due to the diverse publics theology is responsible to, theology can itself be divided among interrelated subdisciplines of fundamental, systematic, and practical theology.

Chapter 3 delves more deeply into a core part of Tracy's theological method, the classic. The classic is described as a powerfully revelatory expression of the truth that is both timely and excessive and that can in some cases be specifically religious in their power to disclose something true about God. Although mostly focused on the great texts and works of art, he comes to recognize the many types of classics (including events, rituals, and persons) and diverse sources (not only the elites but also from the mundane). This ultimately leads Tracy to shift from the classics to a postmodern theology of the fragments. While these carry many of the same theological implications as the classic, they also help him to further emphasize the importance of resistance to totalizing, rigid theologies.

While chapter 3 focuses on the classics as one key source of theological conversation, chapter 4 looks at plurality as a defining feature of both the situation with which theology engages and as a constitutive marker of theological traditions themselves. Plurality describes the diversity that exists in languages, cultures, traditions, and even within the self. Tracy emphasizes not only that such plurality is an inseparable feature of the postmodern world but also that plurality exists even within the early Christian community. As such, one must adopt a critical and engaged posture of pluralism toward this reality in order to effectively witness to the Gospel. The essential Catholic response to such pluralism is the analogical imagination, which takes

Christ as the central or prime analogue that helps human beings to discern truth in a plural and confusing world.

Chapter 5 continues this focus on Christ, investigating how Tracy has sought to make sense of what Jesus means in the Christian tradition. Drawing on insights from his work on the classics and plurality, Tracy describes Jesus Christ as the fullest "re-presentation" of God and as the "form of forms" for divine revelation. While largely side-stepping classical issues (two natures in one person, the psychological self-awareness of Jesus), Tracy delves into the incarnational and sacramental imagery underlying Christology. This leads him to focus especially on the ways in which Christ is revealed in the present, especially through the forms of manifestation, proclamation, and action.

Chapter 6 moves further into the question of the divine by focusing on Tracy's effort to "name God in an age that cannot name itself."[33] Recognizing that this is the more recent formulation of his search and his long-delayed publishing of the "God book," the chapter argues that the effort to name God has been a central, if sometimes over-looked, theme throughout Tracy's theological corpus. Early in his career, this search typically presumed more generic names for God (the "limit-of," the "whole," and "Ultimate Reality"), but a critical reevaluation of the meaning of Christian hope led Tracy to turn more deeply into specifically Christian efforts to name God. Review of a host of these names shows the depth of this search, while also re-inforcing the necessity for thinking about how theological method shapes one's answers to the fundamental questions that make the-ology a public discipline.

The conclusion to the book takes as its lens the famed "Tracy-Lindbeck debate" that was initiated in part by the publication of Lindbeck's *The Nature of Doctrine* in 1984. This dialogue with Lind-beck, as well as with the many commentators who came after, high-lights the interconnections among many of Tracy's theological concerns. Moreover, it showed the importance of public conversation around theology for discerning the distinct, sometimes complemen-tary, sometimes conflicting, commitments and values that diverse theologians hold. The Tracy-Lindbeck debate is a paradigmatic case

---

[33] Gibson, "God-Obsessed," 11; cf. ONP 3.

of how good conversation can sharpen one's understanding of the self and of the other while advancing public knowledge of and engagement with a tradition's beliefs about reality, the self, and the divine.

1

Public Theology

In initially general terms, a public discourse discloses meanings and truths which in principle can transform all human beings in some recognizable personal, social, political, ethical, cultural or religious manner. The key marks of publicness, therefore, will prove to be cognitive disclosure and personal, communal and historical transformation.

—David Tracy[1]

Tracy's claim that theology is a public discipline might seem strange to many at first glance. For decades, religion has often been thought of as a private affair, one of those controversial things (like politics or sex) that one does not discuss in polite company. In countries like the United States, which prizes its separation of church and state and its rejection of an established religion, some argue not only that religion is private but that it should increasingly become so (if not disappear altogether). Major scholars of secularization, such as José Casanova and Charles Taylor, have noted the variety of ways that the perception of religion as a private phenomenon has permeated Western thought (even as they show that this perception is not always accurate).[2] This sense is sometimes challenged, particularly

[1] AI 55
[2] José Casanova, *Public Religions in the Modern World* (Chicago: University of Chicago Press, 1994); Charles Taylor, *A Secular Age* (Cambridge, MA: Belknap Press of Harvard University Press, 2007).

when the faith of political leaders comes up during election years, but even then the discussion often revolves around depicting these commitments as personal and with limited public relevance.

In Tracy's theology, such an approach to the public-private question misses an important opportunity. He does not think the public can be reduced only to the political but must include the cultural, the artistic, and even the religious. At heart is the question of reason and argument: "public-ness" is intimately tied to the ability to make a case for one's beliefs, convictions, and values. Moreover, this case should be accessible not only to those who share one's traditions and context but to anyone who is smart and interested. He asserts that the sort of questions theology responds to—those timeless, deeply human questions about meaning and existence—are so ubiquitous as to beg for public, intelligent conversation around them.

This chapter looks at the idea of theology as a public discipline in two of Tracy's major books, *Blessed Rage for Order* and *The Analogical Imagination*. These texts focus deeply on the questions of what theologians are doing when they do theology, what makes theology an academic discipline, and what responsibilities that grounds for the theologian. At issue is what it means for theology to be a "public" discipline. While Tracy's notion of the public may contrast in some respects with more "commonsense" views, he envisions public-ness as being tied to the making of arguments that could be accessible to any intelligent, reasonable, responsible person. Discussion about theology is thus an open, public conversation, rather than a privatized or members-only one.

Discerning the meaning of that public conversation depends on tracing the trajectory in Tracy's thought as his idea of public-ness, and particularly of the three publics themselves, shapes his approach to theology more broadly. Initially he describes his theology in "revisionist" terms, emphasizing the possibility that the Christian tradition and common human experience might have mutual influence on one another, rather than the unilateral approaches he sees in other theological models. Tracy therefore emphasizes the revisionist theologian's sense of responsibility for both the academy and the church.

While Tracy maintains that effort to correlate aspects of the tradition with the world in which the tradition finds itself, he comes to revise the revisionist approach in light of a broader sense of the responsibilities that theologians have for different publics. Theologians speak to the academy and to the church but also to the wider society. These different audiences come with distinct modes of argument and ethical commitments, which in turn lead to a diversity of ways of doing theology (which Tracy calls the subdisciplines of fundamental, systematic, and practical theology).[3]

With an eye toward how public-ness relates to Tracy's theological method, this chapter argues that there is a meaningful yet subtle shift from the "revisionist" to the "public" modes of theology.[4] "Revisionist" is initially largely identical to "correlation" in terms of significance, but it is also tied clearly to the twin theological commitments to the positive aspects of "authentic secularity" and of "authentic Christianity."[5] Yet as Tracy's approach to correlation develops and his notion of the publics expands, the "revisionist" terminology largely disappears and the notion of "public-ness" becomes the organizing principle and foundation of Tracy's theological enterprise.

[3] The subdisciplines themselves are a focus of the following chapter on theological method.

[4] Gaspar Martinez offers a compelling diachronic reading of Tracy's work on public theology from his Lonerganian background to the work preceding his Gifford Lectures. He largely overlooks the methodological structure in BRO, however, and thus misses the sense in which there is a meaningful shift from revisionist to public theology. See Gaspar Martinez, *Confronting the Mystery of God: Political, Liberation, and Public Theologies* (New York: Continuum, 2001), 176–215. Kristin Heyer recognizes that Tracy started out as a revisionist and seems to move away from that term somewhat, or at least to not fall prey to some of the criticisms directed at other revisionist theologians (Kristin E. Heyer, "How Does Theology Go Public? Rethinking the Debate Between David Tracy and George Lindbeck," *Political Theology* 5, no. 3 [July 2004]: 310, 313). Timoteo Gener's reading of the relationship differs slightly from the one offered in this chapter (Timoteo D. Gener, "With/Beyond Tracy: Re-Visioning Public Theology," *Evangelical Review of Theology* 33, no. 2 [April 2009]: 121–23). Gener subsumes the "revisionist" approach as correlation under the larger heading of "public" theology. This is certainly correct in the sense that revision as correlation remains the process for Tracy in *The Analogical Imagination*. It should, however, be qualified by the recognition that Tracy's "revisionist" only meaningfully has commitments to secular reason (e.g., the academy) and to the religious tradition (e.g., the church). The expansion of the publics to include society in a complete and distinct way reframes the correlation approach and the public commitments.

[5] BRO 33.

Revisionist Theology in *Blessed Rage for Order*

Initial Forays into Public-ness

The public character of theology is a question already in *Blessed Rage for Order*, even as many of the central issues surrounding it are implicit. He opens that text by focusing on the plural context in which contemporary theology is done. This plurality means that there is no singular worldview shared by all; instead, there are a multitude of religious, philosophical, political, and cultural approaches that are all interacting with one another in contemporary discourse.[6] Because of this, theology cannot assume that its place in culture is assured. Rather, it must find ways of arguing for and demonstrating its relevance and its claim to truth. Gaspar Martinez aptly denotes Tracy's move here, claiming, "It is precisely . . . by setting criteria to test the adequacy and truth of theological claims that theology can become public."[7]

For example, consider the question of women's ordination within the Catholic tradition. It is fairly common for theologians, and religious persons more broadly, to appeal to a community's traditions when trying to argue for something. Communities have historically upheld certain texts, believed certain claims, practiced certain rituals, and formed certain habits. Many Catholics will base their argument against the ordination of women on the long-held claim that the apostles called by Jesus were all men, suggesting that had Jesus wanted women to be duly ordained ministers in the church he would have selected women as apostles. If one were an adherent to the Catholic tradition, that claim might be sufficient to find this argument compelling. In the contemporary pluralist context, however, one cannot assume that the conversation partner one speaks with belongs to the same tradition. In the case of the women's ordination conversation, perhaps the conversation partner is Catholic but rejects this specific teaching as unjust toward women when it comes to the role they can play in the church. Or perhaps the person is Muslim and rejects the idea of "ordination" because it introduces a formal and

---

[6] BRO 92–93. The place of plurality and pluralism in Tracy's theology is dealt with more fully in chapter 4.

[7] Martinez, *Confronting the Mystery of God*, 197.

unnecessary separation within the religious community. Or perhaps the person is a secular humanist, who rejects not only ordination but the entire religious sphere of which ordination is a part. The contemporary plural world means that no one can presume that the claims of one's particular tradition will be compelling in and of themselves when others engage them.

Theology therefore needs to make better arguments, ones that are able to engage seriously with the plural world in which theology finds itself. While Tracy maintains a commitment to uphold and engage with faith traditions, he also wants theological arguments that are reasonable to those outside the tradition. The theologian thus needs to be not only faithful but also persuasive. Given his role as an academic, Tracy interprets these two pulls on the theologian as being between two commitments: the "church-community of which he was a believing member" and "whatever community of inquiry . . . [that] aided him to defend and to reinterpret the tradition's beliefs."[8] The theologian has responsibilities both to the "church" (the "community of religious and moral discourse exemplified but surely not exhausted by his own church tradition") and the "academy" ("community of inquiry exemplified but surely not exhausted by the contemporary academy").[9] These two spaces become key *publics* to which theology is responsible.

Five Models of Western Theology

In order to understand the early significance of these publics for Tracy, it is important to look at the different models of theology he initially investigates. He argues that the two commitments the theologian feels, between the tradition and the contemporary pluralist world, shape the essential sources of all theologies.[10] There is a diverse

---

[8] BRO 6. It should be noted also that Tracy's primary focus in this part of BRO is on what he will call "fundamental theology," which he tends to see as the more explicitly academic mode of theology. For more on what is meant by "fundamental theology," see chapter 2, pp. 59–64.

[9] BRO 239.

[10] BRO 23, 43–45. More specifically, the two poles for his revisionist correlation method are "Christian texts" or "Christian theological categories," on the one hand, and "common human experience," on the other. For the latter pole, Tracy sees certain

set of options, however, for how one responds to these twin pulls. Tracy offers five possible responses: orthodox, liberal, neo-orthodox, radical, and revisionist.

First, the orthodox approach holds the faith tradition in high esteem while seeing the contemporary world as not necessarily theologically relevant.[11] There tends to be a strong sense of the timelessness of theological claims, which cannot be changed or abrogated by the sciences (neither natural nor social). Instead, theology (or the faith tradition more broadly) "is the best bulwark" against the dangers of the modern world.[12] The *orthodox* theologian, therefore, is a believing, practicing member of the faith community whose work focuses solely on understanding, explaining, and defending the claims of his or her particular faith tradition.

Second, the liberal approach takes contemporary pluralism quite seriously, often (but not always) to the detriment of the faith tradition. Liberal theology desires to uphold Christian claims and recognizes that these claims sometimes conflict with the claims of modern science, history, and politics. It does not outright reject or ignore the tradition but rather tends to adapt and even change longstanding faith claims in order to accommodate modernity. There is surprisingly little challenge given to the modern world from the religious perspective. The *liberal* theologian thus has a "modern consciousness" that is "committed to the basic values of modernity," and his or her work focuses on restating traditional claims in a more modern way.[13]

Third, the neo-orthodox approach is largely a reaction against the liberal one. The claim here is that liberal theology makes two key errors: it does not really take account of the sinfulness of the world, and it doesn't uphold the belief that justification comes by faith in Jesus Christ.[14] More fundamentally, liberal theology does not grasp

---

enduring and ubiquitous traits despite the profound and extensive pluralism in which human beings live. Chief among these is the experience of the "limit," which reveals to the human person a certain religious dimension to one's existence. See chapter 2 for a more detailed analysis of these two poles.

[11] BRO 24.

[12] BRO 24.

[13] BRO 26. Tracy's key example of the liberal approach is Friedrich Schleiermacher (1768–1834), a German Protestant theologian who is sometimes called the "father of modern liberal theology."

[14] BRO 28.

the *dialectical* character of reality. For Tracy, this means that there is an essential contrast or difference between the God of Jesus Christ, who is the central focus of Christianity, and the fallen, sinful world in which we live. Thus there is an irresolvable tension between the Christian tradition and the contemporary pluralist world in which we find ourselves. The neo-orthodox approach wishes to bring this authentic Christian witness to bear on the human condition, and it is through a dialectical analysis that the deep suffering, sin, and tragedy of human life in modernity is revealed. Neo-orthodoxy rejects the orthodox model's disinterest in the world and the liberal model's simple optimism, seeking instead to engage both the contemporary pluralist situation and the traditions of the faith in an often tenuous, paradoxical grasp. The neo-orthodox theologian is therefore a person of "authentic Christian faith," meaning that he or she embodies "existential attitudes of Christian faith, trust, and agapic love," and the object on which they focus is "the wholly other God of Jesus Christ."[15]

Fourth, the radical approach picks up on this idea of "dialectic" and irresolvable tension and applies it to the Christian tradition itself. The argument here is that the God represented by the other models above was fundamentally alienating to human beings, and thus true human liberation required the death of that idea of God.[16] This does not remove Jesus entirely from the equation; rather, Jesus is the highest example of either "a life lived for others" or of the fully liberated person.[17] The radical theologian, then, is not really a Christian believer at all, but rather one who provides a postmodern analysis of Christian tradition that emphasizes liberation while rejecting God.[18]

---

[15] BRO 29–30. Tracy's key example of the neo-orthodox model is Karl Barth (1886–1968), a Swiss Protestant theologian. While many of his other key examples of neo-orthodoxy are also twentieth-century Protestants (Paul Tillich, Rudolf Bultmann, Reinhold Niebuhr, and Friedrich Gogarten), Tracy also argues that Catholic theologians like Karl Rahner and Gustavo Gutierrez are essentially neo-orthodox.

[16] BRO 31.

[17] BRO 31.

[18] The example of this model is the "death of God" movement, which peaked in the 1960s and 1970s. Here, Tracy mostly mentions Thomas J. J. Altizer (b. 1927), an American theologian, although others are sometimes associated (e.g., William Hamilton, Gabriel Vahanian). This approach is now more commonly called "Christian

The fifth and final option is Tracy's preferred approach, the revisionist model. Like the neo-orthodox, revisionists take both the tradition and contemporary pluralism seriously as places of theological reflection. Revisionists do not, however, see the tension as a paradox. Revisionists focus rather on the method of correlation, whereby both the tradition and human experience each raise questions—of themselves and of each other. Moreover, both of these areas may be able to answer their own questions, or they may be able to answer one another's. What is striking here, for Tracy, is that for the orthodox, the only questions that mattered came from the tradition, and they were answered by the tradition. For the liberals, the modern world answered questions from the tradition and from human experience. The neo-orthodox sought to hold the tradition and modernity together in paradox without any real reciprocity between them. Finally, the radicals thought the tradition offered good moral guidelines, but all other questions would be answered by postmodernity. The revisionist model allows for all of these possibilities, claiming that the tradition may answer some of its own questions and that it may answer some of the questions raised by contemporary pluralism. Similarly, while modern thought may respond to some of its own problems, it might also help to answer questions that come up within a religious tradition. While there may be some significant confrontation between the tradition and the contemporary world, Tracy also holds out hope for "the possible basic reconciliation" between them.[19] This model of correlation, where each source has the potential to be fruitfully critical of one another, is the key insight Tracy sees in this last model.[20] The revisionist theologian, then, maintains commitments to the "beliefs, values, and faith" of both "authentic secularity" and of "authentic Christianity," and their work thus focuses on the ongoing process of critical correlation between these sources.[21]

The question of public-ness may not be immediately apparent in these models.[22] Tracy's interest in outlining them is really about laying the groundwork for the revisionist correlation model and then

---

Atheism," where one practices the moral teachings of Christianity while rejecting key faith claims (particularly the existence of God).

[19] BRO 32.

[20] BRO 43–46.

[21] BRO 33.

[22] "Public" does not even rate a spot in the subject index for BRO.

bringing this model to bear on the question of Christology. Nevertheless, these models reveal something profoundly important about the "public" in Tracy's theology. Each of these models responds to various publics in different ways. His description of the theologian as responsible to both the church and the academy suggests that he sees each of the five theologians listed above as already participating in those two publics, albeit to varying degrees. Each theologian thus has his or her own commitments about what matters most for participating in the church and the academy. For the orthodox theologian, the public of the church is far more significant than the academy, while this dynamic is arguably reversed for many liberal theologians. Moreover, as Tracy is entering into theological questions about modern plurality and what that means for religion, he is implicitly extending the discussion to a public that goes beyond the confines of either church or academy. He hasn't named it as such yet, but Tracy is interested in how the public of the "society" functions in each of these five different models. Although not framed this way, here at the beginning of his constructive work Tracy is taking the underlying idea of the "public" as the organizing principle of his approach to theological method.

Public Theology in *The Analogical Imagination*

In *The Analogical Imagination*, the "public" and "public-ness" become the explicit principle around which Tracy structures his theology. This is most clearly evident in the relationship he forges between the three publics (academy, church, and society) and the subdisciplines of theology (fundamental, systematic, and practical). The parallels between these two triads is intentional, and they become an essential element in his formulation of theological method. Yet this is not the sum total of the effect of public-ness on his theology; two further points must be made. First, Tracy argues that theology must, by its very nature, be public precisely because of its focus on fundamental questions that human beings tend to ask and because of the nature of God as universal. Second, Tracy offers an interpretation of academy, church, and society that goes beyond a common sociology and looks at what theological significance the publics have in and of themselves.

The Nature of Public-ness

While much of the wider discussion about "public theology" tends to focus on the role of religion in politics, separation of church and state, and a variety of policy issues, Tracy is interested in a much more basic set of concerns. He argues that there are two essential reasons for why theology is a public discipline. First, theology is a public discourse because it asks and investigates the "fundamental religious questions" that are common among most people, both around the world and throughout time.[23] Standard examples of these questions include: "What is the purpose of life?" "How should we live?" "What happens after we die?" While theology does not specifically focus on economic, political, or scientific questions, it does ask about the significance of those questions and the values implicit in their questions, methods, and answers. Because these fundamental questions are common to human experience, theology's effort to respond to them contributes to its "public-ness."

Second, theology is public because of the Christian understanding of the reality of God. The Christian claim that God is *universal* means that God cares for the whole of reality. Tracy ties this into how Christianity has traditionally understood the relationship between itself and the world. He pushes the old affirmation "The Christian is *in* the world but not of it" further, saying "the Christian is *released . . . from* the world, *for* the world."[24] While the world in many ways represents fallenness and temptation, Christians nonetheless have a responsibility to love and care for the world and to participate in its renewal. Tracy brings God's universality together with humanity's relationship to the world by arguing that humans are called to have "radical trust and loyalty" in this universal God above all else.[25] Our devotion to God means that we must follow and seek to emulate God's love for all of reality. Finally, because Christians believe in the radicality and universality of God's love, the way Christians are called to *speak* about God must be public and open to all reasonable people of goodwill.[26] The universal character of God makes public speech about God necessary.

---

[23] AI 81.
[24] AI 48.
[25] AI 51.
[26] AI 51.

The Three Publics: Society, Academy, and Church

As he did in *Blessed Rage for Order*, in this text Tracy talks about the publics in terms of the responsibilities of the theologian. While he continues his claim that the theologian has a commitment to the academy and to the church, he also offers a more expansive understanding of what the academy and the church are. Alongside these, he makes explicit the society as a public, distinguishing several aspects within it, and then articulating the responsibility the theologian has to society. In fact, Tracy begins his work on these three publics with society, which is in many ways the broadest or most comprehensive of the publics.

Society: The public of the society is composed of three different "realms" or domains. The first realm is what Tracy calls the "techno-economic" realm. This is made up of all the different social, economic, and technological structures that exist in order to make goods and services available to people.[27] This includes everything from influential technological developments like the assembly line or the computer chip to economic concepts like markets or supply and demand.[28] Because of the techno-economic realm, society is able to make it possible for most people to meet their basic needs and, in many cases, to thrive. Essential to the functioning of society at this level is "instrumental" reason, which is "the use of reason to determine rational means for a determined end."[29] Instrumental reason enables us to figure out the best process, technique, or tool in order to achieve our goals. It does not, however, help us determine what those goals *should* be.

---

[27] AI 7.

[28] It may be helpful at this point to note that Tracy is usually thinking in terms of the global West when he speaks about the techno-economic realm and society more broadly. He references here the "advanced industrial, technological societies with democratic politics and capitalist, socialist, or mixed economies" (AI 6). This does not mean, however, the techno-economic realm is not functional in non-Western societies, but its social, economic, and technological structures may differ. See, for example, Felix Wilfred, *Asian Public Theology: Critical Concerns in Challenging Times* (Delhi: ISPCK, 2010); Edward P. Wimberly, "Unnoticed and Unloved: The Indigenous Storyteller and Public Theology in a Postcolonial Age," *Verbum et Ecclesia* 32, no. 2 (2011).

[29] AI 8.

The second realm is "polity." This term typically refers to how a society is governed, its political institutions, and its laws. For Tracy, the key insight here is about what justice means in a society and how that society uses its power to achieve it. It is on this level that members of society (citizens) are most likely to engage each other in conversation about the political issues that are necessary "for any human polity."[30] Through these conversations, citizens voice their beliefs about the ideals and principles that do, or at least should, govern their society. This discussion is at the level of *practical* reason, as it focuses on goals and values (Tracy gives the example of competing notions of justice). Because it focuses on what society's goals should be, it differs meaningfully from the aforementioned instrumental reason, which seeks the best means for achieving those goals. According to Tracy, in the best societies these claims made about justice and ethics will determine decisions about the best functioning and allocation of resources within society.[31]

Finally, the third realm of society is culture. At this level, society is particularly focused on the relationship between its ethos (the way the citizens of society live) and its worldview (the way citizens envision reality).[32] The conversation here is at the deepest level, where citizens participate in what Tracy calls "critical reflection upon symbols" that reveal what is most meaningful and most valued by the citizens.[33] The primary, though not exclusive, place in which this

---

[30] AI 9. A note on terminology here: the terms used in this section for members of the society ("citizen") and the academy ("intellectual") are drawn from Tracy, although he does not use them consistently. See David Tracy, "Freedom, Responsibility, Authority," in *Empowering Authority: The Charisms of Episcopacy and Primacy in the Church Today*, ed. Gary Chamberlain and Patrick Howell (Kansas City, MO: Sheed and Ward, 1990), 34–47, for "citizen," and chapter 1 of BRO for "intellectual." The choice of "believer" for a member of the church is suggested by Tracy's occasional use of "non-believer," but "believer" is not itself clearly used. I suggest it here both for ease of use and as a parallel to the other two terms.

[31] AI 10.

[32] AI 7. Tracy's argument here is deeply shaped by the definition of culture given by Clifford Geertz: "an historically transmitted pattern of meanings embodied in symbols, a system of inherited conceptions expressed in symbolic forms by means of which men communicate, perpetuate and develop their knowledge about and attitudes toward life." See Clifford Geertz, *The Interpretation of Cultures* (New York: Basic Books, 2000), 89.

[33] AI 11.

symbolic reflection takes place is in art and religion. Through these two, citizens enter into deeper engagement with transcendental ideas like the good, the true, and the beautiful. Both art and religion have value for the society in its coming to understand and ground itself. Tracy recognizes that both art and religion can become private, even solipsistic, but he thinks that tendency devalues the possibilities and purposes of both. The marginalization of either art or religion diminishes the society at large.[34]

As may already be evident, Tracy prefers, and even idealizes, a certain hierarchical ordering of these three realms. At the peak, the symbolic reflection on our religious and artistic traditions of a society helps us to consider the relationship between how we think the world is ordered and how we ought to live in that order. This reflection enables us to better use our practical reason to determine what constitutes justice in our society and what it means to live well as neighbors with one another. Finally, this determination about justice leads us to figure out the best techniques, the best systems, the best means with which to set up markets, allocate resources, and target the development of new technologies. It's possible within this hierarchy for new conversations about justice or new scientific discoveries to ripple up and impact our reflection about values. Nonetheless, the ideal system still places culture above polity and polity above the techno-economic.

Tracy recognizes, however, that this idealized system is often undermined by contemporary events. First, he notes that the success of instrumental reason in the techno-economic realm can lead citizens to think that this should be the dominant form of reason. Instrumental reason is fairly easy to employ and to judge its success or failures, and so it is an attractive model for how to think. But that success can seduce a person into assuming, without critical, practical reflection, that instrumental values like efficiency or measurability are the highest values. The reflection on means (instrumental) then shapes, or even subsumes, the reflection on ends (practical). This trajectory leads almost inexorably to a fairly simplistic "the ends justify the means" mentality *precisely because* the means are *determining* the ends. Tracy describes this as turning a "technological society" into an "emerging

---

[34] AI 13.

technocracy," where the mere fact that we are *able* to do something overcomes any questions about whether we *should* do that very thing.[35]

Second, and related to this glorification of instrumental reason, is a general ignorance about and disinterest in questions of value. Tracy laments that contemporary Western society suffers from an ongoing malaise of practical reason, a malaise that "demand[s] professional competence in every major area of our communal lives except value issues."[36] Similarly, skill in symbolic reflection has largely been set aside from public discourse because certain forms of secularism have made acceptable, and even encouraged, ignorance about religion. Because religion is purportedly in an unending process of decline[37] (while art is allegedly either about narcissistic identity formation or commercial profit), there's no real need for anyone to learn much about it. Indeed, in this mind-set, "religion seems to be the sort of thing one likes 'if that's the sort of thing one likes.' "[38] Whatever value practical and symbolic reflection might have, it is limited to the private, to individual consumption. It is treated as though it offers nothing to the wider society.

Despite these challenges to the second and third realms of culture, Tracy argues strongly for their necessity and inclusion in public theology. True, he acknowledges that for the theologian, the realm of culture is perhaps the one they are most engaged with.[39] The importance, however, extends beyond this. The central issue is precisely the importance of being able to reflect on meaning, value, and truth in ways other than the technical achieving of particular outcomes.

Indeed, consider two examples of how the tensions among symbolic reflection, practical reason, and instrumental reason have persisted in the years since Tracy first argued this. First, contemporary arguments in the United States over the role of torture in national security often oscillate between "these methods provide actionable intelligence that saves lives" (i.e., it is acceptable because of alleged instrumental success) and "this is not who we are as a country" (i.e.,

[35] AI 8.

[36] AI 10.

[37] For a strong critique of this aspect of the secularization thesis, see Casanova, *Public Religions in the Modern World*, 19–39.

[38] AI 13.

[39] AI 11.

these kinds of means misrepresent the practical values and symbolic image of the nation). Second, the role of the liberal arts in Western higher education is often framed in the same instrumental versus goals mentality. Some argue that study in the arts and humanities is valuable because it helps to free one's mind for greater self-understanding and awareness or to become more participatory members of a democracy. On the other hand, many frame the discussion around the relative incomes of individuals with humanities degrees compared to those with business degrees, noting that the former often have higher salaries five years after graduation. While these two outcomes are not mutually incompatible, the framing of the first is more around practical reason while the latter is instrumental. For Tracy, the critical thinking that allows reflection on how a society determines what is valuable is necessary for its own health, but the marginalization of religion has been a central factor in reshaping such thought toward more instrumental approaches.

Academy: The second public is the academy. While Tracy emphasizes the question of theology within the academy, he clearly speaks of this public in ways that are applicable to all disciplines. Indeed, one essential focus for the intellectuals of the academy is determining what makes a field of knowledge into an academic discipline. Within this public, there are strong norms for determining what makes an argument legitimate, what counts as good evidence for that argument, and what criteria are used to make such judgments. The answers to these questions differ from discipline to discipline: sciences like biology or physics tend to have widespread agreement about acceptable methods, while others like psychology or education often feature significantly different methodological schools of thought.[40] Nonetheless, any discipline ought to be able to defend itself to other disciplines within the academy. It must be public in the sense that its arguments for its own approaches and commitments should be open to critique and response from other disciplines.

Theology arguably has a somewhat tenuous position within this. Tracy admits that theology suffers from both a "lack of a clear sense

---

[40] AI 17–18. Tracy draws here on the work of Stephen Toulmin, who distinguished among compact, diffuse, and would-be disciplines. See Stephen Toulmin, *Human Understanding*, vol. 1: *The Collective Use and Evolution of Concepts* (Princeton, NJ: Princeton University Press, 1972).

of disciplinary direction" and "a lack of adequate professional organization for the discussion of new results."[41] Theology as a field does
not have internal agreement about method, criteria, or evidence;
moreover, it is as a discipline distinct from religious studies, with
which it is sometimes conflated. One of the ongoing struggles Tracy
sees is the effort to work out these disciplinary issues and to continue
to defend theology's place in the academy. Its continuing search for
meaning and truth in the conversation between the Christian tradition and the contemporary world benefits from the academy's rigor
and demand for public-ness. Theology as a discipline makes its own
contribution to the academy precisely because of its focus on symbolic
meaning and value. While many other disciplines focus on matters
corresponding to the first two realms of society (the techno-economic
and the polity), theology is able to focus especially on the third.
Theology's contributions to the academy broaden and deepen the
academy's contributions to society.

Church: The third and final public is the church. At a basic level,
the church as public is a largely voluntary association of believers.[42]
Individuals and families choose to be members of the church and
make decisions about their degree of commitment to that choice.
While many come into the church as infants and children who have
little to no say over their involvement, those same kids will eventually make an adult decision about whether or not to continue with
their participation in the church.[43]

As an association of its members, the church functions as an inter-
mediate space between individuals on one side and the larger society
on the other.[44] This mediating role can be performed as a corporate
influence, such as when particular communions or denominations
try to influence public policy at the national or international level.
For example, consider the Catholic Church's work on environmental
and climate change issues. The publication of Pope Francis's encyclical on the environment, *Laudato Sì*, and the subsequent transmission

---

[41] AI 18.

[42] AI 21.

[43] Tracy notes that this idea of "voluntariness" is a largely modern construction, as premodern society and church would have made such participation effectively com-pulsory. The growth of pluralism, especially among religions, has dramatically in-creased this sense of voluntariness.

[44] AI 21.

of its claims and suggested practices through the bishops and local parishes constitutes a communal effort at influencing society.[45] Beyond this corporate approach, Tracy thinks that the church's social influence is more often realized through the efforts of particular members.[46]

As a public, the church is similar to both society and the academy in that it has its own specific commitments and modes of reflection. Society focuses this on questions of instrumental, practical, and symbolic thinking, while the academy is concerned with method and issues of disciplinary status. For the church, the key concern is fidelity. Members of the church have a commitment to their fellow believers, to the traditions that animate the church, and to the practices and claims that come from those traditions.[47] This leads members of the church to reflect on their experiences and relationships through the lens of the tradition. This fidelity to the church need not be in competition with one's commitments to society and/or to the academy, but they do mark the distinctive character of being part of the church. This tension reveals a key point of focus for Tracy: the theologian, as citizen, intellectual, and believer, is a member of all three publics and thus must seek to responsibly balance the various commitments and conversations that are essential to all three.

Finally, it is worth noting here that when Tracy describes the "church" as a public, he does not restrict this to mean the Roman Catholic Church. While his life as a US Catholic theologian means that he encounters the public of the church from this context, he's clear about recognizing that fact. He notes, for example, that his own tradition has a "highly organized church order," which may differentiate it from evangelical and nondenominational Christian traditions that have more diffuse authority structures.[48] Nonetheless, in

---

[45] Pope Francis, *Laudato Sì*, May 24, 2015, http://w2.vatican.va/content/francesco/en/encyclicals/documents/papa-francesco_20150524_enciclica-laudato-si.html.

[46] AI 21. Here, Tracy is drawing on the insights of Vatican II, particularly *Gaudium et Spes*, which argues for how members of the church perform the work of the church through their daily lives. See *Gaudium et Spes*, Pastoral Constitution on the Church in the Modern World (1965), in *Vatican Council II: The Conciliar and Post Conciliar Documents*, rev. ed., ed. Austin Flannery (Collegeville, MN: Liturgical Press, 2014), no. 43.

[47] AI 22.

[48] AI 22.

naming the "church" as one of the three publics, Tracy does clearly have in mind the overall Christian communion. Despite this, one could reasonably extrapolate this notion of public beyond Christianity (e.g., the *ummah* in Islam).[49] The key insight here is that, while religious traditions may differ in various societies, the religious sphere has a particular and privileged place within the larger social order.

Three Perspectives on the Three Publics

Describing the church this way may suggest that Tracy has a reductive vision of the church. If the church is simply a group of people who choose to follow a shared tradition and use that to shape society, how is that really a public? Is it any different from other voluntary associations, like the Republican Party, Greenpeace, or Rotary International? Closer analysis of the three publics reveals, however, that there are three distinct and important perspectives from which one might consider them: sociological, conversational, and theological. Each perspective both expands our understanding of the given publics and offers a deeper insight into how they relate to one another.

The first perspective, the sociological, follows from Tracy's initial focus on the publics. He introduces society, academy, and church in a chapter titled "A Social Portrait of the Theologian," here offering a description of each public in terms of the type of social status and expectations each has. Each public is, in a sense, voluntary. This has already been established for the church, but it's also evident in the academy (there is no real expectation that any given person be an intellectual). Voluntary status is more ambiguous in society (one's existence in a given time and place automatically places one in a particular society), yet the degree of one's active involvement in society or one's commitment to its flourishing is up to each citizen.[50]

---

[49] This issue, though somewhat unexplored for Tracy, is arguably even more pressing in light of his interest in pluralism within societies.

[50] One can also imagine that a person's membership in any particular society is voluntary, at least in the sense that it is for some (but not all) people possible to decide to leave that society and move to another. One might also consider those who "withdraw" from society, such as fourth- and fifth-century Christian monks. Even some degree of dependence on others suggests, however, that one is still a part of a society, no matter how small.

Moreover, there is an intrinsic overlapping among the persons who participate in each public; for example, all the believers in the church and all the intellectuals in the academy are citizens of society, and some persons (i.e., theologians) are members of all three publics. One can envision here a Venn diagram, with the circle of the church overlapping the circle of the academy, while the larger circle of society fully encompasses both. Finally, each public has its own particular goals (society: the common good; academy: the advancement of knowledge; church: witness to the tradition), and in many ways the goals of the academy and the church are believed to promote the goals of society. If taken in isolation, this sociological view could suggest that the church is simply in service of the wider society; Tracy, however, offers other countervailing perspectives on the publics.

This latter point leads to the second perspective, the conversational. Tracy also describes each public as an *audience* that is largely defined by a particular type of conversation that takes place within it. The audience within the academy is composed primarily of scholars, teachers, administrators, and students, and the conversation in which they participate is particularly focused on academic research.[51] This research takes place in a variety of disciplines, ranging from humanities to sciences to education to engineering to business. We can similarly see that the audience within the church is composed of believers in particular traditions, including both clergy and lay, leaders and followers, and regular and less-engaged participants. The conversation here centers around the content of the tradition, including beliefs, symbols, practices, moral codes, and major figures.

In some cases, the work of these conversations may lead to benefits for other publics. Within the academy, there are numerous conversations (e.g., research agenda, institutes, curricula) that have clear connections to promoting society's public good. Researchers pursuing

---

[51] It is worth noting that Tracy does not really give attention within the academy to students, which is evident in his greater attention to questions of research and little reference to teaching. Some might reasonably attribute this to the fact that his entire career took place in a research and graduate student–focused program. We can note, however, that the vast majority of persons involved in or affected by the conversations in the academy are students. Indeed, students contribute to these conversations as subjects of research, participants within research, the intended subjects of college and university curricula, and the (at least purported) purpose of the existence of (most) such schools.

cancer treatments, institutes promoting civic engagement in the political process, and educators developing critical thinking skills through a liberal arts core curriculum are all working toward healthier, happier, and more productive citizens. Similarly, discussions within the church about refugees, the role of women in ministry, and the virtuous use of new technology also work for a better society.

Yet while the audience of a particular conversation may sometimes overlap, there are also conversations that are squarely targeted within a particular public. For example, in mathematics, Fermat's Last Theorem waited 358 years for someone to be able to solve it, but there is no obvious way in which this effort is connected to either society or the church. The intra-Catholic discussion about celebrating mass *ad orientem* (where the priest stands in front of the altar during the eucharistic prayer, simultaneously facing the same direction as the people and standing with his back to the people) is not targeted at larger social discussions (arguably, it is not even an accessible conversation to non-Catholics). These conversations, and many others like them, have value within their primary public but have limited to no relevance for the other two. This suggests that, on the level of conversation, there is important overlap among the three publics but also significant areas of difference (a more traditional three-circle Venn diagram). Tracy's theologian is the person who stands at the center of all three.[52]

The third perspective is both the most important for Tracy and the most overlooked by his readers.[53] He is particularly interested in a *theological* understanding of the various publics, both in themselves and in how they relate to one another. Moreover, this theological perspective will entirely subvert the dynamic of the sociological and conversational perspectives above; rather than offering an over-

[52] Not dealt with by Tracy is the possibility of the devoutly faithful research chemist or engineering professor, who also would be citizens, intellectuals, and believers. He notes that these intellectuals do not have the same responsibility to speak *to* the church, but he does not really account for their being members of the church that *are spoken to* (AI 23).

[53] See, for example, Owen C. Thomas, "Public Theology and Counter-Public Spheres," *Harvard Theological Review* 85, no. 4 (October 1992): 453–66; Martinez, *Confronting the Mystery of God*, 197–206; Heyer, "How Does Theology Go Public," 309–13, 319–24; and Gener, "With/Beyond Tracy," 119–26.

lapping, Venn diagram approach, it reframes their interrelationships through the traditional Christian image of the church and the world.

Tracy's theological description of the church begins with the church as the "gift" that mediates the relationship between humans and God.[54] The use of "gift" by Tracy to describe the church is essential to the theological perspective. First, it emphasizes that the church is a gift of God's grace, a place where God reaches out to the world and seeks to invite us into fellowship with God. As God's gift, the initiative for the church comes from God, not from human beings.[55] Second, as a place of mediation between the divine and human, the church further mediates the grace of God. That the church is a place where people encounter reverence, community, repentance, and liberation speaks to the ways in which God's grace works through it.[56] Finally, the theological image of the church as gift challenges the sociological image of church as voluntary association. While the free choice to be part of the church is important, that free choice is impossible without the prior initiative of God through the church.[57]

This basis in gift leads Tracy into a sacramental model of the church. The traditional definition of a sacrament as "a visible sign of an invisible grace" is reframed for Tracy through the language of representation and participation. By representation, he means some expression that literally re-presents God and divine grace to the world.[58] Clearly, the "decisive" representation, the most fundamental sacrament, is Jesus Christ.[59] Yet whatever re-presents God's love to us is sacramental, including baptism, Eucharist, and the church.[60] Moreover, Tracy's repeated references to participation, both the church's participation in God's grace[61] and the human participation

---

[54] AI 23.

[55] AI 43n90.

[56] AI 50.

[57] One might note here that Tracy's view of gift shares some affinities with the phenomenology of Jean-Luc Marion, who would become Tracy's colleague at the University of Chicago in 1994. The text of AI, however, precedes the publication of Marion's *Dieu sans l'être* in 1982, and Tracy makes no references to Marion's work.

[58] The "re-presentative" language is essential to his Christology; see chapter 5, pp. 124–130.

[59] AI 216.

[60] AI 422.

[61] AI 50.

in "the reality of the whole" as manifested in particular expressions and experiences,[62] connect with the language of participation so strongly emphasized in Vatican II's Constitution on the Sacred Liturgy (*Sacrosanctum Concilium*).[63] Tracy himself notes that the strong emphasis on "participation language" throughout *The Analogical Imagination* is itself suggestive of his preference for a sacramental model.[64]

He describes the church as "the sacrament of Christ and eschatological sacrament of the world."[65] This version of the sacramental model is particularly rooted in his reading of Edward Schillebeeckx and Karl Rahner.[66] By saying "sacrament of Christ," Tracy is drawing on his idea of re-presentation noted above: the church is the primary mediator of Christ's presence in the world. He does not propose this in order to be triumphalist (i.e., an unrealistic exaggeration of the church's greatness in contrast to how terrible everything else is) or monopolistic (i.e., that grace can be accessed only through the visible confines of a particular community or denomination). Rather, the emphasis on sacrament reemphasizes the church as a gift from God wherein divine grace is encountered.[67]

The latter half of his description, "eschatological sacrament of the world," carries two key implications. First, by "eschatological" he highlights both that the person and event of Christ that is mediated

---

[62] AI 175–76.

[63] See Second Vatican Council, *Sacrosanctum Concilium*, The Constitution on the Sacred Liturgy (1963), no. 14.

[64] AI 43n90.

[65] AI 43n90.

[66] Cf. Edward Schillebeeckx, *Christ the Sacrament of the Encounter with God* (New York: Sheed and Ward, 1963), 47–89; Karl Rahner, "Membership of the Church According to the Teaching of Pius XII's Encyclical 'Mystici Corporis Christi,'" in *Theological Investigations*, vol. 2 (Baltimore: Helicon Press, 1963), 1–87; Karl Rahner, "The Church and the Sacraments," in *Inquiries* (New York: Herder and Herder, 1964), 191–257.

[67] It is also worth noting that Tracy has Avery Dulles's *Models of the Church* in mind here, arguing that the sacramental model is capable of including what is necessary from the institution, mystical communion, servant, and herald models. Oddly, Tracy's reference to these models changes "mystical communion" to "prophet" while maintaining the normal names for the other three. This is presumably a typo, as Tracy's understanding of "prophet" is largely similar to Dulles's "herald" (AI 43n90). His reference to the strengths of these other models is partly as a corrective to the issues of ecclesial triumphalism and monopolies of grace mentioned above. See Avery Dulles, *Models of the Church* (New York: Image Books, 2002).

by the church has happened in the past ("always-already") but that its fulfillment has not come ("not-yet").[68] Tracy strikingly claims that the always-already/not-yet of Christ requires that the instrument of mediation, the church, is itself an eschatological reality that is always-already but also not-yet. The church is not final or complete but continually witnesses to the reality of God and of Christ in the world. In fact, it is through the church's own eschatological status that it is able to mediate the eschatological Christ to the world.[69]

The second implication is that there is a *world* that the church is both sacrament of and in tension with. Tracy argues that this world in fact includes the publics of the society and the academy.[70] This is not to say that "the world" is exhausted by these two publics (one might include *non-human creation* as part of "the world," even as it is not exactly a part of human-centric publics) but rather that these two publics are essential to the theological understanding of the world. Despite the fact that these two publics are not defined by the theological focus of their conversations, that they do not necessarily perceive themselves as theological realities, and that many (if not the majority) of their members do not consider themselves believers, Tracy strongly advances his claim that society and academy are "expressions of the theological reality 'world.'"[71]

The relationship between the church and the world is thus the key to understanding this sacramental model of the church. Tracy cautions members of the church from either outright rejecting the world or from fully assimilating into it. On the one hand, the world is a contingent reality that owes its existence to God's creative work, but it is also ambiguous in being an occasion both of sin and of grace. Indeed, within this simultaneous contingency and ambiguity, Tracy describes the world as "loved by God and by the Christian."[72] It is an object of our care and concern but not an object of ultimate faith, hope, and love. Because of this, the believer is someone who is *"released* (the violence of the imagery is exact) *from* the world, *for* the world."[73] His stress on the term "released" comes from this sense of

---

[68] AI 442n29.
[69] AI 443n29.
[70] AI 23.
[71] AI 23.
[72] AI 48.
[73] AI 48.

radical contingency: the world *could be* otherwise, while God alone is necessary. As a result, the believer is freed from any particular interpretation of the world, how it is, or how it should be. This release also empowers the believer to be *for* the world, to fulfill the commandment to love the world as God does.[74]

The theological perspective on the publics both complements and contrasts the sociological and conversational perspectives. Indeed, all three need to be held in tension in order to understand Tracy's public theology. He notes the difficulty of this, claiming that we tend to think of the society and academy only in sociological terms while considering the church only theologically.[75] Attending to all three perspectives provides a fuller understanding of the three publics in themselves as well as in their relationships to one another.

Conclusion

Tracy's revisionist model of theology is in part structured on adapting the great insights of the liberal and neo-orthodox approaches. He wanted a theology that was able to critique the wider secular culture (like the neo-orthodox model) but also one that could critique the religious tradition in light of new insights received from secular culture (like the liberal model). This desire grounds the correlation approach that grounds revisionist theology and that will be a central focus in the next chapter. Moreover, because of its commitments to both the academic work of critical reason and the church work of critical fidelity, revisionist theology has an incipient sense of what it means for theology to be a publicly accountable discipline.

In developing that idea of the public, though, Tracy expands and reframes the focus of his theology. He recognized that theology has a responsibility also for the wider society that extends beyond the academy and the church. The three distinct publics serve as the essential orientations for theology, and the theologian takes on an identity as citizen, intellectual, and believer. Moreover, he reckons more

---

[74] Here, Tracy is consciously echoing both Johannine (John 15:19; 17:6) and Pauline (Rom 12:2) traditions of seeing the Christian as living *in* the world but not being *of* the world.

[75] AI 23–24.

fully with how theology's emphasis on faith and reason are tied to the pervasive fundamental questions that human beings ask as well as the infinite, universal nature of God that the Christian tradition sees at the root of those questions. The public approach holds theology in its diverse forms accountable to the idea that its approach to these questions and to naming God must have an intelligible, reasonable explanation.

The shift described in this chapter, then, is about how the public model for theology subsumes and expands on the revisionist model. Public theology in fact retains the correlation approach that is so central to revisionism, but that process of correlation is expanded. As is shown in the next chapter, the process of correlation comes in different forms: fundamental, systematic, and practical theologies each draw on diverse aspects of the Christian tradition while focusing on the situations of the academy, the church, and the wider society, respectively. The process of correlation is meaningfully restructured around the three publics, which thus serve as the organizational principle around which Tracy's method is oriented. Moreover, it is closely tied to his insight that all three publics are theological *and* sociological realities. This deepens and expands the sense of responsibility the theologian has for the academy from *Blessed Rage for Order* as well as for the wider society introduced in *The Analogical Imagination*.

Finally, because Tracy's conception of public theology is the organizing principle for his theological method, these two topics cannot be completely separated from one another. The role of reason in public discussion, for example, is tied to the types of arguments made in the distinct subdisciplines of fundamental, systematic, and practical theology. Because of this, a fuller critique of Tracy's publics must be deferred to the conclusion of the following chapter.

2

Theological Method

Karl Rahner . . . was right when he stated, "But we cannot spend all our time sharpening the knife; at some point we must cut."

—David Tracy[1]

Tracy's fondness for this aphorism from the influential twentieth-century Catholic theologian Karl Rahner, SJ, belies a tension evident in his own work. Doing theology well requires having the right tools, and method is a central tool, the "knife," for doing so. Yet what is the value of continually refining one's method if one never *does* theology, never "cuts"? On one hand, he rightly sees the importance of the cut: he sought to develop a Christology in the second halves of *Blessed Rage for Order* and *The Analogical Imagination*, while the latter half of his career has been spent writing the "God Book."[2]

Yet on the other hand, Tracy has been known far more often for his work on "sharpening the knife." Early in his career he described

---

[1] David Tracy, "God, Dialogue, and Solidarity: A Theologian's Refrain," *Christian Century* 107, no. 28 (October 10, 1990): 901. Tracy is actually paraphrasing Rahner here, who wrote, "If we want the knife to cut we must first sharpen it. But if we confine ourselves to sharpening the knife alone then we have not yet done any good cutting. It is the same with theology." See Karl Rahner, "Reflections on Methodology in Theology," in *Theological Investigations*, vol. 11 (New York: Seabury Press, 1974), 84.

[2] David Gibson, "God-Obsessed: David Tracy's Theological Quest," *Commonweal* 137, no. 2 (January 29, 2010): 11.

his plan to produce a trilogy featuring successive volumes on the "subdisciplines" of fundamental, systematic, and practical theologies. The first two were completed—*Blessed Rage for Order* and *The Analogical Imagination*, respectively—but the third never came to fruition, with a couple of articles laying the essential outline of what that project would have looked like.[3] Tracy himself has been a proponent of this reading, as evidenced by his descriptions of the two main texts during the period around the completion of the latter.[4] Further consideration of Tracy's work on method, however, exposes some significant cracks in this reading. Review of the development of Tracy's process of critical correlation, and of the "two poles" of that correlation, demonstrates that his ostensible plans for a trilogy fell through even before a third volume on practical theology was set aside. Instead, *The Analogical Imagination* is more of a revision of *Blessed Rage for Order* on the topic of method than it is a sequel. Recognizing this can free Tracy's readers to explore his work on substantive doctrinal questions, which he lamented had been overlooked in favor of a focus on method.[5]

This alternative reading of Tracy's method comes from taking seriously the "conversational" metaphor for theological method. Recognizing how conversation describes the ongoing practice of theology reveals three helpful insights into his work. First, saying one is having a conversation implies that there are multiple people involved. That conversation may be with a friend, an employer, or one's church community; it may even be the interchange one has when reading an interesting book. Ideas are presented, considered, responded to,

---

[3] "The Foundations of Practical Theology," in *Practical Theology*, ed. Don Browning (San Francisco: Harper and Row, 1983), 61–82; "Practical Theology in the Situation of Global Pluralism," in *Formation and Reflection: The Promise of Practical Theology*, ed. Lewis S. Mudge and James N. Poling (Philadelphia: Fortress Press, 1987), 139–54.

[4] See, among others, David Tracy, "The Public Character of Systematic Theology," *Theology Digest* 26 (Winter 1978): 410; David Tracy, "Defending the Public Character of Theology: How My Mind Has Changed," *The Christian Century* 98, no. 11 (April 1, 1981): 352; Tracy, "The Foundations of Practical Theology," 81.

[5] Todd Breyfogle and Thomas Levergood, "Conversation with David Tracy," *Cross Currents* 44, no. 3 (Fall 1994): 301–2.

and challenged in such a conversation. In contrast to simply deliver-
ing a monologue, having at least two participants allows for this back
and forth.

Second, there are numerous types of conversations that we might
participate in. Some of these are very straightforward and practical,
such as what shall we eat tonight or what shall we do about the
plumbing problem in the house. Others ask deeper questions, perhaps about beliefs regarding the best form of government. As we
distinguish different types of conversations from one another, we can
develop a sense for what Tracy means when he talks about the differences among the subdisciplines of fundamental, systematic, and
practical theology.

Third, conversations develop over time. The different types of
conversation sometimes affect one another (my deep beliefs about
religious practices may affect the practical decision about what parish
I belong to and how that shapes my Sunday morning). Discussions
that take place over time have twists and turns, and they shape other
conversations as well (a particular conversation with my wife may
affect future conversations with my wife, and it may also affect how
I dialogue with my students). Moreover, the way I converse is impacted by past conversations, including those with mentors who
shaped my thinking. Thus the content of conversation, and the way
in which we carry it out, may evolve and change. This is certainly
clear for Tracy, whose very description of theological method adapts
throughout his career.

These three features of conversations serve as a useful outline for
thinking through Tracy's theological method in this chapter. The first
section will look at the method of correlation that Tracy uses to place
theological traditions in conversation with contemporary cultures
and contexts. The second section will examine the different types of
conversation that take place within theology, including practical,
systematic, and fundamental theology. Throughout both of these
sections, the question of how Tracy's understanding of theological
method has developed over time, and the ways that some theological
conversations have affected his later work, will be considered. The
chapter closes by returning to the question of public-ness and method
and drawing on some of the critiques of Tracy's approach.

Conversation Partners:
The Evolving Method of Correlation

The Correlation Theologies of Tillich and Niebuhr

The correlation method for theology refers generally to correlating two distinct sectors or sources. There are numerous ways in which such a correlation might happen, but the key insight is that theology takes questions and concerns from one sector and engages them with the resources and responses from the other. Sometimes this correlation is one way, and other times it is bilateral, but the question-and-answer process writ large is essential. Numerous theologians have employed some version of this approach, including Hans Küng and Edward Schillebeeckx, but the most influential on Tracy were the Protestant theologians Paul Tillich and H. Richard Niebuhr.[6]

Tillich writes that his theology follows a method of correlation that "tries to correlate the questions implied in the situation with the answers implied in the message."[7] By "situation" he means the cultural context in which the theologian is working, including the variety of artistic, scientific, and political expressions of that culture.[8] The "message" he refers to is the kerygma or central truth of Christianity. *Kerygma* is the Greek word for "preaching" in the New Testament, but it more broadly refers to the key or essential claims of the Christian faith. As such, Tillich does not want to identify the message with the Bible alone or with the Christian tradition but rather to claim that the message is present within both. Working on a kerygmatic theology therefore means one tries to strip away the historical and cultural baggage that has been added to the Christian message in hopes of reaching the genuine and eternal core of the faith.[9] Although this process will never be fully successful, it challenges the theologian

---

[6] For a critique of correlation methods of theology, see Lieven Boeve, *God Interrupts History: Theology in a Time of Upheaval* (New York: Continuum, 2007), 61–91.

[7] Paul Tillich, *Systematic Theology*, vol. 1 (Chicago: University of Chicago Press, 1951), 8.

[8] Tillich, *Systematic Theology*, 1:4.

[9] Here, one can see echoes of Rudolph Bultmann's "demythologization." See Rudolf Bultmann, "New Testament and Mythology: The Problem of Demythologizing New Testament Proclamation," in *New Testament and Mythology and Other Basic Writings*, ed. Schubert Ogden (Philadelphia: Fortress Press, 1984), 1–43.

not to identify the Christian faith too strongly with any particular historical or cultural instance of the faith. This is even true to some extent for engaging the biblical witness, which Tillich thought was unable to escape "the conceptual situation of the different biblical writers," including their languages, their categories, and their world-view.[10] Thus while the theologian must respond to the questions and concerns raised by one's contemporary situation, this response should always be consistent with the truths of the Christian message. Indeed, it is the message that judges the situation.[11]

While Tillich's method of correlation served as a valuable starting point for Tracy, it was ultimately seen as incomplete. Tracy likes the commitment to two essential sources (situation and message), but he thinks Tillich juxtaposes them rather than correlates them. For Tillich, questions really only arise from within the situation, and answers really only come from the message. Tillich therefore does not actually take the situation seriously in and of itself precisely because there's no real opportunity for the situation to provide the response to its own question (let alone to potential questions that the message might raise).[12] For these reasons, Tracy saw Tillich's method as a valuable, but inadequate, starting point.

H. Richard Niebuhr presents a somewhat different approach to correlation, one that Tracy finds more fruitful overall. In his seminal text *Christ and Culture*, Niebuhr claimed the key challenge facing Christianity is not its relationship with civilization but rather the

---

[10] Tillich, *Systematic Theology*, 1:7.

[11] Tillich, *Systematic Theology*, 1:8. The titles of the five parts of his *Systematic Theology* refer to the situation-message dialectic: Reason and Revelation, Being and God, Existence and the Christ, Life and the Spirit, and History and the Kingdom of God. While he recognizes that the questions and responses are mutually interdependent, the trajectory of his method of correlation is essentially univocal.

[12] BRO 46. It is helpful here to note that Tracy recognizes there are nuanced differences between Tillich's "situation" and "message" with "common human experience" and "Christian texts" (how the poles are described in BRO). While it is unclear whether Tracy would say that the kerygma has questions to which the situation could respond (although my suspicion is that he would), the more important point is that access to the kerygma is always mediated through its historical and cultural accretions. This is a point that Tillich himself recognizes, and thus to argue that his method correlates the kerygma or message directly with the situation seems to be problematic for Tillich's method, even on its own terms.

more fundamental relationship "between the poles of Christ and culture."[13] Essential to this is the question of how one defines each of these poles. While Niebuhr recognizes that there are a variety of ways of understanding Jesus Christ in the Christian tradition, he argues that there is still a "fundamental unity" in that Jesus is a concrete "person with definite teachings, a definite character, and a definite fate."[14] The central insight for Niebuhr is to recall that the power of Jesus to draw us in stems from the double fact that he is "man living to God and God living with men."[15] Niebuhr offers a similarly limited definition of the pole of culture, arguing that one ought to look at the general notion of culture rather than any particular instance. Culture is the " 'artificial, secondary environment' which man superimposes on the natural," including language, beliefs, technology, and values.[16]

The Christian faith is a response to and mediation of the revelation of Christ, but this response and mediation always occurs within some particular culture. The heart of Niebuhr's text is the five-part typology he outlines for understanding that relationship: Christ against culture, Christ of culture, Christ above culture, Christ and culture in paradox, and Christ transforming culture.[17] The first two mark the extremes of this spectrum, between a sectarian rejection of human society (Christ against culture) and a complete accommodation of Christ's message to whatever culture one finds oneself in (Christ of culture). The latter three, however, fall somewhere between these extremes. These three correlations use the question of the relationship between Christ and culture to examine further the relationship between God and the individual human person. Each in its own way recognizes the challenge and the give-and-take relationship between the two poles, and thus each offers distinct ways for believers to think about how they navigate their belonging to both the faith and the particular cultural-historical space they live in.

---

[13] H. Richard Niebuhr, *Christ and Culture* (New York: Harper Collins, 2001), 11.

[14] Niebuhr, *Christ and Culture*, 12.

[15] Niebuhr, *Christ and Culture*, 29.

[16] Niebuhr, *Christ and Culture*, 32.

[17] Chapters 2–6 of *Christ and Culture*, respectively.

Two key elements from Niebuhr's approach to correlation will recur in Tracy's method. First, in contrast to Tillich, correlation itself need not be univocal. Niebuhr does not claim that theological method ought to correlate answers from Christ to questions from culture, but rather that the mode of relation between these two poles is itself the crucial methodological question.[18] Second, Niebuhr recognizes that none of his five correlations are final or definitive.[19] Christianity consists of a plurality of traditions rather than a single, complete response to the event and person of Jesus Christ. Indeed, within each part of his typology, Niebuhr notes relevant scriptural texts, early Christian thinkers, and modern communities that resonate with the particular model under consideration. This acceptance of diversity within Christianity and the need to resist totalizing interpretations became central to Tracy's work.

A First Foray into Critical Correlation in Blessed Rage for Order

The idea of critical correlation in *Blessed Rage for Order* begins with the "postmodern" theologian. While many in this era have challenged, even set aside, hierarchical authority and a belief in objective, autonomous reason, the theologian grows "disenchanted with disenchantment"[20] and faces a pluralistic world in which "he can authentically abandon neither his faith in the modern experiment nor his faith in the God of Jesus Christ."[21] The two core dimensions of

---

[18] A helpful nuance to draw out here is that Niebuhr seeks to correlate *Christ* and culture, whereas Tracy seeks to correlate the Christian tradition with a contemporary situation. While the differences between "culture" and "contemporary situation" are arguably cosmetic, the differences between "Christ" and "the Christian tradition" are substantial.

[19] "Yet it must be evident that neither extension nor refinement of study could bring us to the conclusive result that would enable us to say, 'This is the Christian answer.' Reader as well as writer is doubtless tempted to essay such a conclusion; for it will have become as evident to the one as to the other that the types are by no means wholly exclusive of each other, and that there are possibilities of reconciliation at many points among the various positions" (Niebuhr, *Christ and Culture*, 231). Cf. AI 376, "The phrase 'mutually critical correlations' functions here to indicate that the responses may take any form in the whole range of classic Christian responses analyzed by H. Richard Niebuhr. The particular form will be dependent upon the particular point at issue."

[20] Cf. BRO 33.

[21] BRO 4.

theology, faith and reason, the *fides* and *intellectum* of St. Anselm's great definition, remain essential commitments for the theologian.

Among the greatest achievements of the modern era is the emergence of a rigorous mode of critical thinking that is keen to challenge prior conclusions. Such efforts are most apparent in history and science, and Tracy recognizes that this can be threatening to many Christians.[22] Both of these fields have raised challenges to the faith, especially to Scripture. And these challenges led many (but not all) Christians to respond in one of two ways: either the Christ *of* culture approach, which downplays traditional faith claims in an attempt to make them plausible to a rationalistic culture (e.g., miracles or the resurrection), or the Christ *against* culture route, which embraces a fundamentalism that rejects any arguments or evidence that might contrast with religious claims (e.g., creationism).

Despite these temptations, Tracy emphasizes the Catholic tradition's commitment to both faith and reason. Christian theology is oriented toward the *truth*, and so it must embrace the variety of sources and methods that lead us to the truth. This includes the value of critical postures toward the religious tradition and toward the "secular faith" of modern rationality.[23] Here, "critical" does not connote a *negative* posture but rather a commitment to open-ended inquiry that challenges all sources on their evidence and arguments for the claims made.[24] This process of inquiry, because it is seeking the truth, leads to an ever-deeper appreciation of the truths of both faith and reason.

The theologian's commitment to faith and reason is the basis for Tracy's revisionist model for theology.[25] The revisionist theologian thus relies on two key sources: the "Christian fact" and "common human experience."[26] In his description of these sources, Tracy tends

[22] BRO 6.

[23] BRO 8–9.

[24] BRO 6.

[25] See chapter 1, pp. 20–21, for Tracy's description of this model.

[26] BRO 43. Both for ease of reference and comparison to later developments, these two poles will be called the "religious" and "situational" poles, respectively. There are two things worth noting in how this religious pole is described. First, in his essay "Task of Fundamental Theology," Tracy argues for "fact" over "tradition" or "kerygma" because he thinks the latter two options imply "that the fundamental theologian need be a believing member of the Christian community" (David Tracy, "Task of Fundamental Theology," *Journal of Religion* 54, no. 1 [January 1974]: 14n3).

to focus more on the method of investigating the two poles rather than listing specific texts, rituals, or beliefs that might comprise them. Specifically, investigation of the religious pole relies on a "historical and hermeneutical"[27] approach while the situational pole calls for a phenomenological assessment of its "religious dimension."[28]

The historical-hermeneutical approach is where Tracy's focus on significant texts becomes most clear.[29] He expects theologians to use the best historical-critical scholarship available in order to reconstruct the texts most essential to Christian self-understanding. Based on this historical-critical work, the theologian proceeds to interpreting those reconstructed texts in order to determine their meaning for the Christian community.[30]

As an example, consider Tracy's attempt at a historical and hermeneutical investigation of the traditional Christian claim that "Jesus of Nazareth is the Christ." Here, the historical effort is to establish and reconstruct as accurately as possible the "New Testament christological texts," which would look at the gospels and epistles especially.[31] The work of scriptural scholars in analyzing and critiquing

-----

This question of the role of belief in or commitment to a tradition will recur when we look at the subdisciplines and what it is that defines *fundamental* theology.

Second, in BRO, Tracy initially identified the former pole with Christian *texts*, and indeed texts are his primary source for understanding the Christian tradition(s). He does, however, recognize in BRO that a robust Christian theology must also consider "symbols, rituals, events, witnesses." He claims that the hermeneutical theory he works with in BRO is adaptable to nontextual sources, but it was not yet sufficiently nuanced in that direction (BRO 15n5). As a result, his fuller development of nontextual sources was postponed until AI and its work on the "classic." See chapter 3, pp. 79–80, for more on this litany of sources.

[27] BRO 49.

[28] BRO 47.

[29] BRO 49.

[30] This hermeneutical approach is heavily indebted to Paul Ricoeur's claim that a text has both "sense" and "referents." "Sense" denotes the internal structure of the text and the meaning that can be determined through "ordinary methods of semantic and literary-critical inquiries," while "referents" means the world the text discloses to the reader (BRO 51; cf. Paul Ricoeur, *Interpretation Theory: Discourse and the Surplus of Meaning* [Fort Worth: Texas Christian University Press, 1976], 19–22). This approach marks a departure from romantic hermeneutics, which focuses on the intentions of the author; Ricoeur instead emphasizes the interpreter's use of genres, images, metaphors, and symbols to appropriate the new possibilities disclosed by the text.

[31] BRO 50.

the construction of these texts, their interdependencies, and their social-historical contexts then grounds the hermeneutical task of deciphering what it means to proclaim Jesus as the Messiah. Bringing the historical and hermeneutical together enables the theologian to engage the production of texts about Jesus, their appropriation by the tradition in history, and the existential reality they claim as meaningful in the present day.

The method for investigating the situational pole differs significantly from the religious one. Tracy calls for "a phenomenology of the 'religious dimension' present in everyday and scientific experience and language."[32] Importantly, Tracy is clearly assuming that common human experience has such a religious dimension. He defines this religious dimension by the idea of "limit character": that which discloses the radical finitude, the bounded-ness of human existence. This in turn leads one to acknowledge that there is something beyond the self. Moreover, Tracy argues that the experience of the limit is shared among all human beings, leading to his claim about *common* human experience.[33]

The task of the revisionist theologian is to correlate the key texts of the Christian tradition and common human experience. In the first place, this means that the tradition ought to be able to provide a substantive interpretation of common human experience. Historically, Christian texts have developed a variety of categories and narratives that offer a vision of the Christian life and human existence in relation to the divine. The theologian thus examines the adequacy of these categories and narratives "for all human experience."[34] Should this examination show that the Christian faith does in fact offer a meaningful response to the basic questions of human existence, then this response is capable of going beyond an "inner-theological" conversation and engaging the wider secular world.[35]

For example, consider the category of redemption, which is a central theme both for the Hebrew prophets and for the New Testament

[32] BRO 47. He describes phenomenology somewhat broadly as "mediating the relationship of particular expressions . . . to our immediate lived experience" (BRO 69).

[33] BRO 92–93. For more on the "limit" concepts in Tracy, see chapter 6, pp. 154–57.

[34] BRO 44.

[35] BRO 44.

evangelists. One particular narrative of redemption might then be that of Saul of Tarsus, who experiences a conversion moment that reorients his life and sets him on the path to becoming the great apostle St. Paul. While this redemption narrative has a clear religious dimension, it could also be connected in a meaningful way with more secular redemption stories. One might look at fictional texts, like the stories of Ebenezer Scrooge or Darth Vader, which similarly offer conversion-redemption stories with varying degrees of spiritual depth. Any of these stories could be useful frames for the individual person to think through one's own human experience and to make connections to the experiences of others. The pervasiveness of redemption stories indicates the relative adequacy of this aspect of the Christian fact for understanding common human experience.

Were Tracy's correlation model to conclude after this initial stage, it would simply be a retread of Tillich's method described above. Tracy, however, suggests two changes that will generate a more robust correlation. First, he claims that Tillich's method failed to take the situational pole seriously because it operated in only one direction: the questions came from one source (the situation) and the answers from the other (the message). In contrast, Tracy says the theologian must take the risk of recognizing that the tradition itself might raise questions and that common human experience might provide a meaningful response.[36] In doing so, he argues for a two-way correlation rather than Tillich's unilateral one. The second tweak to Tillich's method is to recognize that each source might actually answer its own questions.[37] This stems from the "critical" element in correlation, which requires that both sources be subjected to modes of critical inquiry. Both tradition and common human experience may raise questions, and both may propose responses. This leads to a more complex and rich engagement between the religious and situational pole than Tillich's approach offers.

---

[36] As an example, Tracy asked, "Why do we not find in Tillich a critical investigation of the claims that either Jean Paul Sartre's or Karl Jaspers's philosophies of existence provide a better 'answer' to the question of human estrangement than the Christian 'answer' does?" (BRO 46).

[37] BRO 46.

Revisiting the Revisionist Method in The Analogical Imagination

Tracy's basic view of theological method remains consistent between *Blessed Rage for Order* and *The Analogical Imagination*, but he develops it much more fully in the latter. As a result, there are four subtle shifts that have significant implications. The first of these has already been reviewed in the previous chapter, as Tracy moves from mainly describing his theology as revisionist to public. While publicness is present to some degree in *Blessed Rage for Order*, and the revisionist method of correlation continues and develops in *The Analogical Imagination*, the more specific framing of theology as public contributes to a reorientation of the method.

The second and third shifts pertain to how he describes the subdisciplines of theology: history moves from a separate subdiscipline to an integral part of the other subdisciplines, while the orientation of the subdisciplines moves from a temporal orientation to a public one. These latter two changes will be analyzed in the second half of this chapter.

The fourth shift reframes his method of correlation. There is a small addition, where he continues his basic approach of bilateral, "critical" correlation, but he adds the qualifier "mutually" (or "mutual") in order to emphasize more strongly that the two poles must respond to (and even correct) each other. More important, though, he changes the two poles that comprise this mutually critical correlation. He moves from "common human experience" and "the Christian fact" to "the contemporary situation" and "Christian classics." While these changes might seem small, they have a tremendous impact on how Tracy does theology.[38]

The shift in the religious pole is the smaller of these two changes. In *Blessed Rage for Order*, he variously uses the "Christian fact" or "Christian tradition," and he focuses especially on central Christian texts.[39] Inspired by Hans-Georg Gadamer, he sometimes describes

---

[38] Here, proponents of the standard reading of Tracy's method might object that the poles of correlation in fundamental theology differ from those of systematic theology, in keeping with their descriptions in BRO and AI, respectively. A close reading of the re-presentation of fundamental theology in AI shows, however, that this new description of the poles pervades all three subdisciplines (AI 62–64).

[39] Indeed, he limits his historical-hermeneutical investigation to texts (BRO 15n5).

these texts as "classical," but in reality this use reads almost more as colloquial than technical.[40] In *The Analogical Imagination*, however, the "classic" becomes the core of the religious pole in correlation. The key claim is that classics are particular expressions bearing an excess and permanence of meaning. These expressions take a variety of forms, including texts, images, symbols, rituals, events, and persons.[41]

A key aspect to classics as constitutive of the religious pole are their integral role in tradition. Classics arise from within a tradition: they are produced in a specific place and time by particular human beings. Because these creators are shaped by the traditions within which they live and work, their classic expressions bear traces of those traditions. Yet the classic, and the truth and challenge it reveals, takes its place within the tradition as something that shapes the future of the tradition as well.[42]

The importance of the classic for the religious pole is precisely because the theologian interprets the classics of the Christian tradition. Tracy again places most of his focus on classic texts, but he also works other modes of expression (image, event, ritual, etc.) more explicitly into his analysis. Most important, he claims that the central Christian classic is the *event* and *person* of Jesus Christ.[43] Christ the classic is not only the norm for all other Christian classics but also the interpretive lens through which Christians come to understand the world.[44]

Reworking the religious pole of correlation to focus on the classics has a significant impact on the situational pole as well. Moving away from "common human experience," Tracy instead turns to "the contemporary situation" of the theologian. Here, he focuses on how one's interpretations of the contemporary situation might raise "fundamental questions on the meaning of existence," the very kinds of questions that ground the public-ness of theology.[45] His correlation

---

[40] BRO 49, 59–60n33.

[41] AI 100, 108. While Tracy recognizes the expansive possibilities of classics, he does remain primarily focused on texts.

[42] For more on this aspect of the classic, see pp. 80–84 in the next chapter.

[43] AI 131.

[44] AI 233.

[45] AI 340–41.

thus engages not just the classics themselves but the specifically religious dimension of those classics.[46] Pluralism is the key facet of the situation for the contemporary theologian, particularly the consciousness of pluralism within culture. Here, Tracy distinguishes the situation he finds himself in from that of only a few decades earlier: there is no single dominant question, not even that elicited by "the profound sense of meaninglessness, absurdity, the radical threat of nonbeing."[47] This lack of unified focus fractures the wider cultural and theological discussion and creates a profound opportunity for the work of correlation.

The diversity presented by the situation of pluralism further pushes Tracy to focus more on the particular than the universal in human experience. While his prior interest in "common human experience" pursued an ostensibly universal encounter with limits, the "contemporary situation" offers a clearer sense of how the particularity of one's context could shape such experiences. For example, the theologian's experience of the event and person of Christ "occurs to the individual theologian in a particular situation."[48] This particularity can enable, rather than hinder, the manifestation of truth in the classic. The reader can see how that particular text speaks to her in her particular context in such a way that it discloses something true about the self, God, and/or reality. Tracy thus does not abandon a sense of universality—he is still concerned with how truth in its deepest sense is encountered—but he reckons more seriously with how that truth is always mediated through particularity.

Finally, Tracy emphasizes that not only is the theologian drawing on the two sources of the tradition and the contemporary situation but also that the theologian is him- or herself embedded within the tradition and the situation. There is no neutral or objective standpoint from which the theologian brings these two sources together, and there is no theology that does not draw in some ways on both of these areas. Intellectual honesty requires the theologian to recognize this and account for it when doing theology: "Every theology lives in its own situation," and so "theologians are no different from other

---

[46] AI 61, 326.
[47] AI 341.
[48] AI 344.

cultural critics who bring their own orientations, questions and pos-sible, probable or certain modes of analysis and response to the situa-tion encompassing all."[49] The work of correlation is thus done while awash in the sources to be correlated.

Method as Conversation

In both *Blessed Rage for Order* and *The Analogical Imagination,* Tracy's twofold effort on method is to describe the process of correlation at the heart of theology and the different types of theology that do this. The formulation he provides *in The Analogical Imagination* largely settles these two issues, and it continues to be a reference point for Tracy's understanding of method throughout his career.[50] Later de-velopments focused less on tweaking mutually critical correlation or the three subdisciplines and more on further refining the theory of interpretation this presumed. This hermeneutical deepening is built on further developing the idea of conversation, already present in *The Analogical Imagination,* into a full-fledged approach to describing method.[51]

This emphasis is apparent in Tracy's later two monographs, 1987's *Plurality and Ambiguity* and 1990's *Dialogue with the Other.* Just as two people might converse with one another, so too does a reader con-verse with a text (and, by extension, the viewer with a painting, the participant with a ritual, and so on).[52] This is an active process whereby the reader raises questions, considers possibilities, and imagines the world disclosed by the text. The text, rather than being

---

[49] AI 339; cf. Second Vatican Council, *Gaudium et Spes,* Pastoral Constitution on the Church in the Modern World (1965), no. 4.

[50] This is evident as recently as 2011 during his public lecture at Loyola University of Chicago: David Tracy, "The Necessity and Character of Fundamental Theology" (Loyola University of Chicago, April 8, 2011), https://media.luc.edu/media/The+ Public+Character+of+TheologyA+Prospects+for+the+21st+Century+Part+1/1_4rta pi8y/21880401 (part 1) and https://media.luc.edu/media/The+Public+Character+ of+TheologyA+Prospects+for+the+21st+Century+Part+2/1_6fldnvrr (part 2).

[51] Tracy's use of conversation in AI is located primarily in the section on interpre-tation of classics (AI 115–24). This is explored in greater depth in the next chapter, pp. 82–84. Cf. Hans-Georg Gadamer, *Truth and Method* (Bloomsbury Academic, 2004), 356–71.

[52] PA 19.

a mute object in one's hands, can become profoundly captivating by suggesting new possibilities of meaning and value. Seemingly connecting it to his method of mutually critical correlation, Tracy even says that "the model of conversation is not imposed upon our experience of interpretation as some new *de jure* method . . . [but] rather the phenomenon of conversation aptly describes anyone's *de facto* experience of interpreting any classic."[53]

For conversation to be genuine, Tracy argues that it must be open, even risky. First, conversation partners risk losing control. The back-and-forth of conversation becomes like a "game" or "the zone," where one loses one's self-consciousness and allows the conversation itself to take over.[54] Tracy compares this to watching a live stage play or seeing athletes in a game. When the actor becomes self-conscious, aware he is playing a role, the performance begins to fall apart. When the soccer player becomes self-conscious, the distraction pulls her out of the game and impedes her play. So too when the conversation partner thinks mainly of what he wants to say next, or about how well the conversation is going, or about maintaining control, the conversation itself can crumble.

Second, conversation partners risk change. The openness to the other that comes from entering into the zone grounds an opportunity for the other to reveal authentically, even dangerously, new possibilities.[55] One's beliefs, pre-understandings, interpretations, and even horizons are placed on the line. For example, the college student who watches the 1986 film *The Mission* one night for a class may be profoundly struck by the bravery of Father Gabriel; this viewing could reveal the new possibility of religious vocation as a way of living a virtuous life. The student's prior, secure plans for his life may be thrown asunder as a new truth about his own existence is shown to him.[56]

---

[53] DWO 63–64.

[54] PA 18.

[55] PA 93, 103.

[56] It is not clear what this would mean in the situation of interpreting a text. While the reader's worldview may be challenged by the text, it's hard to say that the text itself is at risk. Perhaps it might be best to describe reading as conversation in an analogical, if somewhat one-sided, way.

Third, the conversation partners risk interruption. Thus far, this description of conversation is fairly consistent with Tracy's previous attempts.[57] But where *Plurality and Ambiguity, Dialogue with the Other*, and later essays[58] really advance his position is in relation to the notion of "interruption."[59] Those who participate in conversation are impacted by both plurality and ambiguity. Put another way, Tracy is fond of claiming that interpretation is never an innocent activity: the texts and other classics we interpret come from traditions that are plural and ambiguous. For example, religious traditions that may have played an emancipatory role historically inevitably also possess oppressive and violent dimensions as well. That student who was profoundly affected by watching *The Mission* might also recognize that the characters of Fr. Gabriel, Fr. Mendoza, and Cardinal Altamirano each take different positions in relation to the Guarani, positions arrived at in large part because of their particular interpretation of the demands of the faith. Moreover, plurality and ambiguity describe more than the traditions and the classics themselves; they describe the individuals doing the interpreting. Conversation is thus always impacted by suspicion and critique, of oneself and of one's interlocutors.

As much as conversation is Tracy's basic model for hermeneutics, the method of mutually critical correlation is a specific way of enacting that model. The two poles of correlation are in conversation with one another, mediated by the theologian who is employing the method. The two poles are placed at risk, raised by the possibility that the answers to one pole's concerns might come from the other. This mutual critique requires an openness on the part of both poles but also the necessary critique of one's commitments and of the other's. Conversation, and thus mutually critical correlation, are

---

[57] See especially AI 99–107, 154–67, and 345–52.

[58] See especially David Tracy, "Theology, Critical Social Theory, and the Public Realm," in *Habermas, Modernity, and Public Theology*, ed. Don Browning and Francis Schüssler Fiorenza (New York: Crossroad, 1992), 19–42; David Tracy, "Western Hermeneutics and Interreligious Dialogue," in *Interreligious Hermeneutics*, ed. Catherine Cornille and Christopher Conway (Eugene, OR: Cascade Books, 2010), 1–43. In the latter text, Tracy recapitulates this Gadamerian understanding of conversation as his fundamental model of hermeneutics.

[59] PA 32.

therefore fraught with argument, disagreement, and suspicion. Through the openness of the conversation partners, however, there is also the possibility that the back-and-forth will lead to new manifestations of truth.

Types of Conversation: The Theological Subdisciplines

While Tracy sees theology as "a single discipline" in its effort to engage basic questions of existence, he also argues that it can be broken into "distinct subdisciplines" that each emphasize a different focus within theology.[60] In this section, we look at the arrangement of different subdisciplines or types of theology, with a particular interest in how Tracy develops them between *Blessed Rage for Order* and *The Analogical Imagination*. This includes a recognition of the influence of Bernard Lonergan's "functional specialties" along with how Tracy adapts and deviates from his mentor's influence. While the changes in Tracy's method from *Blessed Rage for Order* to *The Analogical Imagination* may seem subtle at first, they signify the importance of public-ness as the organizing principle for theological method.

The Influential Background: Lonergan's "Functional Specialties"

It is not surprising that Tracy's first major work in constructing his own theology should focus so heavily on theological method. He studied with Bernard Lonergan at the Pontifical Gregorian University and later published the revision of his dissertation in 1970 under the title *The Achievement of Bernard Lonergan*. Moreover, while Tracy was studying with him, Lonergan was finishing his own major text on theological method, *Method in Theology*.[61] In many ways, one could argue that the early form of Tracy's method is built on a complex appropriation of Lonergan's method.

---

[60] AI 56.

[61] One can see Tracy's early impressions of Lonergan's method in the final three chapters of ABL. For Tracy's reading of the completed text of Lonergan's *Method*, see David Tracy, "Review of *Method in Theology*, by Bernard Lonergan," *Journal of the American Academy of Religion* 43, no. 2 (June 1975): 380–81.

First off, Lonergan's goal in *Method* was to develop the method that, because it is rooted in the structures of human consciousness, ultimately underlies all of theology—indeed, all of human thinking. He offers the basic definition of method as "a normative pattern of recurrent and related operations yielding cumulative and progressive results."[62] These operations are performed at the four levels of "conscious intentionality" that Lonergan had worked out in his text *Insight*: empirical, intellectual, rational, and responsible.[63] Put simply, these four levels correspond to how humans receive information about the world around and within us (empirical, experience), how we interpret and make sense of that data (intellectual, understanding), how we judge the truth of those interpretations (rational, judgment), and how we decide to act in accord with those judgments (responsible, decision).[64] Again, *all people* have these levels of consciousness; while the specific types of data or interpretations that theologians are interested in may be unique to the discipline, the underlying types of questions (What is it? Is it true?) are common to any human in pursuit of truth.[65] Lonergan calls this method transcendental, meaning that through the process of inquiring about some*thing*, the human who asks questions also becomes present to him- or herself. The process is thus not confined to any particular field but essentially describes the process of all human investigation.[66]

Nevertheless, as a theologian, Lonergan seeks to apply this method to theology itself. Describing theology as mediating "between a cultural matrix and the significance and role of a religion in that matrix,"[67] Lonergan argues that theology is "an ongoing process" that is inevitably conditioned by historical developments within culture. The interrelationship between culture and a religious tradi-

---

[62] MT 4.

[63] MT 9.

[64] For an accessible overview of this aspect of Lonergan's thought, see Mark T. Miller, *The Quest for God and the Good Life: Lonergan's Theological Anthropology* (Washington, DC: The Catholic University of America Press, 2013), 46–62.

[65] One ought to add the caveat here that varying kinds of intellectual disabilities might qualify the degree to which any one person is capable of the different levels of consciousness.

[66] MT 14.

[67] MT xi.

tion leads Lonergan to break out the process of theology into different parts. He identifies eight such parts, which he calls "functional specialties": research, interpretation, history, dialectics, foundations, doctrines, systematics, and communications.[68]

What is most salient here about these functional specialties is how Lonergan organizes them. These eight can be broken into two groups of four, each of which has a specific direction or trajectory. The first four (research through dialectics) are "mediating theology."[69] Here, Lonergan is particularly focused on engaging the historical background of theology. In research, one works to establish the data that will be used in theology, including collecting and (as necessary) reconstructing the texts and sources one works with. Interpretation requires making sense of these sources with respect to their historical context and the intentions of their producers. History seeks to understand history broadly, but in particular it focuses on the "doctrinal history of Christian theology."[70] Finally, dialectics seeks to understand Christian traditions comprehensively and thus to be able to discern the meaningful similarities and differences that exist among them. Lonergan describes these four as having an "upward trajectory," meaning that moving through these four functional specialties corresponds to moving upward through the four levels of conscious intentionality (empirical to intellectual to rational to responsible). Indeed, each of the functional specialties corresponds to one of the four levels.

Similarly, the latter four functional specialties, which he calls "mediated theology," have a "downward trajectory" that moves from the responsible level back down to the empirical level. Foundations seeks to understand the horizon within which theology can be understood. Doctrines make judgments of fact and of value with regard to the Christian tradition and are thus informed by the prior work of mediating theology. Systematics seeks to organize these doctrines, solve inconsistencies, and engage with issues of coherence and adequacy to experience. Finally, communications connects this theological work to the wider world, including other disciplines, cultures,

[68] MT 127–33.
[69] MT 135.
[70] MT 128.

and technologies. Put another way, the upward trajectory of mediating theology is the place where the theologian listens to the preceding tradition, while the downward trajectory of mediated theology is where the theologian takes a stand in the present with regard to what is true, intelligible, and meaningful in the tradition.[71]

Two key features of Lonergan's approach impact Tracy's method. First, it recognizes the variety of disciplines required for the overall conversation of theology. It is not simply a matter of reading texts well or of communicating one's insights; theology must cover a multitude of skills. It might seem especially daunting for one person to take on this task, but both Lonergan and Tracy recognize and affirm the collaborative dimension of doing theology well. Second, Lonergan clearly recognizes the interdependence of engaging with the history of one's tradition and working in one's present context. No credible contemporary theology can be divorced from its past, but theology is not a dead conversation without implications for today. While Tracy's appropriation of these insights will diverge meaningfully from Lonergan's own, the centrality of them will remain clear through the rest of this chapter.

The Revisionist Subdisciplines of Blessed Rage for Order

As Tracy initially conceived of *Blessed Rage for Order* as a work of "fundamental" theology, he spent considerable time developing his theological method and the relevant criteria for assessing theological claims.[72] The goal in *Blessed Rage for Order* was to develop "a model which can be faithful to some of the more important pluralist possibilities of the present day."[73] Part of this is the development of an outline of the different types of theology that one might do and how they fit together. In *Blessed Rage for Order*, he proposes four: fundamental, systematic, historical, and practical theologies. As part of his revisionist project in the mid-1970s, he takes *time* as the organizing principle guiding this outline.

---

[71] MT 267.
[72] BRO 15n8.
[73] BRO 91.

Fundamental theology: The central task of this subdiscipline is to work out the criteria that will be used to make theological claims.[74] For example, what makes for good evidence to support a theological claim? How does one compare and weigh competing arguments? Tracy is driven by the question of criteria in theology because *any* academic discipline has to be able to develop and explain the types of criteria, warrants, and evidence that will be used to make judgments. Tracy wishes to defend the academic rigor and status of theology, so he follows suit.[75]

He develops three key criteria: adequacy to personal experience, appropriateness to the tradition, and logical coherence. In these, we can recognize the tensions within theology as it is pulled between one's present context and experience, on one hand, and the resources of the tradition, on the other. While some other disciplines can, at least theoretically, eschew their past traditions entirely in the pursuit of knowledge, the embedded role of tradition makes this impossible for theology. Theology, however, must be able to offer a reasonable and satisfactory response to what human beings encounter (adequacy) while also being consistent with the theological tradition out of which they are generated (appropriateness). Finally, because these two dimensions need to be held together in a fruitful bond, they must be congruent with one another.[76] When these three criteria are taken together, they form the core convictions of what Tracy calls a revisionist model of theology.[77]

The effort to develop such criteria exhibits a key feature of fundamental theology. Tradition is essential to theology, and fundamental theology is developed from within that tradition. Because fundamental theology is in large part concerned with establishing the grounds for theological claims in concert with secular modes of reason, however, its work "must be conducted on grounds other than [the theologian's] own or his community's vision of faith, or even his own or his community's defense of the continuing existential meaningfulness

---

[74] BRO 250n1.
[75] BRO 55.
[76] BRO 44, 70–73.
[77] BRO 22, 32–34. See also chapter 1, pp. 20–21.

of religious experience and language."[78] Its work on assessing and evaluating arguments leads fundamental theology to encounter other disciplines, particularly philosophy, and thus creates the basis on which the other subdisciplines of theology are built.[79]

Systematic theology: This second subdiscipline draws on the criteria of fundamental theology in order to delve into the doctrinal questions of a particular faith tradition. The standard questions in Christian systematic theology include (among others) the Trinity, soteriology, ecclesiology, and sacraments.[80] In the revisionist approach, traditional formulations of these areas are challenged and reconsidered, potentially undergoing a "hermeneutics of restoration" that factors in common human experience. The theologian must remain open to the possibility that certain formulations of traditional teachings may no longer communicate their underlying truth or meaning to contemporary persons, thus necessitating some translation.[81] Systematic theology is thus at heart concerned with the current moment and with making sense of a particular tradition for contemporary persons.[82]

Historical theology: Tracy described the primary task of historical theology as the reconstruction of texts.[83] Theology depends on historical investigation to determine its sources: the texts, events, symbols, and persons on which and whom theologians build their arguments. Historical theology thus reconstructs the very tradition that theologians work with.[84] The critical task of the historical theo-

---

[78] BRO 147.

[79] Tracy said his view of fundamental theology is roughly the same as the traditional task of "apologetic" theology. The difference, however, is that apologetics was concerned primarily with arguing for the foundational doctrines of theology—revelation, miracles, divine revealer, creation, faith and reason—while Tracy's fundamental theology focuses on the criteria used to judge these claims in light of common human experience (BRO 250n).

[80] BRO 238.

[81] BRO 238–39.

[82] This connects to Tracy's sense that the theologian's commitment to a particular faith tradition must be balanced with the public character of systematic theology. This insight, however, is only hinted at in BRO; its real consideration occurs in AI. BRO 250n1.

[83] Here, one can see echoes particularly of Lonergan's functional specialty "research." Cf. MT 127, 149–51.

[84] BRO 251n8.

logian "*qua* theologian is to decipher how and why past Christian meanings were meaningful and true for a particular cultural situation, and how and why such past meanings either are or are not meaningful and true today."[85] Thus, historical theologians work to make the meanings of texts derived from the tradition available in the present.[86]

Practical theology: This subdiscipline is principally concerned with *praxis*, which Tracy describes as "the critical relationship between theory and practice whereby each is dialectically influenced and transformed by the other."[87] Practical theology is thus focused on what can be done in order to live out the expectations of the tradition more authentically and fully. This is not to say that it's an individual-centered mode of ethics but rather a broader, more social approach. Here, he has in mind the various movements and approaches to liberation from oppressive regimes and systems.[88] Ultimately, practical theology seeks to transform the society and culture in which it is developed.

The organizing principle of this outline thus becomes clear. Under his revisionist model, Tracy arranges the subdisciplines largely on their orientation in time. The historical theologian investigates what past formulations from the tradition meant in their context and what implications that might have for the present. Fundamental theologians work on how theology is done overall, with particular concern for the production and judgment of arguments. Systematic theologians seek to reinterpret the tradition in light of contemporary realities. And practical theologians seek the sorts of future-oriented, transformative actions that the tradition calls for and that might change the world for the better. This *praxis* is rooted in both the *historia* of historical theology and the *theoria* of fundamental and systematic theologies.[89]

---

[85] BRO 239–40.

[86] BRO 240.

[87] BRO 243.

[88] Part of the influence for him here is critical theory and the Frankfurt School, particularly Adorno, Habermas, and Horkheimer, who each saw emancipation as part of the purpose for their philosophical work. When Tracy discusses the connection between theory and practice, this seems to be the primary *theory* he has in mind. Cf. BRO 245–47.

[89] BRO 240.

The Public Subdisciplines of The Analogical Imagination

In following the standard narrative around Tracy's method, commentators often overlook the differences between *Blessed Rage for Order* and *The Analogical Imagination*. As noted above, there is a sizable revision in method between the two, which is perhaps most pronounced with respect to the subdisciplines. Tracy's development of fundamental, systematic, and practical theologies is far more robust, particularly as he looks at the key dimensions that all three have in common. Most notable, he reorients the subdisciplines away from temporal trajectories to public audiences while sublating the task of historical theology into each of the subdisciplines themselves. Key to achieving this for Tracy is his formulation of main characteristics that define each of the three.

First (and most important) is that each subdiscipline has a primary reference group.[90] Fundamental theology is primarily oriented to the academy, systematic theology to the church, and practical theology to the wider society. It is important for Tracy to qualify these as "primary" reference groups, as each subdiscipline is capable of engaging the other two publics beyond its main one. For example, much of the careful work in systematic theology, even as it is oriented to the church, is done by intellectuals in the academy who are conversing with one another as well as with their faith traditions. This primary orientation helps to determine the other four characteristics that Tracy considers for each subdiscipline: the modes of argument each type of theology uses, the ethical commitments they hold, the reality and role of a particular theologian's faith within that type of theology, and how one understands the relationship between "meaning" and "truth."[91]

Fundamental theology: Like in *Blessed Rage for Order*, this subdiscipline is particularly concerned with the norms for argument in academic disciplines. In discussing the academy more broadly, Tracy's working claim is that various disciplines have generally agreed upon understandings of what constitutes criteria, evidence, and good argu-

---

[90] AI 56.

[91] AI 56. For a particularly good chart outlining Tracy's subdisciplines in AI, see Boyd Blundell, *Paul Ricoeur between Theology and Philosophy: Detour and Return* (Bloomington: Indiana University Press, 2010), 17.

mentation. This leads to a focus on methods and the procedures for assessing new approaches. While the internal conversations among intellectuals in these disciplines about the norms and methods are central to the academy, it is also necessary that academic disciplines be able to engage other publics. Put another way, the academy must try to show the relevance and impact of its work for people outside the academy. Moreover, intellectuals who work in specific disciplines ought also to seek opportunities to engage those in other disciplines, including providing grounds for their own criteria, evidence, and methods. Tracy regards such interdisciplinary conversations about the underlying intellectual commitments and assumptions as essential to the academic enterprise.

With regard to fundamental theology itself and its orientation to the academy, Tracy describes this subdiscipline as determining the status, norms, and methods of theology. The mode of argument is public in "the most usual meaning" of having to be open to any intelligent, reasonable, responsible person.[92] Conversation partners should be neither privileged nor excluded based on their religious commitments (or their lack of such commitments) because the claims made in fundamental theology should appeal to that interlocutor's experience, intelligence, rationality, and responsibility. While their religious commitments are not themselves at issue, they must share an ethical commitment to the process of critical inquiry. Fundamental theologians should follow their questions wherever they lead, even if that ends up challenging their religious, political, or other intellectual commitments. For Tracy, it's not about abandoning those commitments but holding them at enough of a distance to be able to critique them.

The result of this open and critical distancing is that the fundamental theologian approaches the relationship between "meaning" and "truth" by focusing on the "adequacy or inadequacy of the truth-claims, usually the cognitive claims, of a particular religious tradition" and of the contemporary situation.[93] Are these truth claims adequate to human experience? This question is more often argued in light of another discipline's methods rather than on the tradition's

---

[92] Here, one again hears the echoes of Bernard Lonergan's transcendental precepts.
[93] AI 58, 62.

own criteria. Typically, fundamental theologians have used philosophy as that other discipline, or perhaps the philosophical aspects of the social sciences or humanities.[94] For Tracy, this makes fundamental theology the theological subdiscipline that works out the basic methods of making theological claims and adjudicates the adequacy of particular claims. The success of any particular theological claims on this level depends on how well they engage with other disciplines, so many of the topics and issues that fundamental theology deals with are not particular to a given theological tradition. Rather, they are often topics that have relevance within and beyond the task of theology.

Systematic theology: Tracy retains systematic theology's close focus on the doctrinal questions of particular faith traditions, but he reframes its focus from a predominantly contemporary *theoria* to public wrestling with the tradition's classics. In part, this is driven by his sociological and theological lenses for understanding the public of the church.[95] Because the church is both a voluntary association of persons and the principal mediator of the human experience of Christ in the world,[96] systematic theology seeks to make sense of the beliefs, practices, and traditions that bind these people together within this mystical body. It is the believers, the members of the church, who are tasked with witnessing to and passing on to others the theological reality. Systematic theology participates in this by seeking to understand that reality in accord with its own public criteria, warrants, and methods.

Because of its orientation to the public of the church, systematic theology focuses on the central claims of particular faith traditions. In terms of its mode of argument, this subdiscipline focuses on the reinterpretation of a particular faith tradition in relation to the believing community's current context. Its public-ness, then, differs somewhat from fundamental theology's interdisciplinary approach; systematics works instead to mediate a given religious tradition

---

[94] AI 62.

[95] See above, chapter 1, pp. 28–30.

[96] AI 50, 236. Elsewhere, Tracy will describe the "tradition" as the primary mediator of this experience (AI 237). This indicates the close interweaving he sees between church and tradition.

within new contexts that the church might enter. At heart is the belief that the revelation to which the church witnesses has an "ever-present disclosive and transformative power" that can speak beyond its original context.[97] One can thus intelligibly speak of a tradition-specific systematic theology (Roman Catholic, Lutheran, or even Christian more broadly) because of its focus on a primary community and its beliefs and practices.[98] Successfully pursuing these lines of argument requires systematic theologians to be acutely aware of how they are located within a particular tradition.[99] They must take history seriously, as both they and the tradition are embedded in particular historical contexts and currents.

The place of the tradition in systematic theology is essential to discerning the ethical stance, the role of the faith of the theologian, and the relationship between meaning and truth. Tracy describes the systematic theologian's primary ethical stance as fidelity to a particular tradition. On one hand, this means that the theologian is a committed member of a given community, largely holding its beliefs and performing its practices. In contrast to the fundamental theologian, the systematic theologian's personal religious beliefs are both valid and necessary sources of argument.[100] On the other hand, this faithfulness is not simply mindless repetition or blind obedience;

---

[97] AI 57.

[98] Tracy does not explicitly raise the question of whether one might also talk of a Roman Catholic or Lutheran fundamental theology in AI. While he elsewhere compares fundamental theology to "apologetics" (BRO 25, 250n1), the difference for him is that fundamental theology "defends" criteria and evidence for making judgments in general, not the criteria or evidence for defending judgments particular to a given faith tradition. Thus one might argue that an ecumenical approach is more structurally built into Tracy's fundamental theology than his systematic theology (although the latter potentially remains open to ecumenical endeavors as well).

Relatedly, one might recognize a parallel between the relationship Tracy casts between fundamental and systematic theologies with Lonergan's general and special categories. The general categories correspond to the human concerns embodied in the contemporary situation while the special categories correspond specifically to Christian tradition. Matthew Lamb suggests that Tracy's method of critical correlation constitutes Tracy's appropriation of Lonergan's distinction between "general and special foundational theological categories" (Lamb, "David Tracy," 681). Cf. MT 271–81.

[99] AI 100.

[100] AI 67.

Tracy describes it as "critical and creative fidelity that takes the tradition seriously while grappling with its development in light of ever-new circumstances.[101] Finally, systematic theology builds on the "truth-bearing character of a particular religious tradition" and seeks to reappropriate those claims within the contemporary situation.[102] More explicitly than any other subdiscipline for Tracy, systematic theology is both embedded within a tradition and in the process of reinterpreting that tradition.[103]

Practical theology: This third and final subdiscipline is oriented to the public of the society. As the previous chapter showed, Tracy thinks of society as comprised of three "realms": the techno-economic, the political, and the cultural. While the former two emphasize instrumental and practical modes of reasoning, culture's focus is on the more elusive symbolic reasoning that engages the basic existential questions that members of society raise. This is evident in Tracy's focus on art and religion within this realm, as these two fields are essential to the larger symbolic system that animates culture. Tracy's ideal society seems to be one where symbolic reflection drives the values and commitments of practical reason, which in turn drive the logistical issues solved by instrumental reason.[104] Of course, this ideal is not always the case, and Tracy laments how symbolic reflection has often atrophied while being displaced by the other two, especially instrumental reason.[105]

The key point of consistency between *Blessed Rage for Order* and *The Analogical Imagination* is that Tracy emphasizes *praxis* as the focus of practical theology. Here, he describes the relationship of theory and practice within practical theology in terms of *praxis* as the "originating and self-correcting foundation" of theory, claiming that good theory depends on particular practices of integrity and critical thinking.[106] Practical theology, then, does take account of more theoretical claims of fundamental and systematic theologies, but he further suggests

---

[101] AI 57.

[102] AI 58.

[103] AI 104.

[104] AI 12–14.

[105] Although not upfront about it, Tracy seemed to suggest that the United States of the late twentieth and early twenty-first centuries falls into this "technocratic" trap (AI 8).

[106] AI 69.

that practical theology actually grounds *and* transforms the theoretical work.[107] The praxis of practical theology is therefore a mode less of arguing than of responding to specific issues in particular contexts that are deemed religiously significant.

Practical theology's orientation to society means that the practical theologian is both engaged with particular social-cultural issues and committed to a particular faith tradition. Tracy describes the practical theologian as having an ethical commitment to involvement in particular social issues, and he focuses especially on the call to be in solidarity with those who are in need of some form of liberation.[108] This may take the form of commitment to a particular praxis movement (e.g., base communities in Latin America, trade unions in Europe, human rights advocacy in Asia), and Tracy names Johann Baptist Metz, Jürgen Moltmann, Gustavo Gutierrez, James Cone, Rosemary Radford Ruether, and Juan Luis Segundo as examples of this.[109] While it is true that anyone could practice such solidarity,

---

[107] AI 57. The extent to which this claim is modeled in Tracy's own work is questionable. One could reasonably read his career trajectory as treating practical theology as an afterthought, given the comparatively sparse treatment he gives it. Beyond the sections in BRO and AI, Tracy's fullest considerations of practical theology are David Tracy, "Revisionist Practical Theology and the Meaning of Public Discourse," *Pastoral Psychology* 26, no. 2 (Winter 1977): 83–94; Tracy, "The Foundations of Practical Theology," 61–82; Tracy, "Practical Theology in the Situation of Global Pluralism," 139–54; and Tracy, "A Correlational Model of Practical Theology Revisited," 49–61.

[108] AI 70.

[109] AI 57. Tracy's highlighting of figures often associated with "contextual" theologies, such as political, liberation, and feminist theologians, has led to a critique that Tracy only sees them as practical theologians while ignoring or overlooking their contributions as fundamental and systematic theologians (see especially Dwight N. Hopkins, *Being Human: Race, Culture, and Religion* [Princeton, NJ: Fortress Press, 2005], 16–23). Such figures seem to be simply prophets within the implicitly normative Western theological tradition. This critique, coupled with Tracy's generally limited engagement with practical theology, contributes to a larger sense that Tracy is not seriously engaged with such thought.

With respect to the theoretical contributions of these other theologians, it is clear that Tracy could do more to engage those seriously (they are largely absent from his work on fundamental and systematic theology, particularly in the 1970s and 1980s), and he could be more attentive to the contextual nature of his own theological work. He did on occasion note his own social location as a "white, male, middle class, and academic" person (DWO 6), but he also tended to lump "political, liberation, and feminist theologies" together without any real distinction or nuance.

It is also worth noting, however, that Tracy does mention that fundamental and practical theologies often intersect, stating, "For many theologians of liberation, for

Tracy argues that the practical theologian's work must be specifically rooted in their social location as members of particular faith traditions and communities. Thus, like for the systematic theologian, religious commitment is a necessary part of the practical theologian's work.

Finally, the understanding of meaning and truth in practical theology is further shaped by the emphasis on praxis. Here, Tracy focuses on truth as a "praxis-determined, transformative" notion that acknowledges the priority of involvement over theory.[110] Practical theology thus explores situations of what he calls "systemic distortion" (e.g., sexism, racism, classism, elitism) in order to determine whether they require theological analysis and a religious response. Put another way, Tracy connects the search for truth in practical theology to the idea of "faith working through love."[111] The theoretical truths worked out by fundamental theology and reinterpreted in systematic theology are thus both grounded on and focused toward practical theology's commitment to situations of praxis.

Development of Tracy: Review of the three subdisciplines in *The Analogical Imagination* reveals how they differ in three significant ways from *Blessed Rage for Order*. First, they are far more substantially developed. In *Blessed Rage for Order*, the description of systematic, historical, and practical theologies is almost entirely left to the final chapter, almost as an appendix to the work of fundamental theology. The process of mutually critical correlation takes place in each subdiscipline, and each one is identified as a hermeneutical exercise that depends on classics and the contemporary situation.

Second, the subdiscipline of historical theology drops out on its own effort. Tracy instead reconceives the historical impulse as part of each of the other subdisciplines. Thus, instead of historical theology doing the history and fundamental, systematic, and practical theolo-

---

example, it follows that the major problematic of most forms of fundamental theology, the problem of the truth-status of the cognitive claims of both Christianity and modernity, cannot in principle be resolved by better theories" (AI 70). Here, he draws on the Lonerganian parallel that intellectual, moral, and religious conversion are the foundation of constructive theology (what Lonergan refers to as "mediated" theology) in recognizing the correctness of these "praxis" theologians' effective advocacy for the priority of lived experience to theoretical reflection.

[110] AI 58.

[111] AI 87n37.

gies doing constructive work in the present and for the future, each of his three subdisciplines in *The Analogical Imagination* has both a historical and a constructive dimension.[112] Tracy recognized that he had made this change in *The Analogical Imagination*, describing it as a "more relatively adequate formulation of the role of 'historical theology'. . . . in *every* theological discipline."[113] Although he argues that this is not a "substantive change" to his method, this claim can be disputed on two grounds. First, it makes the other three subdisciplines significantly more robust in terms of their connection to tradition and to their work in the contemporary situation.[114] Second, as Tracy himself notes, he has shifted from identifying the subdisciplines in terms of "modes of temporality" to modes of public-ness.[115]

Indeed, that last shift is arguably the most important and dramatic of the changes Tracy makes to his method. Fundamental, systematic, and practical theologies have distinct questions and commitments, but even more so they are focused on distinct audiences. The public-ness hinted at for systematic theology in *Blessed Rage for Order* expands into the full-blown public-ness of all theology, even as different subdisciplines concern themselves primarily (but not exclusively) with particular publics. Fundamental theology is written for and in conversation with the academy primarily, while systematic theology goes with the church and practical theology with the wider society. This reorientation shows that the basic organizing principle of his theological method has changed to public-ness, that the core principles underlying theology's public character (universality of God and ubiquity of fundamental questions)[116] are at stake for all types of theology, and that all modes of theology are anchored in their

---

[112] AI 56. Comparison to Lonergan might be helpful here: whereas one might distinguish "mediating theology" as more historically focused and "mediated theology" as more contemporary and constructive, with functional specialties fitting into one or the other, Tracy places a historical and a constructive dimension in each of the three subdisciplines.

[113] AI 84–85n28.

[114] Matthew Lamb is even more emphatic in his insistence that this reorganization of the theological subdisciplines in AI increases the significance of history in Tracy's theological method; he connects this to Tracy's increased reflections "on the diverse social contexts in which theology is practiced" (Lamb, "David Tracy," 689).

[115] AI 84–85n28.

[116] See chapter 1, p. 22.

tradition but also engaged in issues and conversations that are distinct from those traditions.

Returning to the Question of the Publics

The important role the subdisciplines of fundamental, systematic, and practical theology play in Tracy's thought returns the focus to the question of public theology. There are several critiques of Tracy that focus on the relationship between public theology and theological method. The first of these is that Tracy's conception of publicness is ultimately self-defeating when it comes to the purpose of theology. Noting the centrality of argument, criteria, and evidence in Tracy's view of the publics, Timoteo Gener argues that Tracy prioritizes "non-religious criteria . . . over against the public appeal of systematic theology."[117] True public discussion is essentially nonreligious philosophy, and thus only fundamental theology is truly public.[118] It is possible that his privileging of fundamental theology and the public of the academy are tied to his own long career in academic theology.[119] Gener calls instead for a public theology that, while not kept solely within the churches (a move Tracy clearly agrees with), nonetheless moves outward missiologically, seeking to transform the world through communicating the prophetic message at the core of the Christian scriptural tradition.[120] Gener thus wants a stronger systematic and practical theology than Tracy offers while also resisting Tracy's privileging of secular reason as the standard by which public argument is judged.

A second critique follows similar lines, emphasizing the issue of the "ordinary or normal meaning" of the term "public."[121] Owen Thomas argues that the emphasis on arguments, criteria, and evidence that "any reasonable person would accept" certainly means that systematic or dogmatic theology cannot really be considered public, at least not in this "normal" sense. But pushing beyond this,

---

[117] Gener, "With/Beyond Tracy," 130.

[118] Gener, "With/Beyond Tracy," 133.

[119] Kristen Heyer offers a similar objection, claiming that Tracy is fairly thin on engaging the public of the church; see Heyer, "How Does Theology Go Public," 322.

[120] Gener, "With/Beyond Tracy," 135–36.

[121] Thomas, "Public Theology and Counter-Public Spheres," 456.

Thomas also highlights the postmodern and liberationist critiques of reason, which emphasize both the deeply contextualized character of what is seen as "reasonable" as well as the implications of power on discourse and the way that marginalized groups are excluded from the "discussion table."[122] Thomas notes that both of these issues are ones Tracy attended to, particularly in texts published after the public theology of *The Analogical Imagination*, but also that Tracy continues to uphold the necessity of this public approach to reason and argument within plural and ambiguous conversations.

A third critique is that of Jürgen Habermas, who similarly focuses on the character of fundamental theology. His concern has a different focus, arguing that if one aims to provide warrants and arguments that are available to all reasonable persons without the explicit faith claims of a particular tradition, then it's not clear that "theology" is actually adding anything to the conversation. Religion seems generally to include faith commitments, not just reason. Thus to set those faith commitments aside in order to engage the wider audience of the intelligent, reasonable, responsible removes what is distinct about religion. For Habermas, it is therefore unclear what is "theological" about fundamental theology at all.[123] T. Howland Sanks notes that some of Tracy's postliberal critics are concerned precisely with this issue and the possibility that theology will simply be subsumed under a modern, liberal, rationalist project.[124]

These three critiques help to delineate core issues in the relationship between public-ness and method in theology: the relationship of faith and reason, the role of context and particularity, and the limitations of academic theology. In response it is worth highlighting three key points here. First, Tracy's approach to truth and reason largely focuses on the manifestation/transformation view of truth,

[122] Thomas, "Public Theology and Counter-Public Spheres," 462–65. This critique can be connected to Dwight Hopkins's critique of Tracy on liberation theologies and where they fit within Tracy's subdisciplines noted above. See Hopkins, *Being Human*, 20–23.

[123] Jürgen Habermas, "Transcendence from Within, Transcendence Within This World," in *Habermas, Modernity, and Public Theology*, ed. Don Browning and Francis Schüssler Fiorenza (New York: Crossroad, 1992), 230–33.

[124] T. Howland Sanks, "David Tracy's Theological Project: An Overview and Some Implications," *Theological Studies* 54, no. 4 (December 1993): 725.

whereby what is true is disclosed and encountered in life and reso-nates as fundamentally true. When he speaks about the classics and disclosure of the "whole" or the "infinite," this is the model he has in mind. Tying this to his approach to public argument, evidence, and criteria shows that he is not simply considering manifestation or transformation as a relativistic "I'm okay, you're okay" approach to truth. Rather, that manifestation must be defended and argued for. It is not limited to propositionalist or correspondence approaches to truth (more comparable to a mathematical proof than a personal epiphany), but it adapts the concern from those approaches for in-ternal, logical coherence and nonsolipsistic evidentiary support. This complex approach to truth draws on the Catholic tradition's com-mitment to both faith and reason; it does not sever them.

What does this mean for the relative public-ness of fundamental, systematic, and practical theologies? It is true that Tracy does not think one must have a faith commitment to engage in fundamental theology, or at least that one does not use one's faith commitment as a primary source of warrant for theological argument. It is also not the case, however, that fundamental theology has no interest in the-ology at all. Habermas misunderstands Tracy's point, which is not only that religious traditions can make claims but more so that it must be able to articulate the grounds on which one might consider religious claims to be reasonable. Why is it possible that a person might hold these beliefs and yet not be considered irrational? This is essential to fundamental theology's task. It seeks to persuade not the inevitable truth of such claims but rather that such claims can be reasonably held. Further, the very motivation for trying to make this case comes from the religious tradition. Tracy argues that the task of theology making an argument for itself on public, rational, nonreli-gious grounds is evident already in Paul's Letter to the Romans and his Areopagus speech in Acts.[125] He further cites Justin Martyr, Augustine, and Thomas Aquinas as theologians who sought in

---

[125] Cf. Rom 1:20-21: "Ever since the creation of the world, his invisible attributes of eternal power and divinity have been able to be understood and perceived in what he has made. As a result, they have no excuse; for although they knew God they did not accord him glory as God or give him thanks. Instead, they became vain in their reasoning, and their senseless minds were darkened."

various ways to make the case for Christianity to non-Christians on rational grounds.[126]

Moreover, because systematic and practical theologies also maintain the relationship between faith and reason, they too are tasked with making arguments and disclosing truths that may have a transformative impact on one's life. Tracy recognizes that they are public in a way somewhat different from fundamental theology—they do assume commitments to specific religious traditions. Yet this particularity does not make them nonpublic, as all publics are particular and have concrete contexts. This is true of any society, any academy, any church: there is a real, not imagined, public that is the audience and setting of such discussions, and these audiences have general (sometimes explicit, sometimes unsaid) norms about what counts as a good argument. There are implicit power dynamics that shape the conversations of all such publics, which typically does limit the participation of those without power, credentials, or access. That each public can be more inclusive, or at least more representative, is an ideal to which to aspire, not an indictment that it has failed to be public.

Indeed, in contrast to Gener and Heyer, Gaspar Martinez has argued that systematic theology is the "touchstone" of Tracy's public theology.[127] Public-ness is expressed through particularity, and thus the particularity of a given religious commitment becomes one route to genuine public-ness rather than an obstacle. The centrality of classics to this approach to public theology necessitates that such expressions be highly particular. Even the apparent openness of the public-ness in fundamental theology, which is associated with the academy, must be considered in light of the relative narrowness of the academy in terms of its participants, its goals, and its generally accepted modes of argument. Academic discourse can be so rarefied as to be inaccessible to nonexperts; one might then push back both on Thomas's critique and Tracy himself and ask whether academic discourse is really public in the generally accepted sense. Thus, one might instead recognize the particularities of the specific instances of the publics, the emphasis on making a critically engaging presentation of one's claims within that context, and allowing for the

---

[126] AI 63–64.
[127] Martinez, *Confronting the Mystery of God*, 197.

possibility that, like the classics and the fragments, one's claims within that public might be comprehensible and even disclosive beyond the confines of their initial particularities.

One possible issue at hand is a misunderstanding about the relation between theological subdisciplines and their primary reference groups, which we can see in two aspects. First, while the three publics are distinct, they are also interrelated and mutually condition one another. The theologian is not only a member of one public and responsible to one public but instead is responsible to all three. With Tracy himself, it is true that the vast majority of his work is focused on questions of academic theology and was produced for other academic theologians. Much of what he wrote fits most comfortably under the heading of fundamental theology than it does of systematic or practical theology. On the other hand, though, it would be inaccurate to suggest he ignored systematic theology in general or the church in particular. The church occupies an important part of the work of *The Analogical Imagination*, and he made substantial contributions to the volume *Parish, Priest, and People*.[128] Moreover, he was also an active member of his parish, St. Thomas in Hyde Park, and a well-regarded homilist. Tracy wrote about the church, composed systematic theology, and exercised a pastoral role. While it is certainly true that the church and systematic theology are not Tracy's primary focus, to limit his contributions as only being academic, fundamental theology is at best reductionistic.

Conclusion

Conversation is the linchpin to Tracy's theological method. It provides an apt metaphor for thinking through the approach of his method and the various subdisciplines he identifies, but it also explains why his method develops and adjusts over time. While Tracy himself claimed that *Blessed Rage for Order* and *The Analogical Imagination* were intended to be the first two books of a trilogy, in hindsight

---

[128] William C. McCready et al., *Parish, Priest and People: New Leadership for the Local Church* (Chicago: Thomas More, 1981). Tracy was responsible for writing the chapters "Systematic Theology of the Local Community," "Theological Reflection on Local Religious Leadership," and "Local Religious Leadership and Social Justice."

it is difficult to read them this way. Not only did an intended third volume on practical theology never materialize, but the second volume proposes a creative and effective revision of the method outlined in the first. These improvements derived from the influences of other scholars and the conversations Tracy engaged with, and the development of his method actually continued in his later texts.

These conversations are intimately tied to the publics where those conversations take place. Tracy theorized a set of relationships among the publics, distinguished based on the types of conversations, the kinds of arguments and evidence they considered, and the religious and ethical commitments of their participants. Yet he has also participated in a variety of those conversations himself, seeking to model in an imperfect way their concerns while simultaneously engaging and highlighting other figures who sought to do the same. The concept of the public is the organizational linchpin to Tracy's theological method, and thus critical engagement with one cannot be separated from critical engagement with the other.

3

The Classic and the Fragment

So story is real. And music is real, and what is real is an icon of our Creator. . . . A Bach fugue is for me an icon of this reality, and so with my often inadequate fingers I struggle at the piano, in order to get myself back into reality.

—Madeleine L'Engle[1]

As the previous chapter showed, Tracy sees theology as a conversational endeavor between a religious tradition and the contemporary context in which it finds itself. At that level, this conversation can seem abstract, even ephemeral, which for some is a source of difficulty in reading Tracy. To see theology this way, however, misunderstands a core piece of his approach. As a hermeneutical theologian, he is concerned with the process of interpretation, especially with the particular objects that are being interpreted.

The objects of interpretation Tracy focuses on are not chosen at random. Rather, he highlights what he considers the most central, compelling, and challenging sources. Initially calling them classics, he looks to these as revelatory expressions of truth that have resonance beyond the time, place, and tradition that gave them birth. While the vast majority of classics that Tracy focuses on are texts, he also recognizes that the timeless and powerful disclosure of truth can

[1] Madeleine L'Engle, *And It Was Good: Reflections on Beginnings* (New York: Convergent Books, 2017), 48.

be found in beautiful musical performances, major historical events, and lives well lived.

The classic is so central to Tracy's early thought and method that it has practically become synonymous with him. It is also, however, a conceptual tool that he has slowly moved away from, to the point that "classic" almost disappears entirely from his later essays. This is due to a number of factors, including the class implications of calling something a "classic," the challenges of everyday, nonelite sources for theological reflection, and the continuing impact of postmodern modes of thought. These issues lead not to a complete abandonment of the classic, though, but rather its revision and transformation into the *fragment*.

This chapter presents the history of Tracy's classics and fragments. Analysis of his descriptions of these terms will show that both of these concepts describe human expressions that are capable of revealing something universal precisely through their intensified particularity. Yet the term "classic," and Tracy's appropriation of it, come with some elitist connotations that he seeks to overcome by using the "fragment." Furthermore, his insight into the particular as revealing the universal is intimately tied to a fundamentally sacramental worldview that is partially determinative of his approach to theology as conversation.

The Classic in *Blessed Rage for Order*

The classic and its role in theological method are already percolating in Tracy's *Blessed Rage for Order*. As noted in the previous chapter, *Blessed Rage for Order* proposes a method of critical correlation between common human experience and the Christian tradition.[2] In trying to describe this "Christian tradition," he focuses on the role of "symbols and texts of our common life and of Christianity."[3] On one hand, he recognizes that an interpretation of the Christian tradition would need to take into account "symbols, rituals, events, witnesses" as well as texts.[4] On the other hand, he notes that the interpretive

---

[2] BRO 43–46; see chapter 2, pp. 44–48.
[3] BRO 3, 49.
[4] BRO 15n5.

approach he outlines for investigating texts would need serious modifications in order to apply to sources other than texts.[5]

Thus, Tracy's primary sources for investigating the Christian tradition are typically texts. Yet these are not just any texts but rather the "classical Christian texts," those "basic texts of Christian self-understanding."[6] These are the ones that best represent the core commitments, the essential rituals, and the central figures of the Christian tradition. These texts take priority over others because they ground the Christian tradition and shape the trajectory in which the tradition develops.[7] In more than one instance, Tracy uses the phrase "charter document" to describe the essential role of classic texts in founding and perpetuating a tradition.[8]

Tracy's use of the term "classical" here is suggestive of the influence of Hans-Georg Gadamer. In his *Truth and Method*, Gadamer described the classical in the context of tradition. Instead of using "classical" to distinguish a specific period of history that is often held up for acclaim, Gadamer instead uses "classical" as a *normative* judgment that a particular work of art or a text is historically and culturally significant. He argues that the classical endures the ongoing process of being handed through tradition and "allows something true . . . to come into being."[9] This insight about the classical shapes Tracy's adoption of "classical" to describe the essential texts of the Christian tradition. Tracy, however, has not yet fully worked out his particular understanding of what the classic means, and in many ways his use of the term is perhaps more colloquial than technical in *Blessed Rage for Order*.[10]

---

[5] Tracy somewhat lamely notes that limiting this interpretation to texts might be acceptable since Christianity is a "religion of the word" that takes the Scriptures "as at least its charter document" (BRO 15n5).

[6] BRO 49.

[7] Cf. MT 161.

[8] Cf. BRO 59–60n33.

[9] Hans-Georg Gadamer, *Truth and Method* (Bloomsbury Academic, 2004), 288.

[10] Tracy first begins to work this out in his article, "Modes of Theological Argument," *Theology Today* 33, no. 4 (January 1977): 389–92. The key effort in that text is to work on the criteria developed in BRO and how those might shape the role of the classic in a systematic theology. Subsequent refinements of the classic prior to AI can be found in David Tracy, "Theological Classics in Contemporary Theology," *Theology Digest* 25 (Winter 1977): 347–55; and "Theological Pluralism and Analogy," *Thought* 54 (1979): 24–37.

The Classic in *The Analogical Imagination*

By the time Tracy writes *The Analogical Imagination*, the "classic" has become an indispensable part of his approach to interpretation and his theological method. Two full chapters are devoted to explaining the classic and the *religious* classic.[11] Herein he gives his basic description of the classic as an expression that arises from within a tradition and that discloses both an excess and a permanence of meaning.[12] A closer look at the different aspects of this definition can offer a clearer sense of what Tracy intends.

First, the classic is an expression. As was true in *Blessed Rage for Order*, Tracy usually has texts in mind as his default form of expression. Most of the examples that Tracy calls classics are texts, and most of his theological work focuses on surveying arguments by other authors (in texts) over what other texts should be considered classics. Moreover, when he outlines his four stages of interpretation, he gives pride of place to the text as an object of interpretation.

Tracy's privileging of texts does not, however, ultimately rule out other forms of expression. Indeed, Tracy recognized the risk that theologians are "a largely word-oriented bunch" who must remember "the power and the limits of word."[13] Indeed, humans interpret not only texts but also paintings, songs, movies, and even the experiences that make up our lives. Tracy thus often cites the litany of "texts, events, images, rituals, symbols and persons" as sources of potential candidates for classic status.[14] Moreover, Tracy sees a close alignment between religion and art, describing both as indispensable to the realm of culture when he investigated the public of society. This further demonstrates his recognition that nontextual works of art could be considered classics. Finally, Tracy argues that the fundamental classic of the Christian tradition is not a text at all but rather the *event* and *person* of Jesus Christ.[15]

---

[11] Chapters 3–4 of AI, respectively.

[12] AI 68, 102.

[13] William M. Shea, David B. Burrell, Bernard J. Cooke, and William J. O'Brien, "Review Symposium," *Horizons* 8, no. 2 (Fall 1981): 330.

[14] AI 100, 108. Bernard Cooke highlights this as one of the strengths of Tracy's classic, as it "substantially enrich[es] our understanding of Christian tradition and of its relation to scripture." See Shea et al., "Review Symposium," 324.

[15] AI 233. A fair question one might ask about classics and texts is whether it is possible to have *access* to these other kinds of classics without texts. For example,

Second, these expressions arise from within a tradition. In one sense, tradition refers to a particular set of beliefs, attitudes, and practices that are handed down generation to generation. In this sense, the tradition is a *tradita*: an object or a thing that can be passed down. When tradition is seen in this way, all that is necessary is consistent, continual repetition of what was done before. These older formulations do not change, and there's no real sense that the *tradita* can be subject to critical inquiry or engagement. Because it's a clear, objective deposit, there's no sense that new cultural or historical situations might offer different, even challenging, insights into the tradition. Tracy sometimes calls this view "traditionalism," claiming it is a truncated and problematic approach to thinking about tradition.

In another sense, tradition refers to the process of passing on itself. While the particular beliefs, attitudes, and practices are important for the tradition, so too are the ways in which these are handed on to the next generation. This view emphasizes *traditio*, the activity of handing on particular traditions. Because this notion of tradition foregrounds the way one generation passes to another, it is better able to account for how changes in history, culture, and context might impact that tradition. The specific traditions are translated into their new context.[16] In fact, these traditions are themselves historical realities that develop, have particular but changeable trajectories, and engage with their ever-unfolding contexts.[17]

Tracy sometimes uses the life of Saint Francis of Assisi as an example of a classic *person*. In the present day, however, our access to that life depends on texts, including biographies of Francis, collections of his sayings, and reports of his spiritual impact on others. Perhaps one might say that this debate depends on how narrowly or broadly one means the word "text"—St. Francis is also known through oral tradition, children's stories, statues, and stained-glass windows. The first two depend clearly on shared language, but there's not a singular or clear *text* underlying them. The latter two, however, are nontextual works of art. Further, when Tracy describes the life of St. Francis as a classic, he means the *person* himself, not necessarily any specific text or artwork that refers to that life. Thus for many, the encounter with the classic of St. Francis will come primarily through classic rituals of prayer and devotion.

[16] AI 99–100.

[17] Here, one can see the influence of Lonergan, in particular his distinction between "classicist" and "empirical" views of culture. The former, with its notion of "universal and permanent" achievement, contrasts with the latter's recognition of ongoing change, progress, and decline. Traditionalism fits into the classicist notion of culture, while *traditio* is more empirical (MT xi).

Third, classics carry what Tracy calls an excess and permanence of meaning. To say that their meaning is excessive means that there is no single, definitive interpretation for any given classic. Instead, such a classic constantly invites, even requires, reinterpretation. Its questions must be asked again and again, in new historical and cultural contexts, and so must the responses those questions provoke. Since the classic cannot be interpreted in a final, once-and-for-all fashion, there is always the possibility of it speaking truthfully anew. This gives the classic its permanence: classics are not *timeless*, but rather have a "permanent timeliness."[18] Because of this timeliness, a particular classic can also have a profound effect on the shape and development of the tradition that generates the classic.[19] Indeed, the excess and permanence of meaning in a classic grounds the possibility that it could bear meaning for persons in other traditions. Perhaps a Muslim who reads Aquinas's *Summa Contra Gentiles* will be deeply affected by his description of monotheism, or a Western architect who views the Sheikh Lotfallah Mosque in Iran will be taken with how the interior of the dome draws the eyes ever upward. In these and other cases, the classic expresses a profound truth that is, in principle, open to any intelligent, reasonable, and responsible person.[20]

[18] AI 102.

[19] For example, consider the impact of Augustine's *On the Trinity* or *City of God* on the development of the Christian tradition after Augustine. These texts remain classics within that tradition, but they also shape its development and the production of various other classics later on.

Lonergan describes this idea in terms of the classics "ground[ing] a tradition. They create the milieu in which they are studied and interpreted" (MT 161–62). While Lonergan's discussion of the classic is relatively sparse, its place within Lonergan's functional specialty of "interpretation" suggests a clear line of influence for Tracy. For more on the influence of Lonergan's *Method*, see chapter 2, pp. 55–58, on Tracy's development of method.

[20] Cf. AI 233. The ability of the classic to speak beyond its tradition raises the issue of context in a serious way. Insofar as Western culture is widely marked by a consumerist worldview, there exists the widespread practice of shearing religious symbols and other classics from the context that originally gave them meaning (cf. Vincent Miller, *Consuming Religion* [New York: Continuum, 2004]). For Tracy, the interpretation of the classic ought to take seriously its original context, just as the encounter with another person ought to take seriously that person's concrete historicity. Yet he also wants to maintain that if an expression is really a classic, then it must be able to speak beyond the confines of its own tradition.

Fourth, despite resisting a definitive interpretation, Tracy's classic nonetheless provokes interpretation.[21] It pushes its reader, its hearer, its viewer to come to some understanding of its meaning. This provocation is what leads Tracy to outline four key moments that he sees in interpreting the classic.[22] The first moment begins with the interpreter's pre-understanding. We do not encounter classics as blank slates but instead bring with us our past experiences and knowledge. Thus, on reading a classic text for the first time, I might also have in my mind my preconceptions about that text (e.g., I've heard it's a very difficult text, I've already seen the movie version of it, I know that book is my crush's favorite). I might already have some questions or opinions that shape how I encounter it. I might already know a great deal about the classic, including the life of the genius who produced it or its significance for later works. Because this variety of ideas are swirling about in my mind already, I bring them with me when I first engage with the classic.[23]

The second moment is the actual first encounter with the classic. Tracy says that the genuine classic *claims* the interpreter's attention. It provokes, elicits, even demands an interpretation.[24] The experience of being drawn in by the classic might take a variety of forms, "ranging from a haunting sense of resonance and import to a shock of recognition, that sheer event-like thatness," that challenge interpreters in their horizons and offers the possibility of viewing reality in a

---

[21] Here, Tracy seems to diverge from Gadamer on the idea of interpretation and the classic. Gadamer, following Hegel, suggests that the classical is self-interpreting: "The classical preserves itself precisely *because* it is significant in itself and interprets itself. . . . It says something to the present as if it were said specifically to it" (Gadamer, *Truth and Method*, 290). It's not clear that Gadamer rejects the process of interpretation, particularly in terms of coming to understanding as a fusion of horizons, of a classic; instead, he seems to be advocating for the classical as something that communicates itself as classical. Put another way, the classical is self-evidently classical.

[22] Although Tracy describes this process in reference to texts, he believes that these four moments can, at least in principle, be applied to nontext classics like works of art or major events.

[23] AI 118–19.

[24] On this, John Vissers says that Tracy grants the classic "a kind of self-authenticating status," as only the expression that is able to claim enduring and trans-contextual attention should be considered classics (John A. Vissers, "Interpreting the Classic: The Hermeneutical Character of David Tracy's Theology in *The Analogical Imagination*," *Calvin Theological Journal* 25, no. 2 [November 1990]: 198).

new or different way.[25] Going further, Tracy claims that not only does the interpreter interpret the classic but the classic interprets the interpreter. It raises questions for the interpreter about him or herself. In authentic conversation, the individual participants cannot control or manipulate the experience but instead find that it liberates them from their prepared expectations. The interpreter becomes freed from his or her own preconception. Engaging the classic becomes risky, precisely because the interpreter's self-understanding is made subject to change. Even if the interpreter decides to reject the claim made by the classic, this encounter can still disclose a genuinely different possibility that the interpreter is consciously choosing to reject.[26]

In the third moment, the classic grips the interpreter, turning the encounter into something like a game. In a game, one who is truly playing loses any sense of self-consciousness. The player is given over to the game, to its object, and to its purposes. The focus becomes the object at hand rather than the one playing. By giving oneself over to the game, one enters "the zone," allowing the game itself to dictate the direction of play.[27] Analogously, consider actors performing on stage. When an actor becomes self-conscious, aware of performing a role in front of an audience, it ruins the performance for everyone. The purpose of the actor is to break open his or her role and the world it inhabits for the audience and the other actors. Similarly, for the interpreter, the focus is on the subject matter of the given classic, "the 'world' disclosed in front of the text through the text's form."[28]

Finally, in the fourth moment, the interpreter engages with the wider community of interpretation. These classics do not exist in a vacuum; they come from particular times and traditions and have a history of being interpreted by others. One may have a particular take or reading of that classic, but this will both be challenged by how others have read it and challenge those alternative readings. This mutual challenge opens up new avenues of conversation and

---

[25] AI 119.

[26] AI 119–20. Here, Tracy draws on Lonergan's sense that the classic text may challenge its reader, not only to a "broadening of his horizon," but also to "an intellectual, moral, religious conversion" (MT 161).

[27] Cf. Vissers, "Interpreting the Classic," 199.

[28] AI 101, 120.

unfolds potentially new insights into those classics.[29] Taken together, these four moments highlight how Tracy sees interpretation as an ongoing conversation with the classics and with the history of effects of those classics.[30]

While the discussion so far has focused heavily on the reception of classics by their interpreters, this cannot be divorced from their production.[31] Tracy describes two key elements to the production of classics, which he calls *intensification* and *distanciation*. The first, intensification, means that the classic is not a mundane, everyday expression of truth. Rather, it is a radical experience of truth that can reveal the boundaries of everyday life. The classic is an expression that reveals potentially life-altering possibilities, and that can provoke the interpreter to transcend his or her current horizon. As a result, intensification can be demanding, even unpredictable, and what Tracy calls the "journey of intensification" is both desirable and frightening.[32] Indeed, not every text, image, person, etc., that aspires to the level of the classic will achieve it; Tracy says that those individuals who do are the ones we describe as geniuses, heroes, and saints.[33]

The second element of production, distanciation, refers to the creator of the classic surrendering control over it. The classic is released, which allows for the truth disclosed in the classic to be expressed to its potential interpreters. This move is necessary in order "to render . . . a communicable, shareable, public meaning."[34] Distanciation typically occurs with the text when it is published, with the film when it is released to the audience, and with the painting when it is displayed.[35] Similarly, in the example of the classic life, distanciation takes the form of death; for example, saints can be genu-

---

[29] AI 120–21.

[30] AI 100–101.

[31] While Tracy focuses in AI mostly on reception of the classic, describing this as the "major argument of the book," it's worth noting that criticism of the classic often centers on production. This is evident immediately in his exchange with David Burrell (Shea et al., "Review Symposium," 319–23, 333). Yet it is perhaps most manifest in Tracy's own critique and refinement of the classic in PA, as he notes the issues of elitist production of the classic.

[32] AI 125.

[33] AI 125.

[34] AI 126.

[35] Of course, each of these allows for exceptions, including texts being recalled or revised, films being edited or recut, or paintings being touched up later.

inely recognized as such only after their death.[36] So long as the classic expression remains under the control of its creator, it eludes the final form that interpreters will engage with through the various moments of interpretation. Indeed, creators who are unable to cede control of their works have often undermined their reception.[37]

Finally, Tracy builds on this notion of the classic in order to ask what makes a *religious* classic. In the religious classic, the truth that is disclosed is a profound sense of the otherness of what Tracy calls "the whole," a sense that Tracy characterizes as an experience of "radical mystery."[38] The notion that the classic can demand attention from an interpreter is understood in the religious classic to mean that it elicits "a heightened awareness of the reality of what Otto named the 'numinous.'"[39] This claim by the religious classic is not just the claim of a good idea that tugs at your mind. Rather, this disclosure of the reality of the whole that Tracy claims takes place in the religious classic is a disclosure *from* the whole as well. The religious classic is "a genuine manifestation of the whole from the reality of that whole itself."[40] The excess and permanence of meaning in the religious classic comes from the very mystery that such a classic seeks to give expression to.

---

[36] Although related to the Catholic definition of a saint as one who is in heaven, there is a larger point here for Tracy. The meaning of one's life is not completed until death. It remains possible, for example, that one who lives an unholy life may have the sort of late-in-life conversion that leads to being recognized as a classic person. It is only after that life is completed that one can begin to make such judgments.

[37] For example, many believe that the later revisions and alterations made by George Lucas to the original *Star Wars* trilogy have undermined the classic status of the films, in no small part because Lucas has made it so difficult to get access to quality reproductions of the original theatrical releases. This has led to the odd situation where the National Film Registry, which picked the original 1977 release of *Star Wars* for historical preservation, does not have a copy of the film to preserve. See Rose Eveleth, "The *Star Wars* George Lucas Doesn't Want You to See," *The Atlantic*, August 27, 2014, https://www.theatlantic.com/technology/archive/2014/08/the-star-wars-george-lucas-doesnt-want-you-to-see/379184/.

For more on distanciation, see Paul Ricoeur, "The Hermeneutic Function of Distanciation," in *Hermeneutics and the Human Sciences* (New York: Cambridge University Press, 1981).

[38] AI 168–69. As will be shown in the final chapter of this text, throughout AI and its contemporary essays, "the whole" serves as a generic reference for the idea of God.

[39] AI 169.

[40] AI 172.

Critiquing the Classic

Despite the central role the classic plays in *The Analogical Imagination*, Tracy's follow-up text, *Plurality and Ambiguity*, quickly shows his concerns about the term "classic" and its implications. This text continues his focus on hermeneutics and interpretation as essential to theology by more explicitly framing theological method as conversation. In doing so, he retains the important role of the classic, but he also recognizes that these expressions can often be elitist or detached from the lived experience of the faithful.

It will be valuable at this point to recall the previous chapter's claim about the evolution of Tracy's theological method. *Plurality and Ambiguity* takes the reality of conversation as its central concern, making it the lens through which he sees interpretation, tradition, the publics, and method. Indeed, recasting his previous view of method (mutually critical correlation) into conversation is a quite natural development, one that more fully describes the theologian as participating in the back-and-forth between religious tradition and contemporary context. It is this possibility of back-and-forth, the mutual asking and answering of questions, that distinguishes his approach to the correlation model of theology from figures like Paul Tillich and H. Richard Niebuhr.

In this view of theology as conversation, the classic continues to play an essential role. Indeed, in this text he provides his clearest and best description of what the "classic" is:

> an example of both radical stability become permanence and radical instability become excess of meaning through ever-changing receptions. The classic texts are not unique; they are merely the best examples for testing any theory of interpretation because they are the most puzzling examples of the complex process of interpretation itself.[41]

Tracy's view of interpretation remains focused on classics because they are the *best* examples for what his four moments of interpretation are, not because they are the only ones worthy of interpretation. Classics are those expressions that are most provocative, most dis-

---

[41] PA 14.

closive, and most vexing to interpreters. It is because of that category of intensification that Tracy holds on to them while simultaneously recognizing that other, "non-classic" expressions remain valuable.

That being said, Tracy's optimism about the process of interpretation has been tempered by the many challenges interpretation faces. Previously, he would note that theology always needed correctives, whether that be from the historical-critical method that has so impacted study of Scripture or from the suspicious hermeneutics of Karl Marx, Friedrich Nietzsche, and Sigmund Freud. He still held on to the ideals of mutual understanding that could be achieved through an authentic conversation, however, even between two otherwise opposed interlocutors. Yet now, in *Plurality and Ambiguity*, Tracy turns toward the claim that theology, and conversation more broadly, perhaps needs suspicion and critique as much as, if not more than, it needs retrieval of tradition.[42]

Tracy notes that this need for critique and suspicion comes in that very first moment of interpretation. As noted above, every interpreter comes to a text with a pre-understanding. While he had previously emphasized that such prejudgments (or, looking back to Friedrich Schleiermacher, prejudices) were an inevitable part of the ongoing cycle of interpretation,[43] he now also recognizes the ambiguities present in these prejudgments. The view one has of a text, or of an author, or even of the cover can positively and negatively shape how one reads that text. For example, one might assume (wrongly) that Sylvester Stallone's *First Blood* is simply a mindless action film because of the later films in the *Rambo* series, thus missing its serious meditation on PTSD and the experiences of soldiers returning from war. Similarly, one might have an unacknowledged and implicit bias against Muslims that contributes to a critical misreading of Azar Nafisi's *Reading Lolita in Tehran*. Yet more perilously, that same implicit bias might also lead to a critical misreading of one's encounter with a Muslim person in the street, at a store, or at the airport.

Beyond the issue of prejudgments, though, Tracy has a deeper concern about the ambiguity of classics themselves. First, given the reality of human sinfulness, he rejects the idea that interpretations of

---

[42] PA 78–79.
[43] Cf. AI 101.

classics are innocent; rather, they always are inflected in some way by selfishness and disordered loves. Second, and perhaps more important, he rejects the idea that there are any innocent classics to begin with.[44] Classics are produced by fallen human beings who live in times and cultures that are permeated by sinful social structures. Even as these classics can reveal glimpses of "Ultimate Reality,"[45] they are still formulated by imperfect persons. Tracy subtly shifts his prior claim that the classics interpret us just as much as we interpret them, saying instead that "to interpret the religious classics is to allow them to challenge what we presently consider possible. To interpret them is also to allow ourselves to challenge them through every hermeneutic of critique, retrieval, and suspicion we possess."[46] While conversation remains the central metaphor for this encounter, here conversation is more clearly marked by the need for a healthy suspicion both of our interlocutors and of ourselves.

Tracy additionally critiques his view of the classic due to its focus on extremes. He notes that this is in part due to the influence of William James, who thought that "intense instances are the clearest examples of religion as religion."[47] Tracy tries to balance this focus on extremes by also advocating for more attention to the everyday practice of religion by the vast majority of religious believers. He sees himself as a theologian committed to engaging both the pluralism within his own tradition and within the contemporary situation, so the beliefs, attitudes, and practices of everyday believers become important sources for theology that deserve attention. Moreover, attention to extreme forms of religious intensification can lead one to assume that "only a learned elite can read these texts properly" and that "all who wish to enter the discussion should leave the margins and come to the centers to receive the proper credentials."[48] While Tracy and his own works certainly qualify as part of the elite in theology, he has come to recognize that such works are not necessarily more valid expressions of the permanent and timely truths that the tradition is made of. In fact, if the truth manifested by a classic is

---

[44] PA 36–37, 79.

[45] In PA, Tracy typically uses the term "Ultimate Reality" as his general reference for God. For more, see chapter 6, pp. 160–61.

[46] PA 84.

[47] PA 96.

[48] PA 104.

in principle open to any self-reflective person, then the so-called non-elite interpretations of the classics are surely worthwhile conversations to listen to and participate in. Indeed, Tracy thinks that listening to oppressed and marginalized voices and to the everyday classics of their lived experiences will allow a richer understanding of a shared tradition.

Turning from the Classic to the Fragment

The classic is such a recognizable facet of Tracy's thought that some scholars have continued to focus on it for decades after *Plurality and Ambiguity*.[49] This has even been the case despite Tracy's own gradual move away from the term. His concerns about the "classist" undertones of the word itself and the corresponding elitism that accompanies the "classics" in theology led to a serious decline in its use by the mid-1990s.[50] The underlying idea of the classic, however—the particular expression that reveals universal truths—was reformulated and expanded in Tracy's adoption of the term "fragment."

This shift begins somewhat subtly. In his essay "Fragments and Forms: Universality and Particularity Today," Tracy seeks to reconcile the importance of universality in Catholic thought with the realities of diversity and particularity.[51] Recognizing that "catholicity" at its heart means "universality," he argues that true catholicity is always diversity-in-unity. Classics, then, are examples of this fact: "Every classic work of art or religion is highly particular in both origin and expression, yet can be universal in effect."[52] Because a classic reveals the universal in a specific expression, and there are a potentially

---

[49] Cf. Timoteo D. Gener, "The Catholic Imagination and Popular Religion in Lowland Philippines: Missiological Significance of David Tracy's Theory of Religious Imaginations," *Mission Studies* 22, no. 1 (2005): 25–57; David A. Clairmont, "Persons as Religious Classics: Comparative Ethics and the Theology of Bridge Concepts," *Journal of the American Academy of Religion* 78, no. 3 (September 2010): 687–720; Clairmont, *Moral Struggle and Religious Ethics: On the Person as Classic in Comparative Theological Contexts* (Malden, MA: Wiley-Blackwell, 2011).

[50] Notably, Tracy had set out from the beginning to generate a "nonclassicist notion of the classic," but his turn to the fragment suggests that he did not see himself as successful in that goal (AI 100).

[51] David Tracy, "Fragments and Forms: Universality and Particularity Today," in *The Church in Fragments: Towards What Kind of Unity*, ed. Giuseppe Ruggieri and Miklos Tomka (London: SCM Press, 1997), 122–29.

[52] Tracy, "Fragments and Forms," 122.

limitless number of classics, then the classic serves as his paradigm for true catholicity. As such, he maintains that classics bear "an excess and permanence of meaning," and we must therefore be open to the authentic possibilities of existence that they disclose to us.[53]

Nevertheless, while Tracy seems here to reaffirm his idea of the classic, he primarily uses this essay to shift his terminology to the fragment. Here, he is emphasizing that postmodern thought is characterized in large part by a so-called "turn to the other." This certainly includes recognition of the otherness, the genuine difference, of disparate persons and cultures. Yet for Tracy, postmodern concern for otherness helps to reclaim the radical otherness of God and revelation. Much as one might speak of a person from another country as other, Tracy wants to speak of God as Other. Because of this, he claims that "all these expressions of genuine otherness demand the serious attention of all thoughtful persons, especially those in search of Catholic unity-in-diversity."[54] Doing so requires better naming, and the language of fragment becomes a way to name the variety of expressions that come from the sheer diversity and irreducible differences that constitute one's own tradition as well as any other traditions one might encounter.

The concept of the fragment is not new with Tracy, but he does develop a distinct understanding of what it means. To clarify this, he outlines two alternative views of the fragment before defining his own. The first comes out of the German Romantic tradition, particularly the work of Friedrich Schlegel and Novalis.[55] Variously calling it the "conservative," "neo-conservative," or "radical conservative" view, these kinds of fragments sought to resist modernity's worldview that privileged rationality so highly that it left no real room for difference, interruption, or otherness. Drawing on Michel Foucault, Tracy describes such worldviews as a "totality system" that wants to "reduce all . . . to more of the same."[56] Such totalizing worldviews

---

[53] Tracy, "Fragments and Forms," 124.

[54] Tracy, "Fragments and Forms," 125.

[55] David Tracy, "Form and Fragment: The Recovery of the Hidden and Incomprehensible God," in *The Concept of God in Global Dialogue*, ed. Werner Jeanrond and Aasulv Lande (Maryknoll, NY: Orbis Books, 2005), 99.

[56] David Tracy, "African American Thought: The Discovery of Fragments," in *Black Faith and Public Talk: Critical Essays on James H. Cone's* Black Theology and Black Power, ed. Dwight N. Hopkins (Maryknoll, NY: Orbis Books, 1999), 31.

are built on rigid paradigms for seeing reality, so that whenever an event or idea occurs that challenges or interrupts it, the system either seeks to hide that interruption or reveals the worldview's own fragility. For the Romantics, they sought to reclaim the affective and emotional dimension of human existence that they saw modernity as flattening and covering over.

In doing so, however, the Romantics never quite freed themselves from the problem of the modern totality system. Rather, their resistance to Enlightenment rationality was based on their yearning for a prior, different totality system.[57] This use of fragments is fundamentally *nostalgic*, looking backward in hopes of piecing back together a broken but fondly remembered worldview. Tracy frequently invokes the T.S. Eliot quotation "fragments to shore up against our ruin" as the quintessential statement of this longing for a past in the midst of some present decline.[58] While it privileges an earlier totality system over the present one, Tracy highlights that the essential problem is supporting a totality system at all.

Tracy calls his second view of fragments "postmodern." While postmodern thinkers often share the conservative rejection of this modern totality system, their impetus is not the same nostalgic yearning for a long-disappeared past. Rather, the thrust of postmodern thought is to attend and give voice to the expressions of otherness and difference that modern thought had sought to repress, conquer, assimilate, or otherwise ignore.[59] In this vein, Tracy says that modern totality systems are "designed to render all particularities either finally harmless and insignificant or significant and therefore harmful."[60] Fragments, however, are the very particularities that resist being muted or reduced to "more of the same" precisely because they show that it is impossible to create a closed system with no room for

---

[57] Tracy, "African American Thought: The Discovery of Fragments," 31.

[58] Tracy, "Fragments and Forms: Universality and Particularity Today," 126; Tracy, "African American Thought: The Discovery of Fragments," 32; David Tracy, "Fragments: The Spiritual Situation of Our Times," in *God, the Gift, and Postmodernism*, ed. John D. Caputo and Michael J. Scanlon (Bloomington: Indiana University Press, 1999), 174.

[59] Tracy, "Fragments: The Spiritual Situation of Our Times," 171.

[60] Tracy, "Fragments and Forms," 122.

difference.[61] Human existence is messy, such that no perfectly ordered system can fully account for its breadth or complications. The effort to disappear those events, persons, or other expressions of difference that do not fit in leads to a cultural version of repression, if not outright violence. The postmodern therefore sees the encounter with fragments as liberating, freeing people from a false, imposed uniformity and directing them instead toward a universal regard for the irreducible particularity, and dignity, of the other.

This modern effort to control otherness has focused especially on religion. Tracy describes religion as "that other that cannot be assimilated but only at best correlated and, more usually, simply ignored or dismissed."[62] Whether religion was a once-important stage that is no longer necessary (Hegel, Feuerbach) or a disease to be eradicated (Marx), modern thought found religion to be a problem for its systematizing efforts. Tracy thinks the exemplary case for this is the modern debate over the best "-isms" for naming God, such as deism, theism, and panentheism.[63] First, this debate domesticates reflection on the human encounter with the divine by developing an inadequate set of categories into which one marshals an ineffable mystery. Second, this approach does not seriously engage with those religious traditions that resist the "ism-ing" of faith. Buddhism, for example, may have a sense of what is ultimate in existence, but it is not really connected with a sense of a divine being. Buddhism is thus sometimes described as nontheist, but even this fails to grasp the beliefs and practices underlying Buddhism.[64] Indeed, Tracy's current and long-percolating project on naming God tries to retrieve these other and fragmentary namings of God, such as God the Incomprehensible, the Infinite, and the Hidden.[65]

---

[61] Tracy locates the beginning of this use of fragment with Georges Bataille, who "loved extreme fragments as excessive in regard to all order and transgressive of Enlightenment rationality" (Tracy, "Fragments: The Spiritual Situation of Our Times," 176).

[62] Tracy, "Fragments: The Spiritual Situation of Our Times," 176.

[63] Tracy, "African American Thought: The Discovery of Fragments," 31.

[64] One might note here that even in naming this tradition, we call it Buddh*ism*.

[65] Tracy, "Form and Fragment: The Recovery of the Hidden and Incomprehensible God," 108–14. These and other retrieved ways of naming God (e.g., Love, Being, Trinity) are the focus of the latter half of chapter 6 of this book.

Tracy's project to retrieve these ways of naming God relies on his third view of fragments, which he calls theological-spiritual. He defines these as "saturated and auratic bearers of infinity and sacred hope, fragmentary of genuine hope in some redemption, however undefined."[66] These bearers are particular expressions, including texts, symbols, and rituals, yet they carry the possibility of disclosing the infinite, the mysterious, and the beyond to their interlocutors. There is an important distinction here, though, between infinity and totality. Following Levinas, Tracy contrasts them by saying that totality demands closure while infinity remains open to the other.[67] This closed/open distinction is essential to Tracy's claim that the fragment is not only a means of resisting totality but a way of discovering the particularity of one's tradition and of encountering "all the others and the different, in the very same way, as possible disclosures of infinity."[68]

While Tracy thinks there is much to learn from the conservative and postmodern uses of the fragment, he primarily allies himself with the third group. In a debate with Jacques Derrida, he accepted Derrida's claim that the most common use of the metaphor "fragment" implies some prior totality system, like the shattered pieces of a mirror. Yet he maintained that fragments in religion are not primarily tied to totality systems but rather "to something barely nameable, something incomprehensible, the name that must not be spoken." In the theological-spiritual use of fragments, it is precisely the divine that is disclosed, and "God is not a totality."[69] Here, his use of infinity as a way of naming God parallels his prior use of "the whole" in *The Analogical Imagination*.[70]

---

[66] Tracy, "Fragments: The Spiritual Situation of Our Times," 173. Nicholas Collura describes this approach as being "between extreme optimism and extreme pessimism." See Nicholas Collura, "Some Reflections on the Eucharist as Fragment," *Worship* 88, no. 2 (March 2014): 162.

[67] Tracy, "Form and Fragment: The Recovery of the Hidden and Incomprehensible God," 101. Cf. Emmanuel Levinas, *Totality and Infinity* (Pittsburgh: Duquesne University Press, 1994).

[68] Tracy, "African American Thought: The Discovery of Fragments," 30; cf. Ryan P. Cumming, "Contrasts and Fragments: An Exploration of James Cone's Theological Methodology," *Anglican Theological Review* 91, no. 3 (Summer 2009): 416.

[69] Tracy, "Fragments: The Spiritual Situation of Our Times," 183–84.

[70] With similar parallels to the "limit-of" in BRO and "Ultimate Reality" in PA.

In this definition of fragments, one can see both the continuity with the classics as well as a shift in Tracy's influences. Like classics, fragments are particular expressions that come in a variety of types (most notably texts, but also images, rituals, events, and so on). Moreover, while he has shifted from speaking of "the whole" to "infinity," in both cases the particularity of the expression becomes a potential locus for revealing this transcendent reality. Thus the fragment also serves the function of highlighting Tracy's understanding of catholicity, that particularity is the medium through which universality is uncovered.

Crucially, however, one can recognize how the differences in definition illuminate the shift in Tracy's main conversation partners. Whereas the classic is an expansion of concepts already present in Gadamer and Lonergan, Tracy's description of fragments as "saturated and auratic" recalls the work of French Catholic phenomenologist Jean-Luc Marion and German Jewish philosopher Walter Benjamin. Marion first came to the University of Chicago Divinity School in 1994, in part through the efforts of Tracy himself.[71] Marion's work on a phenomenology of religious and theological language, with particular attention to the priority of "givenness," led to his development of the "saturated phenomenon."

Marion's description of the saturated phenomenon relies on the relationship between intention and intuition. Drawing on Edmund Husserl, Marion refers to intention as the idea one has or what one expects, while the intuition is the appearance of some phenomenon that one experiences (particularly, but not exclusively, through sensory experience).[72] Marion critiques Husserl, though, who considered only two possibilities for correlating these. First, if the intention one has is greater or exceeds the intuition one has of something, then the

---

[71] Their mutual regard was well established several years previously, when Tracy wrote the foreword for the 1991 English translation of Marion's *God without Being*, which remains perhaps Marion's best-known work in the United States. See Jean-Luc Marion, *God without Being: Hors-Texte*, trans. Thomas A. Carlson (Chicago: University of Chicago Press, 1995); Tracy's foreword is on pages ix–xv.

[72] Here, one can see both the influence of Immanuel Kant, whose philosophy of human knowing was built on the correlation between the "concept" and the "intuition," and Edmund Husserl, who discussed "intention/intuition, signification/fulfillment, noesis/noema, etc." (Jean-Luc Marion, *Being Given: Toward a Phenomenology of Givenness*, trans. Jeffrey L. Kosky [Stanford, CA: Stanford University Press, 2002], 190).

phenomenon is objectified. One can control or dominate the experience, the text, the person.[73] Second, if one has perfectly aligned intentions and intuitions, then there is a state of "adequation" (such as when one engages in mathematics or formal logic).[74]

Marion, however, proposes a third, more compelling possibility, which is when the intuition exceeds our intentions. This "saturated phenomenon" is not under one's control and cannot be expected or predicted.[75] Indeed, their excess gives rise to an "overflow with many meanings, or an infinity of meanings, each equally legitimate and rigorous, without managing either to unify them or to organize them."[76] The saturated phenomenon thus goes beyond one's horizon, drawing one into engagement with the phenomenon in a way that is beyond one's grasp. It is this latter aspect that seems most connected to Tracy's fragment: the theological fragments he focuses on represent expressions (phenomena) in which the infinite that is beyond human grasp is encountered. The fragment is self-disclosive and exceeds the expectation of its interpreter.[77]

Curiously, the insight Tracy pulls from Benjamin is that of the aura, which the latter effectively describes negatively. In his essay "The Work of Art in the Age of Mechanical Reproduction," Benjamin says the aura is "that which withers in the age of mechanical reproduction."[78]

---

[73] Marion, *Being Given*, 196–97. This correlation might be most evident when one thinks of the objectification of human persons: by seeing the other as something less than a full human being, a "non-person" in the language of Gutierrez, one is enabled to use that person for one's own ends without regard for the other.

[74] Marion, *Being Given*, 191.

[75] Marion, *Being Given*, 199–200.

[76] Jean-Luc Marion, *In Excess: Studies of Saturated Phenomena*, trans. Robyn Horner and Vincent Berraud (New York: Fordham University Press, 2004), 112.

[77] Tracy notes that the key insight of Marion's work on the saturated phenomenon is that "the phenomenological defense of 'revealability' shows the condition of possibility of the 'Impossible' revelation" (David Tracy, "Jean-Luc Marion: Phenomenology, Hermeneutics, Theology," in *Counter-Experiences: Reading Jean-Luc Marion*, ed. Kevin Hart [Notre Dame, IN: University of Notre Dame Press, 2007], 62–63). The reference to the "Impossible" here is to one of the names of God in Tracy's later work; fragments are thus essentially a form of mediation of the divine.

For more on the saturated phenomenon, the clearest analysis and assessment can be found in Tamsin Jones, *A Genealogy of Marion's Philosophy of Religion: Apparent Darkness* (Bloomington: Indiana University Press, 2011), 110–16.

[78] Walter Benjamin, "The Work of Art in the Age of Mechanical Reproduction," in *Illuminations: Essays and Reflections*, trans. Harry Zohn (New York: Schocken Books, 1986), 221.

Because the copy does not have the "presence in time and space," the "substantive duration," or (most fundamentally) the "authenticity" of the original, it has lost—or, more strongly, excised—what makes that work of art powerful. The original work itself has both "uniqueness and permanence," tied to its coming from "the fabric of tradition."[79] Indeed, this original can "absorb" the person who concentrates on it and allows the work of art to engage them. By describing his fragment as auratic, Tracy invokes this image from Benjamin, which is clearly consistent with the above description of classics. Thus the auratic fragment is one that originates within a tradition, is marked by both permanence and authenticity, and draws its interlocutor into conscientious but not self-conscious engagement.[80]

Finally, then, the fragment represents a meaningful recharacterization of the classic. While retaining the essential focus on particular expressions that can disclose transcendent truth, the fragment is also able to move away from the elitism that precipitated around the classic. In looking at the contemporary situation of the theologian, Tracy claims that "what we now possess most clearly are fragments of our heritage and new fragments from new cultural situations," a description that resonates strongly with the two sources of theology he cites in his method of mutually critical correlation.[81] Yet now, instead of correlating the classics of the tradition with the contemporary situation, theology aims instead to gather these fragments without rendering a new totality system.[82]

---

[79] Benjamin, "The Work of Art," 223.

[80] For more on the relationship between Tracy and Benjamin on fragments, see William Myatt, "Public Theology and 'the Fragment': Duncan Forrester, David Tracy, and Walter Benjamin," *International Journal of Public Theology* 8, no. 1 (2014): 85–106. Perhaps most relevant for this discussion is that Myatt focuses on Benjamin's work on the fragment in "On the Concept of History," whereas Tracy takes the influence of Benjamin primarily from "The Work of Art in the Age of Mechanical Reproduction."

[81] Tracy, "Fragments and Forms: Universality and Particularity Today," 126.

[82] Tracy cites liturgy, narrative (e.g., the Gospel of Mark), biblical creeds, and systematic theology as historical forms of gathering the fragments (Tracy, "Form and Fragment: The Recovery of the Hidden and Incomprehensible God," 98–99). Specifically, he cites Aquinas's *Summa*, Calvin's *Institutes*, and Schleiermacher's *Glaubenslehre* as examples of non-totalizing systematic theologies (ibid., 107).

Conclusion

The classic has remained one of the most recognized parts of Tracy's theology. It has occupied a central role in his method, and it is a recurring feature of how Tracy discusses various doctrinal questions in the Christian tradition (most particularly Christology, as will be explored in chap. 5). His concern for engaging those expressions that best disclose the divine in our world and our experience speaks both to his deep regard for the Christian tradition and for the Catholic sacramental worldview that informs his thought.

The significance of the classic does not, however, shield it from Tracy's own critique. Beyond the classist implications of the term itself, Tracy's work often focuses on the most intense and most elite expressions to the detriment of potentially more everyday expressions of excess and permanence. This has often been paired with the expectation that only those so-credentialed as to properly interpret the classics ought to be taken seriously.

In response both to these concerns and to Tracy's engagement with the works of Marion and Benjamin, Tracy sought to develop a theology of the fragment. While this retains the essential core of the classic, fragments help Tracy to see even more broadly the resources of the tradition and to work more on how these fragments disclose new possibilities from within the tradition. Tracy thus endeavors to conserve an essential aspect of his approach to theology while also improving the insights of the argument.[83]

---

[83] The significance of this shift can be best seen in his work on "naming God," his chief project since the mid-1990s. For more on this, see chapter 6 of this book.

4

Pluralism

In the past, then, there has existed a notable pluralism of expression. Currently in the church there is quietly disappearing the old classicist insistence on worldwide uniformity, and there is emerging a pluralism of manners in which Christian meaning and Christian values are communicated.

—Bernard Lonergan[1]

The significance of pluralism for Tracy's theology is obvious: one need look no further than the titles or subtitles of most of his books for evidence.[2] Yet there are subtleties to Tracy's approach that significantly nuance this importance. He draws distinctions between the irreducible fact of diversity, which he calls "plurality," and a positive or optimistic orientation toward that irreducible fact, which is "pluralism" proper.[3] Moreover, the range of topics that he considers in light of plurality and pluralism is itself quite divergent. Throughout

---

[1] MT 328.

[2] *Blessed Rage for Order: The New Pluralism in Theology; The Analogical Imagination: Christian Theology and the Culture of Pluralism; Talking about God: Doing Theology in the Context of Modern Pluralism* (co-written with John B. Cobb, Jr.); *Plurality and Ambiguity: Hermeneutics, Religion, Hope.*

[3] Of note on these terms: earlier in this career, Tracy uses these terms fairly interchangeably. Later, particularly around the writing of PA, he becomes more intentional about distinguishing between fact and posture. In this text, Tracy's usage is retained in any direct quotations, but in the main text follows the distinction described here.

his texts, one can find references to religious pluralism, cultural pluralism, radical pluralism, global pluralism, the pluralism of readings, the pluralism of methods, and so forth. Further, he is critical of many types of pluralism, frequently rejecting "repressive tolerance" and "let a thousand flowers bloom" approaches.[4] He even critiques those approaches to pluralism that he approves of for misunderstanding the reality of marginalization, ultimately advocating for the term "polycentrism" instead.

Indeed, Tracy understands plurality and pluralism in terms of a complex set of phenomena that are essential to the practice and understanding of theology. There are real questions about the "situational" pole in the method of critical correlation, particularly with regard to both past and contemporary situations in which people find themselves. Moreover, one might come to reckon with the plurality that exists within the "religious" pole as well, as the investigation of religious traditions reveals its own diversities and complexities. The fact of plurality challenges one to consider one's response to that fact and to consider what might be the most fruitful theological response.

To engage these questions, this chapter sets out to outline the plurality of pluralisms that permeate Tracy's thought. First, it reviews T. Howland Sanks's schema for understanding pluralism in Tracy, which provides a useful, if limited, map for entering into Tracy's concerns here. Second, it considers how Tracy's appropriation of Lonergan initiates his concern for pluralism. The third part examines how the diverse nodes of pluralism develop in Tracy's thought. This requires both synchronic (different types of pluralism at the same time) and diachronic (how those types develop throughout his career) analysis. Fourth, there are the difficulties Tracy sees within the pluralist project and how those difficulties shape his approach (leading to a necessary reconsideration of Sanks). Finally, the chapter turns toward Tracy's argument for the "analogical imagination" as an essential response to the reality of pluralism that best satisfies his criterion of appropriateness to the tradition.

---

[4] AI xi; David Tracy, "The Question of Pluralism in Contemporary Theology," *The Chicago Theological Seminary Register* 71 (Spring 1981): 31.

The Development of Pluralism in Tracy's Theology

Sanks's Heuristic Typology for Tracy's Pluralisms

Before entering into the complex terrain of Tracy on pluralism, it may be helpful to consult a map. In his essay "David Tracy's Theological Project: An Overview and Some Implications," T. Howland Sanks describes three distinct emphases on pluralism that he sees developing chronologically for Tracy.[5] Sanks argues that Tracy "focused on *pluralism within theology* in *Blessed Rage for Order*, then on *cultural pluralism* in *The Analogical Imagination*, and currently on the *pluralism of religious traditions*" (in the articles and books of the late 1980s and early 1990s).[6] Most obviously, these three descriptors track with the relevant book (sub)titles. Sanks also ties them, however, to the methodological concerns evident in each text.

First, *Blessed Rage for Order*'s description of the "revisionist" model for theology is tied to theological pluralism precisely because of the dual commitments of the contemporary theologian.[7] The theologian is tasked with a multitude of choices in terms of methods and sources for doing theology; moreover, these decisions must be made in concert both with particular religious traditions and in light of contemporary secular models of rational argument. According to Sanks, the pluralism within theology is the *de facto* reality of the multitude of options facing the theologian. Moreover, decisions are not to be made capriciously but must instead rely on genuinely public criteria.[8]

Second, *The Analogical Imagination*'s shift to pluralism in culture is also tied to methodological concerns. Sanks sees this as partly due to the stronger focus on systematic theology, which is always deeply embedded within a particular religious tradition.[9] Sanks notes that Tracy continues his commitment to pluralism, but he also believes that the theologian must not "surrender the pursuit of truth in each

[5] T. Howland Sanks, "David Tracy's Theological Project: An Overview and Some Implications," *Theological Studies* 54, no. 4 (December 1993): 698–727.

[6] Sanks, "David Tracy's Theological Project," 722.

[7] Sanks, "David Tracy's Theological Project," 703.

[8] Sanks, "David Tracy's Theological Project," 706, 713.

[9] Sanks, "David Tracy's Theological Project," 713.

particular tradition."[10] The theologian must therefore engage in "the plurality of religious traditions and cultures" that define reality.[11]

Finally, Sanks notes the greater emphasis on pluralism of religious traditions at the time of *Plurality and Ambiguity* and *Dialogue with the Other* and connects it to Tracy's being "increasingly sensitive to the need to include other voices in the conversation."[12] This draws specifically on Tracy's wider engagement with other religious traditions, seeing "conversation among the religions [as] now a necessity."[13] Moreover, Sanks argues that it builds on the analogical imagination as response to pluralism that Tracy developed in *The Analogical Imagination*.[14]

This typology is valuable for framing Tracy's approach to pluralism. Following closer analysis of Tracy's writings on pluralism, however, the chapter will return to Sanks for critique. In particular, it is not clear that this typology is as clean as Sanks suggests. In fact, his outline arguably conceals some significant dimensions of Tracy's understanding of pluralism.

Science and Pluralism in Tracy's Reading of Lonergan

Lonergan's influence on Tracy has already been clearly established.[15] Although perhaps less pronounced, Tracy's sense for pluralism in the contemporary situation receives its first push from Lonergan's treatment of pluralism in the modern historical context. Tracy's reception of this is evident, if briefly, in *The Achievement of Bernard Lonergan*.

In chapter 4 of that text, Tracy moves from analyzing Lonergan's work on Thomas Aquinas to Lonergan's towering masterpiece, *Insight*. To do so, Tracy must take account of the major historical shifts between the medieval and twentieth-century worlds. Key to this, according to Tracy, is the way that modern persons have a new consciousness of theory and of interiority. Taken together, these shifts

---

[10] Sanks, "David Tracy's Theological Project," 713.
[11] Sanks, "David Tracy's Theological Project," 712.
[12] Sanks, "David Tracy's Theological Project," 720.
[13] Sanks, "David Tracy's Theological Project," 721.
[14] Sanks, "David Tracy's Theological Project," 721.
[15] See pp. 55–58 above.

provide the grounding for the transcendental model of consciousness that Lonergan develops (attention, intelligence, rationality, and responsibility).

Theory is where Lonergan makes his key move with regard to pluralism. Tracy connects the development here to the evolution of science from Aristotle to the modern. He claims that this shift is crucial precisely because today "every theoretician (including the theologian) must sooner or later try to explicitate the scientific ideal and method which structures all his work."[16] Just as Aquinas appropriated the scientific thought of Aristotle as the peak of his era, so too must contemporary theologians take account of the finest approaches to scientific and theoretical thought today.

Tracy notes eight differences between Aristotelian and modern science.[17] Key examples of these changes are the shift from a classical search for certainty to the modern engagement with probability, the classical concern with the changeless and immobile giving way to a modern focus on development and change, and the classic emphasis on necessity moving toward modern emphasis on intelligibility. Collectively, these and the other shifts represent a move away from what Lonergan calls the "classicist" worldview.[18] This worldview saw reality as static and unchanging and thus culture as a permanent achievement rather than an ongoing development.

With regard to the question of pluralism, the relevant difference here is what Tracy describes as the move away from essentialism. The "classical" approach of medieval science would have sought "the one, ultimate, intrinsic ground of necessity, universality, and per-se-ity," which would support the sense of permanent achievement that was common to science of the era.[19] By contrast, modern scientists, and theoreticians more broadly, recognize instead that "the reality under investigation may perhaps be too rich and manifold to be captured in a single essence uniquely formulated."[20] This diversity of phenomena is joined with a diversity of methods, as investigation benefits from "a combination of different approaches."[21] Tracy does

[16] ABL 85.
[17] ABL 85–90.
[18] See MT xi.
[19] ABL 89.
[20] ABL 89.
[21] ABL 89.

not think this pluralism necessarily leads to relativism, suggesting instead that it could lead to a "transformation" of the classicist world-view and a continuation of its pursuit of truth.[22] As will be seen below, these three insights (plurality of phenomena, plurality of methods, and potential issues with pluralism) continue to be core features of Tracy's own appropriation of pluralism into his theology.

Theological Pluralism in Blessed Rage for Order

At the outset, Tracy's *Blessed Rage for Order* upholds the conviction that pluralism defines the current context.[23] He builds the reality of pluralism into the architecture of the text, outlining what he describes as his "two principal assumptions": (1) contemporary theological pluralism allows theologians to encounter a greater diversity of views on both Christian traditions and human experience; (2) in the face of this, each theologian is tasked with developing a method for dealing with tradition and experience that has publicly accountable criteria.[24] Amid a wide diversity of options for how to do theology and what to focus on within that, Tracy thinks the responsible theologian will argue for a particular way forward that takes pluralism seriously. Tracy offers such a way forward through his revisionist approach to critical correlation.[25]

Building on his comments on pluralism in Lonergan, Tracy is careful at the outset of *Blessed Rage for Order* to show that pluralism is not an unalloyed good. Even as theological pluralism offers a "richness of imagination" and "several ways of envisioning the world," it also risks sliding into "lazy intellectual 'tolerance.' "[26] By this, he means that there are numerous pluralist approaches that, rather than seeking the truth presented by diverse modes of thought or traditions, instead accept all of this diversity at face value without further critical rigor.

---

[22] ABL 90.

[23] BRO 3.

[24] BRO 3. Although Tracy does not clearly distinguish between "religious" and "theological" pluralism here, a later essay will describe religious pluralism as the diversity of religious experiences and languages while theological pluralism is the diversity of "second-order reflection[s] upon religious experience and language." See David Tracy, "Theological Pluralism and Analogy," *Thought* 54 (1979): 25n2.

[25] See pp. 20–21 and 44–48 above.

[26] BRO 3.

They are, in other words, relativist, unwilling or unable to make reasoned defenses for particular commitments. He notes two such versions early on in *Blessed Rage for Order*: the "consumer society" model, which leaves all questions of truth to simple matters of preference, and "common-sense eclecticism," which assembles an array of options without regard to their context or coherence.[27] The temptations of these kinds of pluralism are a recurring concern for Tracy, which is closely connected to his demand for criteria and argument. One's engagement with the present pluralism must therefore "risk . . . an interpretation" of the reality at hand and provide an "initial defense" for one's way forward.[28] This is what makes for a responsible, rather than lazy, pluralism.

Similarly, Tracy connects the pluralism of the current context to scientific modes of reason. In considering how the theologian is to make publicly defensible arguments, he notes the different moralities one can see between traditional Christian theology and modern natural and social sciences. Here, he claims that traditional (in contrast to revisionist) theologians took their primary ethical commitments to be obedience to the tradition and its claims, such that the authority of the tradition is sufficient to establish the claim's veracity.[29] By contrast, the modern scientist's ethical commitment is to the method of inquiry relevant to that field or discipline. As such, prior scientific claims about particular phenomena are always subject to revision, pending new insights that result from application of the scientific method.[30]

---

[27] BRO 3. In a later essay, Tracy expands on his argument against "eclecticism," stating that these sorts of pluralists "never met a position they didn't like." Indeed, their "critical sense" is unable to make clear and important distinctions, nor can it articulate criteria by which such judgments are made. By contrast, according to Tracy, "every *responsible* pluralist has met positions she/he didn't like" (emphasis mine). See Tracy, "The Question of Pluralism in Contemporary Theology," 31.

[28] BRO 3–4.

[29] BRO 6.

[30] One might note here, however, that Tracy does not make explicit that the scientific method itself is, strictly speaking, a tradition, passed down from scientist to scientist. And while scientists might, in principle, be open to revision of the method itself, this possibility does not seem to be seriously considered here. Tracy has an opportunity to include this later in BRO when he considers limit-questions in science, but this limit-question does not substantively appear there either (see BRO 94–100).

In his revisionist paradigm, Tracy argues that theologians must maintain the dual commitment to both the religious faith tradition out of which they are working and the "morality of scientific knowledge of [their] contemporaries."[31] This latter commitment means critical engagement with the tradition that, rather than accepting it at face value, instead pursues an open-ended inquiry into its claims to meaning and truth.[32] Critique therefore is not inherently negative, nor does it *de jure* or *de facto* require rejection of traditional claims. Tracy does not see these commitments as hierarchical (with faith commitment superseding scientific) but rather as coequal in the larger theological effort. In fact, although he does not explicitly put it this way, Tracy suggests that this dual commitment is a contemporary mode of understanding the Catholic tradition's longstanding commitment to the mutual complementarity of faith and reason.[33]

Tracy focuses the revisionist model and its critical correlation on fundamental theology in *Blessed Rage for Order*. He thus argues that his model of fundamental theology "can be faithful to some of the more important pluralist possibilities of the present day."[34] To do so, he notes that his fundamental theology engages "specific material positions from a broad spectrum of traditions," which is suggestive of the plurality of phenomena both within and among religious traditions.[35] In working through the correlation of Christian fact with common human experience, he arrives in part 2 of *Blessed Rage for Order* at three cascading questions:

> How and in what senses is the religious interpretation of our common human experience and language meaningful and true? How and in what senses is the theistic interpretation of religion meaningful and true? How and in what senses is the christological interpretation of theistic religion meaningful and true?[36]

These three levels—religious, theistic, christological—indicate a move from more general to more specific with the Christian tradition (e.g.,

---

[31] BRO 6.
[32] BRO 7.
[33] BRO 8–9.
[34] BRO 91.
[35] BRO 91.
[36] BRO 91.

one cannot have a christological interpretation that is not religious, but one can have a religious interpretation that is not christological).

Yet on each level, Tracy engages with the larger reality of pluralism. Following this breakdown, Tracy immediately enters into the contested question of what makes a phenomenon "religious." While he draws heavily on Clifford Geertz's definition, and advocates for limit language as a "key (but not exhaustive) category" for the religious, in so doing he recognizes the often irreconcilable diversity of so-called religious experience.[37] Even this idea of limit, further broken out into limit-to and limit-of, admits a multitude of ways that such limits are encountered: limit-language, limit-experience, limit-question, limit-situation, limit-concept, and limit-possibilities.[38] The phenomena that count as religious, and the ways in which human experience encounters those phenomena, are plural.

Further, in shifting to the theistic level, Tracy continues his use of "limit" as a way of surveying a number of responses to the question of God (from within the Christian tradition). While he offers his own argument in favor of a process theology view of God (drawn particularly from Schubert Ogden), he notes other approaches that help to illuminate the relationship between metaphysical (philosophical) and symbolic (scriptural) descriptions of God.[39]

Finally, at the christological level, Tracy notes a plurality of methods for coming to a deeper understanding of Christ and what Christ represents for Christian self-understanding. He describes the work of figures like Friedrich Schleiermacher and Karl Rahner as "psychologizing . . . the ontological high christology of Chalcedon," while more recently Gerhard Ebeling and Ernst Fuchs use hermeneutic methods to seek out "the earliest christologies, implicit and explicit, in the synoptic accounts."[40] Tracy himself proposes a more symbolic analysis of Christ, such that "his words, his deeds, and his destiny, as expressions of his office of messiahship, authentically represent as real human possibilities for genuine relationship to God."[41]

---

[37] BRO 92–93.

[38] Cf. BRO 78, 93, 174, and 206.

[39] BRO 149. In this chapter he mostly works with Ian Ramsey, Frederick Ferré, and Anders Nygren.

[40] BRO 217.

[41] BRO 218.

While these show only a small number of the approaches to the christological question, they are indicative of Tracy's commitment to accounting for a plurality of methods within theological endeavors.[42]

Tracy concludes his consideration of pluralism in *Blessed Rage for Order* by noting the purpose of an open and engaged posture toward the plurality of religious and theological phenomena. Referring again to his mentor Lonergan, he notes that Lonergan saw one of the fruits of his method to be the possibilities and necessity of critical collaboration.[43] Theology cannot be done in a vacuum, nor can any one person individually manage the diverse corpus that theology reflects on. This collaboration ought to be authentic and critical, meaning that it does not "rest content in the merely aesthetic pleasure of a pluralist world" but rather continually seeks the truth that is revealed in Christ.[44] The simple fact of plurality requires that, if theology is to be done well—indeed, at all—it must be done together.

Cultural Pluralism in The Analogical Imagination

Even as Tracy's theological method developed between *Blessed Rage for Order* and *The Analogical Imagination*, many of his basic convictions about the plural context remained the same. He continued to push back against bad forms of pluralism. He noted that underdeveloped notions of pluralism might "mask a repressive tolerance where all is allowed because nothing finally is taken seriously," or where pluralism is used to "cover a genial confusion."[45] He thus also continues his conviction that in the context of plurality, one must still seek what is true while developing and arguing for criteria and methods for demonstrating that truth. Moreover, he adds to this concern, rejecting secularizing calls for a marginalized religion and syncretistic efforts to settle for a "lowest common denominator" approach.[46] Indeed, the shift to a more robust public theology enables Tracy to engage the question of pluralism and truth even more cogently, thus strengthening his rejection of weak pluralisms.

---

[42] See also Tracy, "The Question of Pluralism in Contemporary Theology," 31–33.
[43] BRO 249.
[44] BRO 249.
[45] AI xi.
[46] AI xi.

There are also, however, key ways in which his approach to pluralism in *The Analogical Imagination* shifts slightly. Some of this stems from methodological shifts noted previously.[47] The stronger focus on the contemporary situation as one pole of critical correlation grounds a stronger interest in the "culture of pluralism" in the subtitle. At the same time, the more robust notion of the classic, tied to a better hermeneutical approach to the Christian tradition, enables Tracy to better express the pluralism that is, and always has been, present in Christianity. Finally, these pluralisms further coalesce into an intriguing recognition of the plurality that exists within the individual self.

By cultural pluralism (or pluralism of culture), Tracy is trying to connect the power of the classic with the fact of their particularity. He notes that classics always come from particular cultures and are deeply shaped by those cultures. For example, he sometimes references his own Irish-American Catholic background to make a connection with Eugene O'Neill's *Long Day's Journey into Night*.[48] This text is deeply embedded in the culture that gave birth to it, but that particularity is what grounds the possibility of its revealing truth to those who are not from that culture. The "otherness . . . even its interruptive alienness" of the classic powers its disclosure of reality, even—perhaps especially—to those who are not originally from the culture of origin for that classic.[49] He thus contrasts the classic with the "period piece," the latter being those expressions that downplay the particularity of their creator's context in order to try to be "universal.[50] Cultural pluralism effectively grounds the possibility and power of the classics, precisely because it is within this diversity that particular expressions arise that are able to disclose universal truth.

---

[47] See chapter 2, pp. 49–50.

[48] David Tracy, "Ethnic Pluralism and Systematic Theology: Reflections," in *Ethnicity*, ed. Andrew M. Greeley and Gregory Baum, *Concilium* 101 (New York: Seabury Press, 1977), 94.

[49] Tracy, "Theological Pluralism and Analogy," 30. See also David Tracy, "Christianity in the Wider Context: Demands and Transformations," in *Worldviews and Warrants: Plurality and Authority in Theology*, ed. William Schweiker and Per M. Anderson (Lanham, MD: University Press of America, 1987), 15. In AI itself he makes a similar claim with respect to James Joyce's *Ulysses*, although there he does not make the explicit connection to his own background (AI 132).

[50] Tracy, "Ethnic Pluralism and Systematic Theology," 94.

Tracy notes that the cultural pluralism he is talking about is best recognized in a historically conscious culture. In that context, he says cultural pluralism is simply accepted as a fact, a given part of reality.[51] For people in the contemporary West, cultural pluralism is already abundantly evident in the diversity of food, music, and clothing that are widely available. For some, the interpersonal encounter with people from other cultures gives the first embodied contact with that pluralism—perhaps through a college roommate, a coworker, or a new neighbor. Because of these encounters, Tracy sees cultural pluralism as an opportunity to reflect on our similarities and differences with the cultural other.[52] He contrasts this with previous eras, which likely would have thought of "one's own culture as civilization and others as barbarism, regression or distortion."[53]

Cultural pluralism is not the only mode of pluralism that Tracy emphasizes in *The Analogical Imagination*. A second and important insight for him is greater attention to the pluralism within Christianity. In a sense, this is already referenced in *Blessed Rage for Order*, particularly as he works through the three levels of questions he raises with regard to religious, theistic, and christological experience. But the focus here in *The Analogical Imagination* has a different purpose. Here, Tracy highlights not only the present pluralism of Christian traditions but also the pluralism that was present in Christianity at its beginning. He describes the New Testament as containing a "rich diversity of forms . . . grounded in the unifying unity of an event seeking a response of personal faith."[54] It is comprised of numerous forms, specifically "proclamation, narrative, symbol, and thought," which sprawl out from the person and event of Jesus Christ and seek to witness, in myriad ways, his incarnation, ministry, crucifixion, and resurrection.[55] Christ is what unifies the pluralism in the New Testament and (at least potentially) the traditions that spring out from that original witness.[56]

[51] AI 108.
[52] AI 105.
[53] AI 105.
[54] AI 308.
[55] AI 309.
[56] AI 310, 322.

That qualifier—at least potentially—indicates Tracy's concern that pluralism, especially a christological pluralism, not give in to the lazy, eclectic pluralism he has resisted throughout. As such, he again returns to the question of criteria, demanding that all christological interpreters make their case for the "relative adequacy" of their understanding of Jesus.[57] By describing such interpretations as "relatively adequate," Tracy hopes to uphold the "ultimately inexpressible *event*" of the Word made flesh, a reality that can only be fully expressed in the event and person of Jesus Christ.[58] Rather than discouraging interpretation and argument, Tracy thinks this high bar of mystery encourages, or even demands, the effort to try to make sense of it through some personal faith response and through theological reflection on that response. And because all these responses can only be "relatively adequate," there is ultimately an opportunity to debate, to compare, and to judge some responses closer to the mark than others.[59] Moreover, it compels us to recognize that there is no singular way of responding to the Christ event and to accept that the range of possibly acceptable responses is broad indeed.[60]

Finally, Tracy's model of pluralism also expands to recognize what might be called internal or individual pluralism. Tracy connects this claim to his argument for public theology, and specifically for the three primary publics of the theologian: the academy, the society, and the church. Early on, he describes these as a "plurality" of publics that are internalized by theologians.[61] Indeed, he suggests that one might even refer to this as "several internalized selves," further noting the difficulties a theologian might face as a result.[62] This internalization might make it difficult for theologians to make sense of who their work is oriented toward, or even what that work ought be trying to achieve. The commitments to intellectual inquiry of the academy, to creative fidelity in the church, and to responsible action in society can at times pull the theologian in different, even divergent, paths.[63] As with other modes of pluralism, internal pluralism requires

[57] AI 319.
[58] AI 312–13.
[59] AI 319–20.
[60] AI 372.
[61] AI 3.
[62] AI 6.
[63] AI 29.

reflection and serious consideration in order to avoid the "genial confusion" that typically marks lazy pluralism.

While this framing initially emphasizes the internal pluralism of the theologian, Tracy recognizes that this fact is not limited to him or her. In fact, he notes that the theologian is "like any other human being," precisely because he or she has "been socialized into a particular society and a particular academic tradition and [has] been enculturated into one particular culture."[64] While this claim certainly needs nuance and qualification,[65] the central insight here is that a common (if not universal) feature of human experience is a diversity of commitments that have specific mores or scripts and that can, at times, conflict, sometimes subtly, sometimes explicitly. Thus for Tracy, pluralism is not merely a fact of theology, of culture, or of the Christian tradition; it is a fact about the very self.

Religious Pluralism in Later Tracy

Beginning in the late 1980s with *Plurality and Ambiguity* and continuing in the early 1990s with *Dialogue with the Other* and *On Naming the Present*, the focal point of Tracy's approach to pluralism shifts more to the idea of religious pluralism. It is not because this is a new insight for Tracy—the diversity of religious traditions beyond Christianity is an evident concern for him already in *Blessed Rage for Order* and *The Analogical Imagination*—but rather because of his own encounters with Buddhist-Christian dialogue.[66] His participation in

---

[64] AI 25. Here, we might also note that, in principle, Tracy's three publics of the theologian might also be publics for other intellectuals who are not theologians. A professor of chemistry, for example, would also potentially have the publics of the academy and society to consider; were that professor also a believer, he or she might have the church as well.

[65] For example, what about those who, by upbringing or experience, are enculturated in two or more cultures? Or what about those not explicitly or apparently brought up in any academic tradition (or is "academic" here significantly broader than modern Western educational systems)?

[66] In addition to *Dialogue with the Other*, see also David Tracy, "The Christian Understanding of Salvation-Liberation," *Buddhist-Christian Studies* 7 (1987): 129–38; David Tracy, "Kenosis, Sunyata, and Trinity: A Dialogue with Masao Abe," in *Emptying God: A Buddhist-Jewish-Christian Conversation*, ed. John Cobb and Christopher Ives (Maryknoll, NY: Orbis Books, 1990), 135–54; David Tracy, "Some Aspects of the Buddhist-Christian Dialogue," in *The Christian Understanding of God Today*, ed. James M. Byrne (Dublin: Columba Press, 1993), 145–53.

such conversations led him to a greater appreciation for religious pluralism and the positive role he thought it might play.

Several of the key features of Tracy's view of pluralism develop in conversation with this wider religious focus. He continues to find little fruit in attempting a rigid definition of religion. After considering the potential for recognition of similarities-in-differences between religious traditions through authentic conversation, he notes that we might sometimes use a "family resemblance" model for talking about these.[67] For example, diverse forms of Judaism still have enough in common to be recognizably Jewish, even if those similarities cannot be boiled down to a few lowest common denominators. Similarly, the different religious traditions themselves bear family resemblances to one another, whether that be concern with Ultimate Reality or myriad ways of conceiving of "transformation."[68] Even with such family resemblances, however, Tracy is adamant that "there is no single essence, no one content of enlightenment or revelation, no one way of emancipation or liberation, to be found in all that plurality."[69] Indeed, the diversity of religions is simply a fact that one must reckon with.

As he works through his more robust sense of religious pluralism, Tracy more clearly articulates the important if subtle distinction between *plurality* and *pluralism*.[70] *Plurality*, as per the title of the text, refers to the fact of diversity, of myriad possibilities, of a variety of interpretations. It is, essentially, an empirical or descriptive claim about reality.[71] One can see this fact of diversity not only in the various religious traditions, or the diversity within those traditions, but also in the variety of phenomena these traditions and others reflect on or the range of methods employed in that reflection. When Tracy speaks of plurality as an "interruption" to conversation,[72] he is highlighting the fact of the real other, the difficulty of our different languages, and the necessity of reckoning with those differences in order to offer a plausible, responsible interpretation of reality.[73]

---

[67] PA 94–95.
[68] PA 89–90.
[69] PA 90.
[70] PA 90.
[71] Tracy, "Christianity in the Wider Context," 8.
[72] PA 32.
[73] PA 82.

This idea of "reckoning with those differences" brings us closer to what he means by *pluralism*. By this term, he means "one of many possible evaluations" of the fact of plurality.[74] It is, at root, an attitude or posture toward diversity that is open to engaging the possibilities that diversity reveals.[75] Tracy argues that, with this attitude, we as individuals and as communities are more open to growth and development and are better enabled to seek the truth.[76]

That reckoning still requires a critical lens, criteria, and commitment. Tracy's regular inveighing against lazy pluralism or eclecticism takes a more suspicious turn. Noting that even his own past affirmations of pluralism can risk turning into "simply a passive response to more and more possibilities, none of which shall ever be practiced."[77] Responsible pluralism requires at the outset one's openness to learn from other traditions, texts, and figures, including those who are not themselves pluralist. In a striking example, Tracy asks, "Does anyone really wish that Luther, instead of simply stating, 'Here I stand; I can do no other,' had added *sotto voce*, 'But if it really bothers you, I will move'?"[78] Authentic, responsible pluralism requires the pluralist to, at some point, commit to a particular interpretation of reality and defend it, respectfully, in light of other possibilities. Without this "Here I stand" moment, Tracy claims, the pluralist "prove[s] unfaithful to the demands for critical assessment."[79]

While religious pluralism is deeply important to Tracy, the place of pluralism of language must not be overlooked during this period. The third chapter of *Plurality and Ambiguity* focuses on the question of language. While initially this plurality of language might seem obvious, given the thousands of languages that people speak and write in, Tracy has something deeper than a linguistic version of cultural pluralism in mind. Keeping with the theme of "interruption" and what challenges the "ideal speech situation," Tracy argues against views of language that see it only as a tool (the "instrumental" understanding) or as a "system."[80] Instead, language is "discourse,"

---

[74] Tracy, "Christianity in the Wider Context," 8.
[75] PA 90; Tracy, "Christianity in the Wider Context," 9.
[76] Tracy, "Christianity in the Wider Context," 9.
[77] PA 90.
[78] PA 91.
[79] PA 92.
[80] PA 49–51, 53–56.

meaning that "someone says something about something to someone."[81] By this phrase, Tracy wishes to show that language is not simply about the words, their specific usages, or grammar but rather that it shows a world full of explicit and implicit meanings. This world is built on difference, on plurality, and it is only through the interplay of that plurality that one can communicate meaning to another.[82] Through a hermeneutical "discourse analysis" approach to language, it becomes possible to affirm and engage the plurality inherent in language.

Taken together, both religious and linguistic pluralism underlie a larger factor of pluralism: otherness. A key concern for Tracy is to recognize the other as *authentically* other in contrast to a *projected* other.[83] By projection, Tracy focuses on the risk of taking one's own fears, hopes, or expectations and using those as the rigid filter through which the encounter with the other is mediated. This filter prevents the other from being encountered as he/she/it actually is: a person who reveals a possible way of being in the world, a tradition that offers a different worldview, or a text that proposes a new interpretation of existence.[84]

The encounter with otherness is thus a way of framing religious pluralism and the encounter with other faith traditions. In *Dialogue with the Other*, Tracy gives particular attention to Buddhist-Christian dialogue and Jewish-Christian dialogue.[85] In both cases, he emphasizes how these different traditions offer opportunities for each to learn more fully about itself. For example, he discusses the Buddhist teaching of the no-self as a way of further understanding Christian freedom and its opposition to "possessive individualism . . . [and] the culture's terror at its own transience."[86] He notes in doing so that the no-self idea is not a doctrine *per se* (a far more Christian term) but rather a "realization of emptiness and dependent co-origination" within the Buddhist tradition.[87] By participating in this conversation

---

[81] PA 61.
[82] PA 65.
[83] DWO 4.
[84] PA 93; DWO 41.
[85] Chapters 4 and 5, respectively.
[86] DWO 76.
[87] DWO 75.

with an "other" tradition, the Christian can come to a deeper understanding of that other and also of oneself. This realization comes only
when one lets the other be authentically other *and* lets oneself be
authentically oneself.

Moreover, this sense of otherness is connected to Tracy's idea of
internal pluralism. In contrast to the integral, autonomous self as-
sumed by Enlightenment thought, Tracy posits that we have come
to recognize the "split self" that characterizes postmodernity.[88]
Through deeper reflection on that self, one can come to recognize
"the radical otherness not only around us but within us," which Tracy
names the "unconscious."[89] In going beyond the possibilities that
emerge outside of ourselves, presented by other persons and traditions, Tracy alerts us to the unconscious parts of ourselves that are
not entirely under our control. As a result, he insists that human
knowing is limited to relative adequacy and our self-understanding
and self-control are ultimately limited by the lack of "transparency
of consciousness to itself."[90] Thus the interruption of plurality affects
more than religious traditions and language; it affects our very selves.
As a result, the "split self" of postmodernity will, at best, achieve a
"rough coherence: interrupted, obscure, often confused, self-conscious
of its own language use and, above all, aware of the ambiguities of
all histories and traditions."[91]

Finally, engagement with the other leads Tracy to tentatively move
beyond the language of pluralism and plurality. He notes that while
the language of pluralism and the other might help us to pay greater
attention to the marginalized, in reality it reinforces the sense that
"we" are at the center of things. This literal self-centering contributes
to that danger of the "projected" other.[92] He therefore introduces
"polycentrism" as a way of describing this plurality. This term maintains the diversity and range evident within the world, but it also
recognizes that there is no one center around which all is arrayed.[93]
It challenges the pluralist posture to recognize its own otherness and

---

[88] PA 77, 82.
[89] PA 77.
[90] PA 78.
[91] PA 83.
[92] ONP 4.
[93] ONP 5.

particularity. With respect to the Christian tradition, then, one must be open to the existence of "each center of Christian theology in our situation," which though varied and contentious are also united in their orientation to the church, to Christ, and to God.[94]

Sanks and the Problems of Pluralism

Returning to Sanks's schema, it is clear that he successfully paints the broad strokes of pluralism for Tracy.[95] In both his major texts and his articles, Tracy does give significant focus to theological, cultural, and religious pluralism, respectively. Yet there are important places where Sanks's typology falls short. First, his periodization of Tracy is not as clean as he suggests. While it is true that Tracy emphasizes theological pluralism in *Blessed Rage for Order*, the insight into religious pluralism extends as far back. Moreover, the idea of pluralism within theology extends forward, particularly in his insights about the plurality within the early Christian tradition and how that continues to the present.

Second, Sanks misses a crucial distinction in Tracy between pluralism and plurality. The fact of diversity and the way in which one responds to that diversity are different, and Tracy argues in favor of pluralism as one particular posture to adopt. This approach pushes the individual, the community, the tradition to be authentically itself while also being open to the possibilities and challenges presented by the other. Nonetheless, one can reject the posture of pluralism without denying the fact of plurality. In defense of Sanks, Tracy did not make this distinction explicit until later,[96] but it is a necessary distinction for understanding the path Tracy pursues.

Third, Sanks overlooks other key aspects of pluralism for Tracy. The plurality of methods and readings is a crucial foundation for many of the other types of plurality. The internal pluralism that impacts individual persons is essential to Tracy's theological anthro-

---

[94] ONP 18.

[95] Following the publication of *On Naming the Present*, none of Tracy's essays offer new insights into his views on pluralism, neither by development nor by expansion. Thus there is no need to go beyond the periods outlined by Sanks in his essay.

[96] See PA 90 and Tracy, "Christianity in the Wider Context," 8.

pology. As for language, Tracy sees the plurality of language as one of the most central interruptions to conversation, and thus as a major concern for the entire enterprise of theology itself. Tracy's sense of plurality is tremendously broad, and it puts us into the difficult position of learning how to navigate it. Indeed, it makes it difficult to discern rightly what is true. He offers us the analogical imagination as the best way forward in that endeavor.

An Analogical Imagination as Catholic Response to Plurality

There are several options one might pursue for engaging this fact of plurality. One option, frequently criticized by Tracy, is the lazy or eclectic approach, which prefers to avoid critical judgments of other commitments, cultures, and modes of thought. He often derides this as the "let a thousand flowers bloom"[97] approach, which is ultimately unable to make any kind of claims of truth, nor can it even defend the criteria and warrants needed for truth claims. This approach tends toward univocity and the assertion of irreducible sameness. Given how much of Tracy's work, particularly in theological method, is built on developing the necessary tools for productive, intelligent conversation and argument, his rejection of lazy or eclectic pluralism is obvious.

A second option would be to reject all that is different, to see it as simply false on its face. This approach has no room for the diversity that exists within one particular faith tradition, let alone among a multitude of traditions and cultures. Tracy sees this approach as one that does not give texts like the Bible their due regard, as it commits to a hermeneutical reading divorced from the text and then imposes it on the text. This approach is unable to find the seeds (or even the growing plants) of truth that may be present in traditions and communities other than one's own. This is essentially the more equivocal approach, which is unable to allow for any similarity amid the overwhelming differences.

[97] AI 319.

Tracy opts instead for a third approach for engaging pluralism, which he terms "the analogical imagination."[98] He describes analogical language as "a language of ordered relationships articulating similarity-in-difference."[99] An initial sense of analogy, then, might be similar to the types of questions sometimes included on standardized tests: A is to B as C is to D, or Obi-Wan Kenobi is to Luke Skywalker as Duncan MacLeod is to Richie Ryan. We use this ordered relationship to recognize what the pairs hold in common while also acknowledging the differences between them. Thus in this example, broad familiarity with the mentor-mentee relationship between the two characters from the *Star Wars* franchise can help readers learn that there's a similar mentor-mentee relationship between the latter two *Highlander* franchise characters. Yet there are significant differences between these relationships: the Obi-Wan/Luke relationship falls under the shadow of a third figure, Darth Vader, while the MacLeod/Ryan relationship builds on one training the other to survive "the Game" by learning to fight to the death with swords. Tracy sees this analogical process as key to learning and understanding: by making comparisons to what we already know, we can come to understand what we do not yet know.[100]

This basic sense of analogy allows Tracy to get into a deeper and more fundamental mode. Recognizing that theology is, at its root, a

---

[98] One might reasonably argue that Tracy sees the analogical imagination as more than a response to contemporary plurality, and, in a sense, that would be correct. For Tracy, the analogical imagination is the focal insight into how Christians broadly, and Catholics specifically, understand reality. To restrict the analogical imagination, which Tracy explicitly connects to the theologies of St. Thomas Aquinas and the First Vatican Council, to current concerns would be foolish (see David Tracy, "The Catholic Analogical Imagination," *Proceedings of the Catholic Theological Society of America* 32 [1977]: 237–40).

One ought also to recognize, however, that Tracy does not really consider plurality to be solely a contemporary or new phenomenon. As this chapter has endeavored to show, Tracy thinks that diversity and particularity are inevitable features of reality, that human knowledge and understanding does proceed and always has proceeded through analogical thinking, and that the prime, fundamental analogue in existence is the event and person of Jesus Christ. Thus the analogical imagination is, in a sense, more than a way of engaging pluralism, but in another sense plurality is a timeless and ever-timely fact of human existence.

[99] AI 408.

[100] AI 447.

second-order reflection on religious experience, he argues that theology is seeking to develop ordered relationships that help to make sense of religious experiences in light of the divine (or, as he refers to it in *The Analogical Imagination*, "the whole").[101] Building on the longstanding kataphatic approach in the Christian tradition, he claims that what is specific to the theological mode of analogy is that the "order among the relationships is constituted by the distinct but similar relationships of each analogue to some primary focal meaning, some prime analogue."[102] Theological reflection on religious experience thus describes these relationships around their connection to the "prime analogue," which in the Christian tradition is Jesus Christ. Indeed, he argues that the whole effort of systematic theology itself is built on Christ as this prime analogue.[103]

The key to this claim is that Christ is the incarnation of God. Through Christ, the divine is most perfectly mediated to created reality. As religious experience brings us into contact with the divine, the relative adequacy of religious claims is measured according to how it relates to the prime analogue that is Christ. Amid the plurality of human experiences, traditions, and communities, it is through their particularity that one finds the ordered relationships that connect it to the divine. Tracy does not see this as saying that all claims to religious experience are equal or that any interpretation of divine revelation is as good as another. Rather, it is insofar as these particular expressions disclose the universal that they are better or worse analogies to the revelation in Christ. The analogical imagination is, most basically, an incarnational and sacramental imagination that sees the inbreaking of God into the world through the particular traditions, experiences, and expressions of human life.[104]

He contrasts analogical language with dialectical language. The essential aspect of dialectical theological language is "the necessity of radical theological negations to constitute all Christian theological language."[105] This approach can lead one to a host of "negations":

[101] AI 408.
[102] AI 408.
[103] AI 421.
[104] Tracy, "The Catholic Analogical Imagination," 236, 239.
[105] AI 415.

rejecting any continuity between faith and culture, denying the ability to save oneself apart from God, opposing anything but infinite difference between the Creator and creation. Tracy most clearly connects this theological language to the twentieth-century neo-orthodox theologians (Barth, Tillich, Gogarten), but its roots clearly extend back through the long apophatic tradition in Christianity. This language disrupts ordered relationships, especially any efforts that might smack of Bonhoeffer's "cheap grace."[106]

Where the relationship between analogical and dialectical languages becomes clearest for Tracy is when it comes to the question of imagination. Human imagination is not simply about creating something new; it is about taking what one knows or has experienced and reconfiguring that reality, leading to some new possibility from that. An imagination that is built solely or primarily on dialectical language becomes unable to see the similarities and relationships between the divine and the created, between Christianity and its context. On its own, according to Tracy, "a theological negative dialectics" leads eventually to "the chaos of pure equivocity."[107] By contrast, Tracy fears that if one's imagination is formed only by the similarities in analogy without taking account of the dissimilarities, one lurches toward "an atheological vision of a deadening univocity."[108] In his desire to avoid both equivocal and univocal responses to pluralism, then, Tracy argues for an analogical imagination that integrates the negating edge of dialectical language. The analogical imagination makes it possible to "literally reimagine reality as a new series of ordered possibilities."[109] Imagination allows one to come to a new, better understanding of reality; the analogical part recognizes that the key to that is the focal point that gives meaning to that reality.

A simplistic reading of the analogical and dialectical imaginations might conclude that they describe Catholic and Protestant worldviews, respectively. There is a kernel of truth in this: Tracy describes the analogical imagination as the "family resemblance of what con-

---

[106] AI 417.
[107] AI 421.
[108] AI 413.
[109] Tracy, "The Catholic Analogical Imagination," 235.

stitutes Catholicism" rather than as its defining, fundamental feature,[110] while many of his key examples for illustrating dialectical language are Protestant.[111] But in some cases, Tracy treats it more as a question of emphasis: his reading of liberation theologies (both Catholic and Protestant), for example, notes their strong dialectical edge, manifested in their critique of the present order of the world and its opposition to the Gospel.[112] Even in such cases, however, he reads this dialectical move as occurring within the larger "context of analogical imagination because they seek to reimagine reality."[113] The move to a praxis of transformation shows the larger hope in the possibility of a different ordering to reality. Tracy sees the potential for various theologies to employ different balances of these theological languages, but he ultimately argues that the more analogical approach is the best for systematic theology.

By attending to the prime analogue that is Christ, Tracy believes that we can come to a deeper understanding not only of ourselves but of our relationship both to God and to the world.[114] To some extent, this must always take account of our present selves and our present world, which is why the theologian seeks a more relatively adequate theology in his or her particular situation.[115] This approach—constructing one's theology (especially systematic theology) around this prime analogue—allows the theologian to respond to the particular situation from within a given tradition. Put another way, the analogical imagination describes a worldview that allows one to recognize and come to some relative understanding of the infinite, universal God within the particularities of one's context, community, and experience.[116] Given the diversity of such contexts, communities, and experiences, the analogical imagination serves to find the similarities that connect a plurality of theologies together.

---

[110] Tracy, "The Catholic Analogical Imagination," 234–35.

[111] Beyond the neo-orthodox theologians listed above, he also references Søren Kierkegaard and Jürgen Moltmann (AI 415–16).

[112] AI 419–20; Tracy, "The Catholic Analogical Imagination," 238.

[113] Tracy, "The Catholic Analogical Imagination," 238.

[114] AI 425.

[115] AI 421–22.

[116] AI 429.

The analogical imagination thus describes the very approach that leads one both to a sacramental worldview and to rely on classics for one's theology. The sacramental worldview sees how particular, concrete symbols make manifest the universal love of God in the life of the church. It presents a series of ordered relationships (e.g., between bread and wine and body and blood) that both signify and make present the incarnate God (i.e., Christ, the prime analogue). These sacraments are themselves classics, in Tracy's sense, precisely as they are permanent and excessive expressions from within a tradition that, through their particularity, reveal the universal God. Sacraments, and the classics more broadly, are both deeply analogical dimensions of the Christian faith.

Conclusion

While Sanks's typology for assessing Tracy's approach to pluralism has much to commend it, the focus on pluralism within theology, cultural pluralism, and the pluralism of religious traditions leaves out several key aspects of his thought. The separation of periods in Tracy's thought obscures the long arcs of different aspects of pluralism, the relationship between plurality as a fact and pluralism as a commitment and approach is ignored, and other aspects of pluralism are simply overlooked. Perhaps the most foundational claim about plurality that Tracy wishes to make clear is that such plurality is not a new fact of reality but rather an ever-present one. Not only is it evident within theology, culture, and religious traditions, but it is also clear in our languages, our interpretations, and our core texts. Tracy's emphasis on how rigorous analysis of New Testament texts and the early church reveal the plurality present at that time underscores our present plurality; indeed, it directs us to consider that plurality with renewed eyes.

The analogical imagination allows for theological appreciation of this plurality while also offering a way forward. The diversity of interpretations, sources, traditions, and claims need not be accepted uncritically or rejected out of hand. Rather, by seeking what they share in common and how they relate to the revelation of God in Christ, the theologian can appreciate the plural expressions within and among religious traditions.

5

Christology

To state "I believe in Jesus Christ" is to affirm that, in whatever form of mediation I have experienced this event, the event itself as the decisive event of God's self-manifestation in Jesus Christ takes primacy.

—David Tracy[1]

In an exchange in the Gospel of Mark, Jesus asks his disciples who other people have been saying he is (Mark 8:27-30; NAB). They rattle off several possible options: John the Baptist, Elijah, or some other prophet. Jesus then pivots the question, asking the disciples what they think. This question—"Who do you say I am?"—effectively encapsulates the central question of Christology. Theologians must reckon with the question of who Jesus is and what makes him so essential to the Christian tradition.

Although it is a typically overlooked aspect of his theology, Tracy does offer an answer to the Markan question. While other theologians might investigate questions around the union of humanity and divinity or Jesus' self-awareness of his mission, Tracy focuses on the role of mediation in the life of Christ. He investigates this mediation in two senses: what it means to see Christ as the essential mediator between the divine and the human and also how Christ is himself mediated in the present moment. This approach can aid in understanding how other Christologies analyze the presence of Christ in

[1] AI 329.

the church and the world today, but Tracy's efforts have been largely ignored. Discerning the reason for this neglect requires looking back into the arc of his Christology, particularly the key dimensions of Christology that he returns to again and again.

This chapter proceeds in four movements. First, it examines Tracy's initial forays into Christology in the latter half of *Blessed Rage for Order*, specifically his focus on Christ as "re-presentative" of God. Christ here serves rhetorically to support the transition from religious and theocentric language about God to the specifically Christian means of approaching God. Second, it outlines how the re-presentative Christ is reframed in Tracy's language of the classic and the "prime analogue." The emphasis on the classic here supports Tracy's development of what he calls the classic Christian forms of mediation: manifestation, proclamation, and action. Third, the chapter considers how the emphasis on Christ as mediator shifts in Tracy's later writings in light of the development of fragments and his theocentric turn. In this context, Tracy continues his focus on Christ as liberating, not only from political and material oppression, but also from a certain conceptual totalitarianism. Finally, the chapter argues that the scant attention Tracy's Christology receives is the result of numerous factors, including that rhetorically Christ often functions as much as an example of other concepts in Tracy as he does a central focus in his own right and that the claims Tracy makes about Christology are not significantly innovative or different from other more robust and more explicit Christologies. While Christ is at the nexus of much of Tracy's theology, Christ is sometimes a secondary focus in his theology.

Christology in *Blessed Rage for Order*

The core of Tracy's christological work in *Blessed Rage for Order* is in the ninth chapter. Here, he pursues a detour in his larger fundamental work to see how the ideas of fact and fiction could illuminate the image of Christ as re-presentative of God. Unpacking this approach requires first explaining his somewhat idiosyncratic understanding of fact, including three key facts about human existence he thinks shape reception of the New Testament narratives about Jesus. Following this, Tracy develops the idea of re-presentation as his way to talk about Christ as the mediating figure between God and humanity.

First, by "fact," Tracy means something that is a particular way but, at least theoretically, could have been otherwise. For example, the Apollo 11 moon landing, led by Neil Armstrong and Buzz Aldrin, is a historical fact. The events could have unfolded differently—perhaps different astronauts, a different date, or even a failed mission—but they did not. Fact, in this sense, is basically what has traditionally been called "contingent." Tracy contrasts facts with metaphysical realities, which are necessary and could not be otherwise.[2] With respect to Tracy's Christology, what is at stake here is that, in Christ, there is a collision between these senses of fact and metaphysical reality. While Christ is a re-presentation of the universally metaphysically necessary God, Christ is also the historical manifestation of the same who became incarnate in a particular body, a particular place, a particular time, any of which could have been otherwise.[3] By saying so, Tracy seeks to preserve divine freedom: there is no compulsion in God's incarnation in Christ but a free, gratuitous decision about how it was to take place.[4] Moreover, the incarnation ties in with Tracy's emphasis on the tension between the universal and the particular: the historical self-revelation of Christ is a particular expression of the universal God. And because God is universal, this revelation potentially has existential meaning for all of human experience.[5] The fact of Christ is a centrally effective means of encountering the metaphysical necessity of God.

This notion of fact leads Tracy to some key facts of human existence that till the ground in which the seed of Christology is sown. The first of these is the fact that humans need and perhaps best understand through "story, fiction, and symbol."[6] Here, he emphasizes strongly the term "fiction," at turns provocatively and unproductively describing the narratives about Christ as fictions that can be revelatory of

[2] BRO 205.
[3] BRO 205.
[4] Here, one can see parallels to St. Anselm's argument regarding antecedent and consequent necessity, the latter of which sounds much like Tracy's "fact." See *Cur Deus Homo* 2.18.
[5] BRO 206.
[6] BRO 205.

new possibilities.[7] He does not appear to use the word "fiction" to mean false or made up but instead as a "redescription of what reality is and might be."[8] In this he seeks to recapture the value of narrative in theology as often more effective than "careful analytical discussions."[9] This does not preclude the value of such rigorous analysis or of the doctrines and teachings it can produce. It simply means that while both narrative and doctrine are required, human experience attests to the transformative power of stories for understanding such doctrinal claims, for understanding ourselves, and for imagining how reality might be better.

His second fact is the reality of evil in human existence.[10] Again he references the fact/metaphysical reality distinction, noting that if evil were necessary it would entirely undermine the claim of human freedom and responsibility (such freedom, in fact, he does consider a metaphysical necessity).[11] Evil is instead an *inevitability*, as the Christian tradition describes evil and sin as an inescapable condition of human existence.[12]

The third and final fact is something of a feint: Tracy wishes to distinguish between facts that are actualizations of possibilities and facts that are re-presentations of possibilities.[13] The former category of facts are, according to Tracy, the standard Aristotelian understanding of act and potency: when something moves from being a possibility to an actuality, it has become a fact that precludes other possibilities.[14] For example, when LeBron James is considering

---

[7] BRO 207.

[8] BRO 208. Writing about various types of narrative theology, Gary Comstock picks up on this, describing fiction as "a way of construing the world." He goes on to say "all narratives are fictions, constructions of the human imagination. To infer that this means they are false, however, is to commit the genetic fallacy. The origin of a story is not necessarily relevant to deciding whether it is true or false" (Gary L. Comstock, "Two Types of Narrative Theology," *Journal of the American Academy of Religion* 55, no. 4 [Winter 1987]: 696, 705n17).

[9] BRO 208.

[10] BRO 205.

[11] BRO 212.

[12] In this section, Tracy considers a few different attempts to explain the fact of evil, particularly medieval and Niebuhrian accounts, but largely only in passing. His central goal in this section is simply to establish the long Christian tradition of seeing evil as a fact but not a necessity of human nature.

[13] BRO 214–15.

[14] BRO 214.

whether to remain on the Cleveland Cavaliers or go to the Miami Heat, he has two possibilities in front of him. By deciding to take his talents to South Beach, one of those possibilities has become actual while the other is neither actual nor possible. Tracy's latter category, the re-presentation of possibilities, is much more significant for Christology. What he argues here is that symbolic language, whether that be religious, ritualized, or fictional, offers to its practitioners and recipients a "re-presentation" of possibilities. Such re-presentations connect the person to real possibilities that they can actualize in their own lives.

Tracy is adamant that such re-presentations are not "mere possibilities" but must be described as "facts."[15] At issue in this claim is that the re-presentation goes beyond a mere claim about some past event or text. He references, for example, Martin Luther King Jr. On one hand, Tracy notes the historical fact of King living a good life dedicated to a righteous cause. In this way, the fact of King is a person who actualized a particular possibility for himself. On the other hand, re-presentative, King becomes a symbol for the rest of humanity, demonstrating a real possibility for how one might now choose to live one's own life in the face of injustice. The power of King's life goes beyond the specific fact of his own. The symbolic representation that one might receive from that life offers a new "possible mode-of-being-in-this-world."[16] Moreover, Tracy notes that, to some extent, a figure like King could fall short of really fulfilling the good possibilities of his own life and still serve as a powerful symbol. This is a part of Tracy's claim that there is a difference between the fact as actualization of a possibility (King living a holy life in opposition to injustice) and fact as symbolic representation (King's example disclosing new possibilities for the rest of humanity in how to oppose injustice).[17]

---

[15] BRO 215.

[16] BRO 216.

[17] Tracy does not drive that example through King himself, making no reference to evidence of King's infidelity as an example of his own failure to actualize his possibilities. Rather, Tracy notes, in the example of sacraments as re-presentations, that the principle of *ex opere operato* means that even if the priest confecting the sacrament is not living a good and holy life, it does not in the least take away from the symbolic power of the sacrament to re-present a mode of holiness in the world for the recipient of the sacrament (BRO 215).

Tracy's approach to Christology in *Blessed Rage for Order* rests on this distinction between two kinds of facts. He claims that the first kind, which would focus on how Christ actualizes certain possibilities in his life, would emphasize those questions about Jesus' psychological state, such as his awareness of his divine nature or his knowledge about his future mission. Such an approach would involve significant historical and hermeneutical evaluations of Christ in the New Testament, which is valuable and necessary work. Instead, Tracy focuses on the second kind as he seeks to investigate what is revealed in Christ about "the truth of human existence."[18] The main work of a contemporary Christology would be to determine what all this groundwork, Christ's "words, his deeds, and his destiny, as expressions of his office of messiahship," would reveal about the human relationship to God.[19] In the context of Tracy's revisionist approach to theology in *Blessed Rage for Order*, the heart of christological language is discerning what the fact (*not* metaphysical necessity) of God's becoming human in Jesus of Nazareth reveals for humans in the present day about how one ought to live and how one is related to God.

In the final few pages of the chapter, Tracy finally offers the Christology he's been building the intellectual substructure for. Recognizing, first, the fact of human need for narrative to understand oneself, one's traditions, and one's God, and, second, the fact of human sinfulness, Tracy recapitulates the narrative depiction of Christ in the New Testament with a specific emphasis on three christological symbols. First, the ministry of Christ, both in word and deed, represents to us today his focus on "eschatological 'Kingdom' language" that discloses "the promise of a new righteousness for humanity."[20] Christ lives the sort of life that humans are called to, a life at the limits of human possibility. Humans are called to take the risk of self-sacrificial love, the same risk Jesus called his first disciples to, and serve others the way Jesus did. The fact of Christ's ministry discloses this possibility for human existence.[21]

---

[18] BRO 216–17.
[19] BRO 218.
[20] BRO 219.
[21] BRO 219.

Second, Tracy ties the ministry of Christ to his crucifixion. That ministry led almost inexorably to the "dishonorable and obscene fate of crucifixion."[22] The key possibility represented in the symbol of the cross is that the life Jesus modeled and called others to live is countercultural, contrary to the powers of the world. The cross is a result of the fact of sin; it stands in opposition to and in judgment of that sin.

Third, the symbols of the ministry and the cross lead to the resurrection. Tracy interprets the resurrection as evidence that "the representative words, deeds, and teachings of this representative figure, this Jesus as the Christ, can in fact be trusted."[23] The resurrection validates the life, ministry, and death of Christ and thus supports the possible way of living that Christ models for all other persons. Moreover, Tracy takes the resurrection as further support for one's basic faith in the God that takes on flesh in Christ, as Christ's "words, deeds, and destiny" reveal God to be a "loving, righteous Father" who desires the liberation and salvation of all persons.[24]

These three symbols together form the core of Tracy's Christology in *Blessed Rage for Order*. He describes the Christian tradition as "radically christocentric," seeking to show that the way in which Christ represents "the only God there is" is essential and fundamental to Christianity. The three symbols of ministry, cross, and resurrection, taken collectively, reveal "the presence of the righteous, loving, gracious God re-presented in Jesus the Christ."[25] All who hear the call of Christ are invited "to risk living a life-at-the-limits," one that is committed to the sort of self-sacrificial commitment to others that Jesus had.[26] He notes the tension between "exclusivist" and "inclusivist" understandings of Jesus, arguing for the latter because Jesus discloses all reality and is meaningful for common (not only Christian) human experience.[27]

His Christology, then, has both a sacramental and an anthropological bend to it in *Blessed Rage for Order*. Tracy does not expend significant effort here to consider psychological questions about the

---

[22] BRO 219–20.
[23] BRO 220.
[24] BRO 220.
[25] BRO 221.
[26] BRO 221.
[27] BRO 206.

consciousness of Christ, metaphysical questions about the hypostatic union of divine and human nature, or ecclesiological questions about the relation between the material and mystical bodies of Christ. Rather, he focuses on what he means by Christ as "re-presentative" (i.e., Christ as a particular yet full mediator of the agapic love of the universal God) and how that re-presentation is significant for human beings (disclosive of genuine possibilities for living a holy life). The issue of mediation is thus at the heart of Tracy's early Christology.

Christology in *The Analogical Imagination*

Christology continues as a significant focus in *The Analogical Imagination*, and it retains the core concerns of *Blessed Rage for Order*. Tracy's response to the question of "Who do you say I am?" continues to focus on Christ as mediator of God and as the disclosure of a possible way of living. Yet his development of the classic provides a more robust intellectual framework within which to think about Christ as mediator, and his greater attention to systematic theology enables critical engagement with the contexts and forms in and through which this mediation occurs. As a result, Tracy both expands on and pulls away from some of his christological concerns in *Blessed Rage for Order* while still upholding his core commitments.

To begin, *The Analogical Imagination* recapitulates Tracy's language of "re-presentation" for talking about Christ as mediator. He writes that Christians must recognize Christ as "the decisive re-presentation in both word and manifestation of our God and our humanity."[28] While the significance of "word and manifestation" will be examined below, here it is worth noting the fuller sense of mediation that Tracy imbues re-presentation with. Throughout *Blessed Rage for Order*, "re-presentation" consistently refers to the idea of Christ as the fact, narrative, and symbol that both reveals God and also exhibits a new way of being human in the world. Here, Tracy maintains the idea that God is mediated to humans through Christ, but he also casually references that Christ also re-presents "humanity." This draws on the traditional Chalcedonian Christology of the full divinity and full humanity of Christ and the concomitant recognition that Christ medi-

---

[28] AI 218.

ates human nature to God.[29] His approach to mediation here is more explicitly, if cursorily, bilateral than in *Blessed Rage for Order*.

Further, Tracy continues his emphasis on Christ as a model of human living. He again references the gospel narratives and the variety of central symbols in Christ's life as markers of possibility for all other human beings. He connects this to "our deepest yearnings for wholeness," which are grounded in God's own desires for our flourishing.[30] In pursuit of this, Tracy challenges us to accept that Christ's life is one of love that goes beyond "sentimentalized notions" and enters into "preference for the outcasts, the poor, the oppressed" and "love of the enemy."[31] He describes this life as one in contrast to what Bonhoeffer calls "cheap grace," as this life makes demands and places the self at risk. Tracy considers such a life to be possible so long as one "trust[s] in the God who is Love and whose decisive re-presentation is Jesus Christ."[32] The notion of trust references here the language of "basic faith" from *Blessed Rage for Order*: Christians have a "fundamental faith" in the "all-pervasive reality of the God of love and power disclosed in Jesus Christ."[33]

Christ the Classic

Tracy's understanding of Christ as mediator and model is developed far more robustly through Tracy's concept of the classic. As previously mentioned, classics are particular expressions that disclose both an excess and a permanence of meaning. When used as a lens for understanding Christ, Tracy emphasizes the *religious* classic, where the truth disclosed in the classic is connected to "the whole" and a sense of "radical mystery."[34] He describes Christ as the classic

---

[29] Tracy never really investigates the Chalcedonian concerns about nature, person, or the hypostatic union; these, much like the questions surrounding Christ's divine self-awareness, are simply not his focus. It is apparent that he accepts the Chalcedonian formulation and that his argument about Christ as re-presentative of God depends on that claim.

[30] AI 329.

[31] AI 330.

[32] AI 330–31.

[33] AI 51.

[34] AI 168–69.

par excellence, because Christ is the standard by which all other Christian classics are judged.[35] Put another way, all Christian classics seek to disclose something true about the universal God through a particular expression. Christ, as both *event* and *person* (two of the types of classics Tracy frequently references), is such a particular expression: the Word made flesh.[36] Moreover, Christ, who re-presents the divine to humanity, is the fullest and most complete expression of the very truth that all other Christian classics seek in some way to communicate.[37]

Tracy's success in this claim hinges on his categories of "event" and "person." These two terms are consistently linked for Tracy whenever he describes Christ as a classic. This is striking in his work, as the form of classic that he overwhelmingly focuses on is *texts* (as might be expected of an academic). The emphasis on event and person, however, is necessary in order to do justice to how the classic of Christ is encountered by Christians.

"Person" is fairly straightforward for Tracy, typically referring to an individual human person. *Classic* persons would be those who, through the particularity of their lives, disclose a potentially universally accessible truth. The saints and mystics are in many ways the paradigmatic examples of persons as classics for Tracy.[38] One might consider the life of Mother Teresa, whose life's work revealed a profound commitment to the marginalized and ignored. As a person, she herself re-presented central truths of the Gospel, but in such a way that she also touched the lives of persons who were not Christian, who were not part of the particularities of her culture and location.

Christologically, Tracy does not delve deeply into the meaning of the term "person," sidestepping doctrinal questions about divine and human natures and the hypostatic union. It's not that Tracy provides

---

[35] AI 233.

[36] Anthony J. Kelly draws on Tracy's description of Christ as *the* classic as part of his argument for how Christology can reinforce the concreteness of Christian belief (Anthony J. Kelly, "Refreshing Experience: The Christ-Event as Fact, Classic, and Phenomenon," *Irish Theological Quarterly* 77, no. 4 [2012]: 335–48).

[37] See Second Vatican Council, *Dei Verbum*, Dogmatic Constitution on Divine Revelation (1965), no. 2.

[38] AI 381; here, he mentions Francis of Assisi as such an example.

any grounds on which to question his acceptance of such teachings: his description of Christ is evidently orthodox. Rather, the point here is that these doctrinal questions seem not to be a driving question in his work. Simply put, his use of "person" here is consistent with the larger tradition, and it is tied specifically to his focus on Christ as mediator. It is in Jesus that one finds "the person in whom God's own self is decisively re-presented as the gift and command of love."[39] His use of "person" seems largely to be for reiterating that Jesus Christ lived a real human life in history and in a particular place, which is a *sine qua non* of the Christian tradition.

Jesus Christ as classic person is tied intimately to Jesus Christ as classic event. "Event," too, seems to have a largely straightforward if not carefully delineated meaning: events are simply things that have occurred. For example, the past event of Chuck Yeager breaking the sound barrier can potentially be named a classic precisely because that event disclosed truth about the human experience of boundaries and the desire to transcend them. It was an event deeply shaped by its historical and technological context, but it can serve as a potent expression of how the finite pursues transcendence.

What is striking in Tracy's christological and religious use of "event" is how it ties the *past* dimension of the event into the *present* experience of the event. There is an already/not yet character to the Christ event that connects one's present encounter with Christ with the historical reality of Christ's incarnation, ministry, crucifixion, and resurrection. The Christian believer, then, is someone "for whom that event has happened and does happen."[40] This differentiates it from the typical sense of event (such as the Chuck Yeager example above): the Christ event is "an event *from God* and by God's power" that is experienced anew in the present day.[41] Event and person are in fact tied together precisely because the *event* aspect of Christ as classic links past and present to the *person* aspect of Christ in whom God has chosen to fully and completely reveal God's presence, power, and love. This reality of God, disclosed in the event and person of

[39] AI 234.
[40] AI 234.
[41] AI 234–35.

Christ, is thus mediated now to any persons who encounter Christ in contemporary realities.[42]

Contexts and Classic Forms of Mediation

This raises the essential question that occupies much of the latter half of *The Analogical Imagination*: Where and how does this mediation occur? There are two senses in which Tracy talks about the mediation of Christ. First, he names the church, the tradition, and the Scriptures as central places or contexts in which Christ is mediated to the person. All of these are understood to be witnesses to Christ, but they are also normatively judged by Christ. Second, he describes three different expressions or modes in which the mediation takes place: manifestation, proclamation, and action. His descriptions of these almost sound like different languages, in a way comparable to analogical and dialectical languages. As will be shown, however, these three modes of mediation are not reducible to either analogical or dialectical imaginations.

As was noted previously, Tracy describes the church, along with the society and the academy, as one of the three publics for theology.[43] It is, in a meaningful sense, a social institution that depends on one's choice to be a member. In this way, the church is comparable to other membership-based organizations, such as unions, fan clubs, and cooperatives. Yet Tracy also wants to argue that the church cannot be reduced to this "sociological" reality because, more fundamentally, the church is a gift that participates in "the grace of God disclosed in the divine self-manifestation in Jesus Christ."[44] Indeed, he names it as the "primary mediator" of that gift—of the event and person of

---

[42] There are some grounds for distinguishing person and event for Tracy, where person corresponds to Jesus and event corresponds to Christ; see especially AI 235–36. The idea here is that the *Christ* event is about the event of divine revelation, then and now, while the *Jesus* person is about the specific individual in whom that *Christ* event occurs. Tracy does not really push this distinction too strongly, as he wants the emphasis to far more strongly rest on the claim that *Jesus is the Christ*. The revelation in that event and person is both unified and unique, and so the value of distinguishing them in this way is limited.

[43] See pages 28–30 for Tracy's understanding of the church in the context of public theology.

[44] AI 23.

Christ.[45] In contrast to more individualist approaches to Christianity, Tracy argues that Christians come to believe in Christ because their "present experience of the Christ event" is always "mediated by the whole community of the Christian church."[46] Without the community called together by Christ and guided by the Holy Spirit, there can be no authentic communication of Jesus Christ.[47]

The church cannot be separated from a second context of mediation, the tradition. Tradition for Tracy is, at heart, the ongoing conversation among the members of the church about the plural beliefs, practices, rituals, and commitments that make up the Christian faith. It cannot be limited simply to the things passed on (the *tradita*) but includes also the process of that passing on (the *traditio*).[48] This process continually requires taking account of the new historical and social contexts in which the tradition finds itself while holding onto its core. Through this tradition, the Christian is able to experience Christ in the present through "word, sacrament, and action."[49] These three aspects of the tradition are indeed central to both what the tradition communicates about Christ and how it communicates. One's faith in or fidelity to Christ therefore is based in a real sense on one's trust in the reality of Christ as the tradition has carried it.[50]

Indeed, the tradition and the church are not so much separate contexts for mediation as interconnected realities. They represent distinct ways of talking about the essentially communal and diachronic reality of the Christian faith. The present experience of the event of Christ requires as a condition of possibility that the past event and person of Christ be communicated, shared, and passed on from the originating historical event and person, through the community of believers in their texts, rituals, and practices. The tradition has an intrinsically "communal character," and the community cannot sustain itself without the ongoing shared practices and beliefs that are central to the tradition.[51] Tracy cautions against "the familiar

---

[45] AI 50.
[46] AI 428.
[47] AI 328–29.
[48] AI 100.
[49] AI 234.
[50] AI 322–23.
[51] AI 322.

distortions of that faith into ecclesiolatry and traditionalism," in which one improperly orders the relationship of Christ to these twin contexts of mediation.[52] While the encounter with Christ is mediated through the church and the tradition, these two realities are always in fact measured against the norm of Christ.

Often implicit in this for Tracy is the normative role of Scripture as well. While he works on Christology in the latter half of *The Analogical Imagination*, Tracy focuses especially on different sections of Scripture and what they reveal about Christ. As he enters into these interpretive sections, he states that "these scriptures will serve as finally normative" for one's understanding of the tradition.[53] As much as the tradition is necessary for the ongoing transmission of Scripture, it is Scripture as the original textual witness to the event and person of Christ that will be the standard by which later tradition is judged. In staking this claim, Tracy is careful still to note that Scripture itself remains a "more relatively adequate" set of narratives and texts about the revelation of God in Jesus Christ.[54] The phrasing of "relative adequacy" is not meant to be dismissive but instead denotes Tracy's way of saying that even the most important source in the Christian tradition still does not attain the level of perfect and complete revelation of God that the event and person of Christ does. Scripture assuredly is the most important witness to that central mystery of the Christian tradition, but it is still only a witness to it. As norm for tradition, and by extension of the community of the church, Scripture too serves as a central context in which the mediation of Christ to human persons occurs.

While church, tradition, and Scripture may be described as *contexts* of mediation, Tracy also discusses particular *forms* of the mediation of Christ: manifestation, proclamation, and action. In describing these three as "forms," Tracy seems to mean that the person experiences the encounter with divine truth in a way distinct to each form. As a way of clarifying this, consider his reference to manifestation and proclamation as "classical forms of religious expression" and distin-

[52] AI 322.
[53] AI 249.
[54] AI 248.

guish that from other uses of "the classic."[55] Most basically, classics are the particular expressions themselves, such as the Gospel of John or Martin Luther King Jr. Those expressions can be grouped by the particular type or genre of classic that he so often mentions in litany: "text, image, event, symbol, person."[56] Thus, the Gospel of John is a classic text whereas King is a classic person. In this section, though, with the emphasis on forms, the question becomes how those particular classics (regardless of genre) disclose truth from and by the "power of the whole."[57] Tracy categorizes the Gospel of John primarily (but not exclusively) as taking the form of manifestation,[58] whereas King's life would seem more to be an example of the form of proclamation. The key here is not whether one engages the classic as an image or an event but how that engagement is revelatory.

Further, manifestation, proclamation, and action are described more specifically by Tracy as *religious* classical forms. Recall that all classics result from the dialectic between intensification (the "journey into particularity" that generates an authentic expression of truth) and distanciation (separation of that expression from its producer).[59] With religious classics, the truth that is revealed is from God, and it is revealed by the power of God (which Tracy refers to as "the whole" in this context). With respect to these three classical religious forms, the issue is how the person who receives that disclosure of truth interacts with that reality.[60]

Manifestation names what happens when intensification leads primarily to a profound experience of participation in the reality of the whole. The classic expression in the form of manifestation becomes saturated with the power of the whole, leading the recipient into sacred space that is beyond the normal experience of space and time. For example, manifestation is what Tracy sees primarily occurring when one participates in sacraments and rituals, listens to the great myths, or has mystical experiences.[61] In these, the power of

---

[55] AI 202.
[56] AI 233.
[57] AI 248.
[58] AI 281–87.
[59] AI 125–30.
[60] AI 203.
[61] AI 205.

manifestation is disclosed specifically to those who enter into the sacred time and space. Tracy is influenced in this by the work of Mircea Eliade, explaining that only through such participation can "we impoverished and parochial Western moderns be freed . . . from ordinary time and space, indeed from history itself."[62] The classic expressions of manifestation engender this participation and, in so doing, put people in contact with the whole.

Proclamation also discloses the power of the whole, but it does not lead to this sense of participation. Rather, Tracy describes it as an address to the receiving self that shatters one's sense of participation in the whole.[63] There is a profound recognition of the radical difference between the self and the whole that undermines one's confidence in the relative adequacy of one's rituals, sacraments, myths, and symbols. Proclamation confronts both the community and the self by demanding fidelity "through word and deed in this time and this history to the God who gives that word as enabling command."[64] In this way proclamation reveals the radical estrangement of the self from the whole.[65]

These two classic religious expressions are distinct but basic ways of conceiving the relationship between humans and the divine. While both manifestation and proclamation reveal the whole, they are related to different aspects of the divine-human relationship. Manifestation emphasizes the profound connection between humans and God through human participation in the whole through ritual, symbol, and myth, leading Tracy to describe "religions with a mystical-priestly-metaphysical-aesthetic" emphasis as more likely to recognize divine manifestation.[66] Proclamation, on the other hand, shows the radical alienation of the human from the divine, especially as regards the finite individual self, thus favoring "religions with a prophetic-ethical-historical emphasis."[67] Manifestation and proclamation need each other because neither is sufficient on its own to articulate this relationship. Indeed, only in concert with each other can the real

---

[62] AI 206.
[63] AI 209.
[64] AI 210.
[65] AI 211.
[66] AI 203.
[67] AI 203.

ambiguity about the divine-human relationship become clear: "the significance and goodness of history, the estrangement and sin in self and society, the ultimate incomprehensibility of self, society and history, the hope for a really new future, the radical affirmation of world that is released by radical world-negation."[68]

Curiously, action as a classical form is inconsistently presented by Tracy. His initial analysis of manifestation and proclamation includes no reference to action, nor is there a clear place for action in the dialectic of "participation-nonparticipation" that defines manifestation and proclamation.[69] Previously in *The Analogical Imagination*, he had discussed the meaning of *praxis* in theology with reference to the subdiscipline of practical theology, but this analysis made no apparent connection to manifestation or proclamation.[70] The first indication that action is also a classical form comes when he says that the event of Jesus is mediated "in the present through word, sacrament, and action."[71] This is suggestive of some sort of triad because Tracy had previously ascribed "word" to proclamation and "sacrament" to manifestation.[72]

The case he does make for the importance of action as a mediation of the event and person of Jesus Christ is built largely on his reading of liberation, political, and feminist theologies.[73] He claims that in these theological approaches, events of manifestation or proclamation lead one to recognize the need for action in the church and in the world.[74] Praxis is taken as primary, and it has the potential to discourage or undermine theologies of manifestation or proclamation that tend toward individualism or quietism.

His description of action does have a few key differences from manifestation and proclamation. First, he tends to see it as much more

---

[68] AI 213.

[69] AI 176.

[70] AI 69–79.

[71] AI 234.

[72] AI 203.

[73] It must be noted, though, that he will also group all of these as "theologies of liberation," given that all have some focus on the problem of oppression. Tracy would likely thus also include postcolonial, womanist, mujerista, queer, and ecological theologies under this heading as well.

[74] AI 390.

future (or, really, eschatologically) oriented.[75] The work of action envisions a future that can only be realized by the divine but that also demands "the struggle for justice now."[76] This leads to a second difference: the key classic genre for action is the event "of liberating praxis" not a text, image, ritual, or person. He specifically makes this claim with regard to the theologies of liberation, which both work and wait "for communal, societal and ultimately global liberation."[77]

Tracy's treatment of action does raise a few key questions. First, is there a place for action in the dialectic of participation and non-participation? Action seems to fit in a real sense into both. A recurring theme in theologies of liberation, and in Tracy's own treatment of action, is that the sought-after liberation is a "kairotic event" that cannot be achieved without the work of the divine, yet it also demands the efforts (i.e., participation) of the people of God. Liberation from oppression seems to be an essentially cooperative project between the divine and human. Yet Tracy also connects proclamation (and its alienation from the divine) to the prophetic tradition, which is marked by judgment of the variety of ways in which the people of God fall short of their responsibilities for one another. Given the centrality of "participation-nonparticipation" for how Tracy conceives of classical forms of religious mediation, greater clarity for how "action" as a form fits in would be helpful. Perhaps action is located within the hyphen between participation and nonparticipation?

A second question is related: Does Tracy consider action to be a "classical form" at all? Even as he introduces action, he again explicitly describes manifestation and proclamation as "classical routes," by extension suggesting that action is not such a classical route.[78] This is a strange implication by Tracy, as a particular act in history that is potentially disclosive of truth, which is completed by its agent, would fit his usual definition of classic. He seems to fall prey to terminological slippage here, as his use of "classical" in this sense sounds more like the idea of something old or longstanding rather than the technical focus on intensification and distanciation. Moreover, action is

---

[75] AI 431. Intriguingly, this is one way in which the temporally focused orientations of the theological subdisciplines from BRO continues, given the close connection between action as mediation here and the role of praxis in practical theology.

[76] AI 434.

[77] AI 398.

[78] AI 390.

itself old and longstanding within the Christian tradition anyway, extending back at least into the prophetic tradition's concern for the poor. Tracy's apparent distinction of action from the other two classical forms is inconsistent in his larger argument.

The third question returns us to the question of how Tracy thinks about theologies of liberation. As was previously noted,[79] he is sometimes critiqued for lumping such contextual theologies into the subdiscipline of practical theology and ignoring their fundamental and systematic dimensions. His approach to practical theology and his understanding of action as mediation are tied together by his view of *praxis*, so it is reasonable that the question of liberation theologies is engaged in both sections. His claim that the "classic of liberation theologies is . . . an event" raises a paradox for Tracy and his critics: What is one to make of the great texts of liberation theology? For example, Gutierrez's *A Theology of Liberation* is arguably much more a text than an event of liberating praxis, and Tracy would assuredly consider it to be a classic text at that.[80] Does its being a text mean it fits more as a classic expression of fundamental or systematic theology in Tracy's schema? Or does the significance of its publication, surely an event within twentieth-century Catholic theology, connect it more to practical theology's focus on events? What this example points to is that while there is a connection between practical theology and liberation theologies in terms of proclamation and prophetic critique, Tracy's strong emphasis on working with texts, coupled with action as a form of mediating Christ, suggests that he would not simply subsume theologies of liberation into practical theology. It seems more the case that Tracy is here trying to critique the many theologies that are *not* focused on liberation for their neglect of the power of action to reveal Christ. Referring back to the second question, Tracy seems to argue subtly that most Christian theology tends to be manifestation- or proclamation-focused theologies that fail to challenge the radical, systemic injustices of the world. His work on theologies of liberation and action is thus not really about the limitations of those theologies but rather of those that do not lead to action.

---

[79] See page 67, footnote 109.

[80] Gustavo Gutierrez, *A Theology of Liberation: History, Politics, and Salvation*, trans. Caridad Inda and John Eagleson (Maryknoll, NY: Orbis Books, 1988).

Ultimately, Tracy sees manifestation, proclamation, and action as three forms in which the truth of the divine reveals itself. These forms can be expressed in a variety of genres, including texts, events, and persons. But the encounter with the divine might lead to a sense of participation, a sense of alienation, or a command to act in the world for the world. Recall that Tracy's primary understanding of truth is based on disclosure (where something is no longer concealed or hidden) and transformation (whereby one's encounter with such a disclosure promotes conversion to the other).[81] God is mediated to the human community through the event and person of Jesus Christ, and Christ himself is mediated through the classical forms of manifestation, proclamation, and action. One's openness to and encounter with these mediations reveals something true about God, commands a change of life, and empowers the possibility of such a change.

A Fragmented Christology

Following *Blessed Rage for Order* and *The Analogical Imagination*, Christology became less of a focus in Tracy's thought. The rest of the 1980s are bereft of any meaningful texts from him on the topic, and in the early to mid-1990s he turns his focus more and more to fragments and the question of naming God. Both of these shifts show subtle resonances in his later Christology. Indeed, it is striking that as he delves more deeply into the Christian tradition's various images of God, his work on the figure of Jesus Christ who mediates that God remains largely the same. The main themes initiated in *Blessed Rage for Order* and developed in *The Analogical Imagination* continued (Christ as mediator, the central importance of Christ in the Christian tradition), but his further expansions are mostly minor and at the margins. Reviewing the subsequent literature exhibits three valuable christological points in conversation with his previous work.[82]

---

[81] AI 62–63.

[82] There are four main articles where Tracy does this work: David Tracy, "Fragments and Forms: Universality and Particularity Today," in *The Church in Fragments: Towards What Kind of Unity*, ed. Giuseppe Ruggieri and Miklos Tomka (London: SCM Press, 1997), 122–29; David Tracy, "Trinitarian Speculation and the Forms of Divine Disclosure," in *The Trinity: An Interdisciplinary Symposium on the Trinity*, ed. Stephen Davis, Daniel Kendall, and Gerald O'Collins (New York: Oxford University Press, 1999),

First, Christ as the mediator of God remains the underlying emphasis of his Christology. Again, the claim here is that the "Christian understanding of God" is defined by believing God to be "the One who revealed God-self in the ministry and message, the cross and resurrection of Jesus Christ."[83] The whole existence of Christ is the disclosure of God, and the Christian understanding of God cannot therefore be separated from the historical Christ event. He does not focus as strongly on the claim that this event is re-presented today as he did previously, but his continued use of "event" language is suggestive of its importance.

Tracy does, however, raise questions (somewhat circuitously) about the emphasis of a "mediator Christology." In a later article on Augustine's Christology, Tracy names the "typical view" of Augustine's Christology as "a traditional mediatorship christology."[84] Tracy critiques that description of Augustine, saying that the "cruciform Christ form" breaks a Christology reduced to "mediatorship,"[85] although it's not entirely clear what he means by this. First, he does compare Augustine's view of mediation to his neo-Platonic contemporaries: Augustine saw Christ as the one mediator between the divine and creation, whereas "the pagan neo-Platonists kept . . . multiplying the forms of mediation" from the One.[86] So it is possible that what he means by "traditional" here is the neo-Platonic tradition that influenced Augustine. If, however, he means something else by "tradition" (such as the subsequent Christian tradition in its diverse incarnations), it's not clear what that is. That he sees the cross as specifically challenging, even shattering, is consistent with his language about fragments and "totality systems." But, as he says, the cross is one among several central christological symbols, and in true

---

273–93; David Tracy, "Forms of Divine Disclosure," in *Believing Scholars: Ten Catholic Intellectuals*, ed. James L. Heft (New York: Fordham University Press, 2005), 47–57; David Tracy, "Augustine's Christomorphic Theocentrism," in *Orthodox Readings of Augustine*, ed. George E. Demacopoulos and Aristotle Papanikolaou (Crestwood, NY: St. Vladimir's Seminary Press, 2008), 263–89.

[83] ONP 31; cf. Tracy, "Trinitarian Speculation and the Forms of Divine Disclosure," 285.

[84] Tracy, "Augustine's Christomorphic Theocentrism," 275.

[85] Tracy, "Augustine's Christomorphic Theocentrism," 275.

[86] Tracy, "Augustine's Christomorphic Theocentrism," 276.

fragmentary fashion, any of them should shatter complacency or totality with respect to one's understanding of Christ. Third, as has been shown throughout his work, Tracy's own Christology is effectively a mediator Christology. Such a Christology need not be considered some kind of totalizing discourse but rather an essential recapitulation of the ineradicable role of Christ in revealing God within the Christian tradition.

Second, Tracy does budge somewhat on the language of christocentrism. As noted previously, this term means that Christ is the central focus of the faith. Tracy had previously described the tradition as christocentric, but he later turns to the term "theocentrism" instead.[87] The distinction between christocentrism and theocentrism may be subtle, given his tying Christ and God together through his work on mediation and re-presentation. He is in no way denying the importance of Christ but rather seeking to shift the point of emphasis. In fact, he considers this to be an essentially christological move, claiming that it makes it so that "no single symbol or doctrine . . . can be adequately understood without explicitly relating the symbol to the reality of God as disclosed in Jesus Christ."[88]

Third, the real valence in the theocentric shift is his introduction of the term "christomorphism." The "morphism" derives from the Greek word *morphé*, meaning "form." Tracy's argument here is that Christ is the "form" that Christian theocentrism takes. Moreover, Christ is the "form-of-forms" and the "divine-human form."[89] Much as Tracy had previously described Christ as the "classic *par excellence*" or as the "prime analogue" in the analogical imagination, here Christ is the superlative form that "gathers all other forms to name God."[90] Connecting this with *The Analogical Imagination*, Christ would be the form of forms that is the standard by which the further mediating forms of manifestation, proclamation, and action are judged. Thus as *the* Christian form for God, Christ is also the mediator that forms

---

[87] Compare BRO 206 and 237 with AI 51–54.

[88] ONP 32, cf. Tracy, "Trinitarian Speculation and the Forms of Divine Disclosure," 283.

[89] Tracy, "Trinitarian Speculation and the Forms of Divine Disclosure," 280; cf. Tracy, "Forms of Divine Disclosure," 54.

[90] Tracy, "Augustine's Christomorphic Theocentrism," 273.

Christians and is the key to Christians' having faith in the God that Christ reveals.[91]

Tracy's new term, "christomorphic theocentrism," is an apt summation of the whole thrust of his work in Christology. First, it enables him to name the relationship between Christ and God in such a way that it preserves his mediator Christology: Christ is the "form," the *morphé*, of God that Christians encounter. Second, it also tiptoes a somewhat delicate line between an exclusive Christian stance (Christ is the only form for God) and an interfaith/religious pluralism (Christ is one form among many for God). This is a dialogical move for Tracy because it affirms the distinctiveness of Christian belief, and the necessity of Christians holding that belief, but it also draws lines for productive conversation with members of other traditions. Third, it maintains the significance of Christ within the Christian tradition while resisting the sometimes Western temptation to christomonism (whereby the emphasis on Christ is so strong that it ignores the Father and the Holy Spirit). Thus, "Christomorphism" is a trinitarian move for Tracy, for whom naming God as triune depends on encountering God in Christ.

A concluding question on Tracy's later Christology is how precisely the language of "fragment" fits into it. When his career was built on the classics and classical forms, he had a well-developed analysis of the relationship of Christ to them. Christ was *the classic*, the particular expression that disclosed the universal whole both permanently and excessively. Does his reformulation of the key insights of the classic into the fragment lead to his describing Christ as the fragment *par excellence*? Tracy does not seem to make this shift.

In his essay on Augustine's "christomorphic theocentrism," Tracy does refer to "Christological fragments." He claims that developing a complete view of Augustine's Christology depends on gathering "many different fragments of Augustine's christology scattered throughout his oeuvre."[92] These fragments include the different major Christ-symbols (e.g., ministry, crucifixion, resurrection). In this sense, he seems to draw on the first of his three approaches to fragments (reassembling the broken pieces of a prior whole) while orienting

[91] Tracy, "Augustine's Christomorphic Theocentrism," 273.
[92] Tracy, "Augustine's Christomorphic Theocentrism," 274.

that toward the third (particular expressions that excessively reveal the infinite).[93] This does not make Christ the fragment *par excellence* but rather simply argues that one's Christology must take account of the diversity of christological symbols.

The language of fragment largely comes into play in this later Christology via the idea of the "fragmenting form." Just as manifestation, proclamation, and action were *classic* forms of mediation of Christ, Tracy here looks to Christ as the fragmenting form that undermines and critiques "totality systems." Thus, his description here of Christ as the "Form of Forms" recalls and updates the "classic *par excellence*," emphasizing the indispensable place of Christ in the Christian's understanding of God, the self, and reality. These fragmenting forms help us to discover the universality of the divine while evading rigid uniformities that elide "otherness, difference, diversity."[94] In fact, Tracy's "Form of Forms" recalls the "prime analogue" description of Christ as well: Christ is the expression of God by which all other divine-creation relationships must be measured. Christ is not precisely a fragment himself but instead the form to which other fragments point (insofar as they are bearers of infinite meaning) and by which such fragments are assessed.

Assessing the Marginalization of Tracy's Christology

The Markan question—"Who do you say I am?"—is a significant concern in both *Blessed Rage for Order* and *The Analogical Imagination*, and it's one Tracy returns to in subsequent articles as he delves deeper into his project on naming God. Yet people who are familiar with Tracy's work tend overwhelmingly to focus on the topics of public theology, theological method, the classics, or pluralism. His fellow scholars have done virtually no significant analysis of his christologi-

---

[93] More technically, with regard to the first type of fragments, Tracy is arguing that there is not a preexisting totality for Augustine's Christology, as "Augustine's christology unfortunately was never expressed systematically in a single treatise" (Tracy, "Augustine's Christomorphic Theocentrism," 274). Rather, Tracy more generally here is pulling together the various pieces of an expected unified vision of Christology on Augustine's part, with that unified vision being the "bearer of infinity."

[94] Tracy, "Fragments and Forms: Universality and Particularity Today," 128.

cal work and contributions.[95] Tracy himself has expressed confusion and disappointment at this neglect, saying in an interview:

> At least half of [*Blessed Rage for Order* and *The Analogical Imagination*] is methodological and the other half substantive, though many seem to read only the methodological parts, strangely and sadly enough for me, because I still fundamentally hold to the substantive Christology developed in both of them.[96]

While it is worthwhile here to consider why his Christology has garnered little attention, the answer to that might be more fruitfully discerned by considering how his Christology fits into his larger work.

One starting point for this is to consider how Christology fits into Tracy's distinctions between fundamental and systematic theologies. At first blush, Christology seems to be essentially a systematic question. Systematic theology focuses on the ongoing interpretation of a particular religious tradition's classics within its contemporary context, with the primary audience for that conversation being the church itself. Christ is the central classic or form for the Christian understanding of God, self, and reality, and thus the christological question of "Who do you say I am?" is an indisputably systematic one. The

---

[95] There are a few exceptions to this. One early example is Charles A. Wilson's "Christology and the Pluralist Consciousness." There, Tracy is a key example of larger christological trends among theologians who were moving away from beginning with the historical-critical approach to Christ. Yet even still, references to Tracy are mostly in the footnotes, while Schillebeeckx is taken as the paradigmatic example of the trends Wilson analyzes. See Charles A. Wilson, "Christology and the Pluralist Consciousness," *Word & World* 5, no. 1 (Winter 1985): 68–77, especially pages 73–75.

More recently and substantively, Andrew C. Forsyth has investigated the relationship between Tracy's Christology and epistemology (Andrew C. Forsyth, "The Implications for Christology of David Tracy's Theological Epistemology," *Scottish Journal of Theology* 63, no. 3 [2010]: 302–17). Here, he emphasizes the importance of particularity for engaging pluralism, holding up the particularity of Christ as essential to that. Moreover, he argues that "christology must be focused on the present," drawing on Tracy's mediating forms and how they mediate Christ *now* (Forsyth, "The Implications for Christology of David Tracy's Theological Epistemology," 317). That focus enables the "dangerous memory" of Christ to continue to lead people toward love and liberation.

[96] Todd Breyfogle and Thomas Levergood, "Conversation with David Tracy," *Cross Currents* 44, no. 3 (Fall 1994): 301–2.

systematic theologian therefore must take account of their tradition and maintain fidelity with that tradition; here, this means upholding the ineradicable place of Christ as the central mediator of the divine.

On the other hand, Tracy's development of his Christology has always been in service of developing and explaining his fundamental theology. In *Blessed Rage for Order*, Christology is a fairly small part of what was intended to be a text on fundamental theology. It is almost exclusively considered in the second half of the book, which focuses on religious, theistic, and christological limit-language.[97] After first arguing for the limit-character of human existence and how it gives rise to religious limit-language, he turns to the specifically *theistic* type of religious limit-language.[98] He argues that all religious limit-language refers, whether explicitly or implicitly, to God. It is only following two chapters on theistic limit-language that he turns to Christology, which he describes as the "re-presentative limit-language" for talking about God.[99] Thus in *Blessed Rage for Order*, Christology is the final, specifically Christian refinement of religious limit-language. Tracy's intent in this chapter is to make sense of the way Christians speak about Christ within the larger human experience of encountering one's finitude. It serves within the larger text as one example of how his revisionist model of correlation for theology would proceed, but it is nonetheless not "a fully developed fundamental theology, much less a systematics."[100]

In *The Analogical Imagination*, the Christology developed in the second half is clearly developed by working through his revised method of mutually critical correlation. That method is structured on the conversation between the classics of the Christian tradition and the contemporary situation. Chapters 6 and 7 are on two dimensions of the christological classic: Christ as revealed in Scripture and Christ as revealed in the present day. Chapter 8 seeks to describe the contemporary situation, which he names "the emergence of the uncanny." It is then in chapter 9 that the correlation of these two takes place, finding the heart of his Christology here in the classical forms

---

[97] BRO 238.
[98] BRO 109; cf BRO 54, 91.
[99] BRO 218.
[100] BRO 238.

of manifestation, proclamation, and action. The final chapter and the epilogue then turn to the idea of the "analogical imagination" itself, positing this as the core insight of a specifically Catholic systematic theology. Yet in doing so, he also notes that "in an already lengthy work, it would be inappropriate and impossible to attempt a full systematics."[101] Christology in *The Analogical Imagination* serves almost as a proof of concept for the theological method and how one might develop a systematic theology, but it is not a full systematic theology in itself.

Reviewing the Christologies presented, and the way in which they are presented, in *Blessed Rage for Order* and *The Analogical Imagination* raises two helpful points. First, he really does understand Christology to be a question of systematic theology. He argues in both texts that the Christian tradition is necessarily "christ-centric," and thus Christ is the obviously distinct religious and theistic claim for Christianity. As such, Christology is engaged with questions around the doctrinal claims of a specific faith tradition. Even as his formulation of the subdiscipline "systematic theology" evolves from *Blessed Rage for Order* to *The Analogical Imagination*, this focus on a particular tradition remains constant.

Second, while these two texts contain Tracy's most developed work on Christology, it suffers from being a systematic topic used primarily to illustrate fundamental theological questions. Each of these christological efforts is built on illustrating the relevant methods (the revisionist method of correlation in *Blessed Rage for Order* or the expanded public method of mutually critical correlation in *The Analogical Imagination*). He recognizes that both represent limited efforts at systematic theology that cannot be completed in the space he allows; they seem instead to serve as the prelude to some text to come later. Yet it is unclear whether he thought such a later systematic treatise would have a more developed Christology as a part of it (along with its ecclesiology, soteriology, trinitarian understanding, and so on).[102] As illustrations intended to flesh out what he meant by

---

[101] AI 421.

[102] The fact that Tracy's Christology develops in some key ways from BRO to AI suggests that, had he worked out a more thorough systematic theology, the Christology would have grown as well. The subsequent articles examined in this chapter tend to corroborate that conjecture.

fundamental theology, the systematic Christologies offered in these texts are simply incapable of being fully realized responses to the great christological questions. Had Tracy more fully entered into the world of systematic theology, he may have engaged on a deeper and more sustained level the main christological symbols he names (ministry, crucifixion, resurrection) or the host of christological questions he sets aside (e.g., divine-human union, consciousness of Christ).

One might, by way of contrast, consider other significant Christologies that were contemporaneous with Tracy's. Between 1970 and 1985, preeminent texts on Christology were published by John Howard Yoder, Jürgen Moltmann, Edward Schillebeeckx, James Cone, Karl Rahner, Jon Sobrino, Schubert Ogden, and Virgilio Elizondo (among others).[103] Many of these figures and texts are referred to in Tracy's major constructive works, often as examples of particular concepts or approaches Tracy describes.[104] Yet Tracy's Christology does not evoke the critical response (positive or negative) that so many of these classic texts do. Perhaps it is that most of these texts inhabit their particular moment and context more fully than Tracy's does (e.g., Sobrino's liberation Christology amid the upheavals and oppression in El Salvador and other Latin American countries in contrast to Tracy's somewhat genial Western pluralism). Perhaps it is that Tracy's claims are less provocative than others (e.g., Cone's connection between the crucifixion of Christ and the lynching of African Americans in the United States). The nonresponse to Tracy's Christology offers no clear explanation for itself. It seems likely, how-

---

[103] John Howard Yoder, *The Politics of Jesus* (Grand Rapids, MI: Eerdmans, [1972] 1994); Edward Schillebeeckx, *Jesus: An Experiment in Christology* (New York: Seabury, 1979) [originally published in Dutch in 1974]; Edward Schillebeeckx, *Christ: The Experience of Jesus as Lord* (New York: Crossroad, 1980) [originally published in Dutch in 1977]; James H. Cone, *God of the Oppressed* (Maryknoll, NY: Orbis Books, [1975] 1997); Jon Sobrino, *Christology at the Crossroads: A Latin American Approach* (Maryknoll, NY: Orbis Books, 1978) [originally published in Spanish in 1976]; Karl Rahner, *Foundations of Christian Faith: An Introduction to the Idea of Christianity*, trans. William V. Dych, rev. ed. (New York: Crossroad, [1978] 1982) [originally published in German in 1976]; Schubert Ogden, *The Point of Christology* (San Francisco: Harper & Row, 1982); Virgilio P. Elizondo, *Galilean Journey: The Mexican-American Promise*, trans. Eva Fleischner, rev. and exp. ed. (Maryknoll, NY: Orbis Books, [1983] 2005).

[104] Many of them occupy what Tracy would likely consider a mixed space of fundamental, systematic, and practical theologies.

ever, that a combination of Tracy's narrow focus on the question of how Christ mediates and is mediated, along with his more thorough development of questions of method, the publics, and the classic, led to an overall neglect of his specific claims about Jesus.

Conclusion

Theological method, public theology, the classics, pluralism. These are all well recognized as essential aspects of Tracy's theological work, and they are almost certainly the contributions he is best known for. What is so easily overlooked, though, is how central Jesus Christ is to Tracy's development of these aspects. Christ is *the* Christian classic, indispensable for one's public conversation with the contemporary situation. Christ is the prime analogue that makes it possible for us to find truth in an ever-changing, divergent, plural world.

The consistent heart of Tracy's Christology is that Christ mediates God to humanity. This mediation takes place historically in the event and person of Christ in Israel in the first century, but it continues to occur into the present day. The mediation of God through Christ must be further considered as Christ is mediated today through Scripture, tradition, and the church and as that mediation takes the forms of manifestation, proclamation, and action. The centrality of form for mediation shapes the continued development of his christological thought. While this Christology has garnered little attention, certainly when compared to his other theological emphases (or to the Christologies of other theologians), it nonetheless offers a critically engaging reflection on what it means to describe Christ as present in the contemporary situation. It also maintains a deep fidelity to the distinct claims of the Christian tradition, which anchors Tracy as he wrestles with the fundamental-systematic tension surrounding the question of God.

6

God

As I suspect is obvious by now, my own hope is grounded in a Christian faith that revelations from God have occurred and that there are ways to authentic liberation.

—David Tracy[1]

In 1999 and 2000, David Tracy gave the prestigious Gifford Lectures at the University of Edinburgh. His plan was to publish these lectures under the title *This Side of God* within a few years of giving them.[2] His plans for the text eventually evolved past the Gifford Lectures themselves, expanding into three projected volumes: on naming God; on Christology, Trinity, and anthropology; and on the Holy Spirit and Christianity's relations with other religions.[3] Yet while

---

[1] PA 113.

[2] In his 2002 interview with Tracy, Scott Holland mentions that University of Chicago Press was planning to publish the lectures "sometime next year." See Scott Holland, "This Side of God: A Conversation with David Tracy," *Cross Currents* 52, no. 1 (Spring 2002): 54.

[3] Lois Malcolm, "The Impossible God: An Interview with David Tracy," *Christian Century* 119, no. 4 (February 13, 2002): 30. Later, it reads as though Tracy was considering two volumes, to which he gave the titles *This Side of God* and *The Gathering of Fragments*. See David Tracy, "Form and Fragment: The Recovery of the Hidden and Incomprehensible God," in *The Concept of God in Global Dialogue*, ed. Werner Jeanrond and Aasulv Lande (Maryknoll, NY: Orbis Books, 2005), 98–99.

the plans for this work, generally referred to as the "God Book,"[4] have expanded, its publication has been continually deferred.

Even as interested scholars wait for Tracy's magnum opus on the divine, many overlook the significant work he has already published on naming God. His essays on fragments and forms began in earnest in the 1990s, almost as a prelude to the Gifford Lectures, and have continued in the decades since. Many of these seem to be based on some of the lectures themselves. Later essays have focused on the questions and figures that arose for Tracy post–Gifford Lectures, the same questions and figures that seem to have contributed to the publication delay.

While it is tempting to see this as a "turn to God" in Tracy's thought, his question about the most adequate and appropriate ways of naming God has been an enduring, career-long question for Tracy. His major constructive texts (*Blessed Rage for Order*, *The Analogical Imagination*, and *Plurality and Ambiguity*) have each posited ways of naming God that are essential to their project. Some of these attempted namings have been explicit (the process theology portion of *Blessed Rage for Order* or the Triune God that is mediated through Christ in *The Analogical Imagination*), but the more central namings to those texts are more subtle than that. There is a certain vagueness to these ways of naming God, which arguably makes them more conducive to certain types of interdisciplinary and interreligious conversation.

This chapter proceeds in three main movements. The first considers the ways of naming God proposed in those first three constructive texts: the "limit-of" in *Blessed Rage for Order*, the "whole" in *Analogical Imagination*, and "Ultimate Reality" in *Plurality and Ambiguity*. Each one will be connected to explicit or apparent conversation partners that shape Tracy's language about God, even as core features of his theology of God remain the same. The second movement looks at the shift after *Plurality and Ambiguity* in how God is named, which is carried out through a long series of essays that develop and explain the diverse fragmentary forms for naming God. The final part of the chapter seeks to explain the apparent shift, arguing that it is more

---

[4] David Gibson, "God-Obsessed: David Tracy's Theological Quest," *Commonweal* 137, no. 2 (January 29, 2010): 11.

basically a methodological shift from doing fundamental theology to doing systematic theology.

Tracy's Early Efforts to Name God (1968–1990)

Naming God as the Limit-Of in Blessed Rage for Order

The concept of the "limit" is an important piece of the revisionist fundamental theology in *Blessed Rage for Order*. Recall that in the theological method from *Blessed Rage for Order*, one of the poles is common human experience, more specifically the religious dimension of common human experience. The "limit-character" of one's experiences is what distinguishes the religious dimension. By "bumping up" against one's limits—physically, mentally, emotionally, spiritually—one comes to recognize the existence of reality beyond the self.[5] Further reflection can then lead one to recognize the finitude and contingency of everything that exists as we know it, even the vast expanse of the universe. This encounter with our limits alerts us to the possibility of transcendence, of something beyond.

---

[5] In his understanding of the limit, Tracy is influenced by Søren Kierkegaard, largely via Karl Jaspers. Kierkegaard offered early existentialist analyses of the bounded-ness of human persons and their consequent inability to exercise total control over their fate (BRO 107). There is still some degree of freedom, but there is also a deep well of anxiety in the face of that freedom. Anxiety, in contrast to fear, has no specific object; it is "freedom's actuality as the possibility of possibility" (Søren Kierkegaard, *The Concept of Anxiety: A Simple Psychologically Orienting Deliberation on the Dogmatic Issue of Hereditary Sin*, trans. and ed. Reidar Thomte [Princeton, NJ: Princeton University Press, 1980], 42). Although freedom does not necessitate sin, it makes sin possible, and humans become sinners through the exercise of their freedom (Kierkegaard, *The Concept of Anxiety*, 22). Kierkegaard's understanding of anxiety illuminates the radical limitations on the human exercise of freedom (BRO 106–7).

This view of anxiety comes to influence Tracy through the interpretation of Jaspers, who built on Kierkegaard's sense of bounded-ness. Jaspers claims that humans encounter "boundary situations" when something changes in one's life that leads us to "a wall we run into" (Karl Jaspers, *Philosophy*, vol. 2, trans. E. B. Ashton [Chicago: University of Chicago Press, 1970], 178–79). The most common of these are suffering, guilt, and death—unchanging, inevitable experiences that humans encounter in everyday life (Jaspers, *Philosophy*, 2:178, 184). The encounter with such boundary situations enables the self to become "aware of being," both in one's immediate situation and ultimately in the "universal boundary situation of all existence" (Jaspers, *Philosophy*, 2:179, 184).

Tracy then distinguishes between what he calls the "limit-to" and the "limit-of." The "limit-to" is a collection of different kinds of encounters with the limit. The more or less generic version of the "limit-to" is the "limit-experience," which is any moment or event in one's life that engages the transcendent and that manifests our experience of bounded-ness. These limit-experiences can take a variety of forms, but two in particular recur with the most significance.[6] First, Tracy discusses the "limit-question," those questions that help one to recognize not only the bounds of one's own understanding but the bounds of human understanding at all. He reviews at length several specific limit-questions, such as, "Why is there something rather than nothing?" "Why should one be moral at all?" or "Why is the universe intelligible?"[7] These questions neither have self-evident answers nor are problems easily solved with further data.

Second, Tracy considers the "limit-situation." He defines these as those situations in which "a human being ineluctably finds manifest a certain ultimate limit or horizon to his or her existence."[8] Drawing on the existentialist philosophies of the nineteenth and twentieth centuries, he distinguishes between "negative" or "boundary" limit-situations and "positive" or "ecstatic" limit-situations.[9] Boundary situations are typified by the experience of guilt, anxiety, sickness, and death, which confront the person and reinforce the limited degree to which humans have control over their lives.[10] The boundaries can be stark and thus frightening. Ecstatic situations, by contrast, are more those of joy, love, and creation. These limit-situations open up "moments of self-transcendence" that "cannot be adequately stated in the language of ordinary everyday experience."[11] One way of distinguishing between boundary and ecstatic experiences is that the former bluntly force the individual to question the meaningfulness

---

[6] Tracy has several other "limit-" terms (*inter alia* limit-character, limit-concept, limit-dimension, limit-meanings, and limit-possibilities), but these are fairly minor tweaks on the core ideas presented by the "limit-" terms discussed here.

[7] BRO 95–102.

[8] BRO 105.

[9] See the note above on the influence of Kierkegaard and Jaspers.

[10] BRO 105.

[11] BRO 105.

of existence, while the latter gestures toward a reality beyond human limitations that may ground an affirmative answer to that question.

Tracy connects these limit-experiences with the concept of "limit-language." By this, he means the modes of speaking and writing that help to communicate the experience of finitude intended by one's communication of limit-experiences, questions, and situations. He connects this to Ricoeur's language of "sense and referent," where "sense" describes the "internal structure and meaning of the text" and "referent" describes the "mode of being-in-the-world which the text opens up for the intelligent reader."[12] For Tracy, limit-language is the sense while the various limit-experiences are the referents.[13] Put another way, limit-language itself connects us with our finitude precisely as it allows us to struggle through the experience of articulating our experience of our limits.

Again, each of these different "limit-" terms are variations of what Tracy calls the "limit-to," which refers to experiences that lead the person to become aware of their own bounded-ness. The "limit-of," on the other hand, discloses the fundamental reality that grounds all of existence. It "functions as a final, now gracious, now frightening, now trustworthy, now absurd, always uncontrollable limit-of the very meaning of existence itself."[14] His use of "limit-of" serves as a way of denoting the horizon of one's ordinary existence, the grounding reality that gives both existence and meaning to human lives.

As the ground or horizon of experience, Tracy argues that the religious person's relationship to the limit-of reality is essentially one of "basic trust" or "confidence."[15] He claims not only that this basic faith is the reality to which "the religions" attest but that basic faith is the most "authentic mode of being in the world."[16] Moreover, it is the "limit-to" experiences, questions, and so forth that bring a person to consciousness of something beyond the self, and the need to articulate this is the source for religious language that individuals use to

---

[12] BRO 51. Cf. Paul Ricoeur, *Interpretation Theory: Discourse and the Surplus of Meaning* (Fort Worth: Texas Christian University Press, 1976), 19–22.

[13] BRO 75–79.

[14] BRO 108. Tracy will link this to Lonergan's concept of the "formally unconditioned" in BRO 98.

[15] BRO 153.

[16] BRO 134.

describe the "final dimension to our lives."[17] Indeed, he claims that the "objective referent of all such language . . . is that reality which religious human beings mean when they say 'God.'"[18]

Therefore it is clear that "limit-of" is the underlying form of naming God for Tracy in *Blessed Rage for Order*. While it is not the only form of naming God he uses in the text, it is central to *Blessed Rage for Order*'s argument for the religious dimension of human experience as an essential source in the revisionist model of theology. Moreover, the "limit-of" is not a specifically Christian way of naming God but rather a generalized, largely vague, way of describing the ground or horizon of being that is both reconcilable with the Christian tradition and accessible to other religious and philosophical traditions. Even as Tracy references or develops other more or less adequate ways of naming God in *Blessed Rage for Order* (e.g., process theology's dipolar God, the God of classical theism, the triune God in Christianity), this concept of the "limit-of" remains the basis for understanding the strengths and weaknesses of these other approaches.[19]

---

[17] BRO 107–8.

[18] BRO 109.

[19] Some figures have noted the important role of process theology in BRO and from there extrapolated an alleged centrality of its approach to Tracy's overall theology. It is true that the process understanding of God as dipolar, and thus "*both* absolute *and* supremely relative" to all of reality, is a core example of his work on God-language early in his career (BRO 177–79). In the context of this chapter, it must be recognized that the dipolar God serves as an excellent example of the "limit-of" approach to naming God, and Tracy clearly considers it to be a superior example to classical theism (BRO 172).

The importance of process theology to Tracy is, however, easily overstated. The focus it receives in BRO is not sustained in his later texts. A few of his articles make reference to it, but generally in passing (e.g., David Tracy, "Does God Exist? An Answer for Today," *New Republic* 183, no. 19 [November 8, 1980]: 29; Tracy, "Christianity in the Wider Context," 12; David Tracy, "The Hermeneutics of Naming God," *Irish Theological Quarterly* 57, no. 4 [December 1991]: 256–57). His most substantive post-BRO article on process thought was published ten years after BRO, and it largely rehashes the argument of that text. It then goes further in depth in order to offer insight and critique about the work of Charles Hartshorne in light of Tracy's understanding of analogy and metaphor (David Tracy, "Analogy, Metaphor and God-Language: Charles Hartshorne," *Modern Schoolman* 62 [May 1985]: 249–64).

His last significant reference to process theology was another ten years later in 1995 (David Tracy, "Evil, Suffering, Hope: The Search for New Forms of Contemporary Theodicy," *Proceedings of the Catholic Theological Society of America* 50 [1995]: 15–36). There he reviews what he saw to be its positive insights: that the biblical view

Naming God as the Whole in The Analogical Imagination

As has been previously noted, *The Analogical Imagination* continues many of Tracy's same concerns from *Blessed Rage for Order* even as it shifts and rearticulates some of his answers. As his method shifts from emphasizing "common human experience" (the religious dimension of which is so rooted in the concept of the limit) to "the contemporary situation," he also mostly moves away from focusing on the "limit-of" and "limit-to" categories. Yet even as his terminology shifts here, there is significant continuity in the underlying insights of his new way of naming God, "the whole."

Tracy's discussion of "the whole" is rooted in his public theology, in particular his discussion of the relationship between culture and religion. In his analysis of the three publics of church, academy, and society, *culture* is the highest level or realm of *society*. Here, Tracy draws on the work of anthropologist Clifford Geertz on culture and religion, arguing that culture passes on both an ethos and a worldview.[20] *Ethos* in this case means the style of how a people lives, including their attitudes, characters, and values, while *worldview* refers to the underlying sense of how reality in fact works.[21] Subsequently, Tracy will argue that religion (which is connected for him to the realm of culture), and specifically the religious perspective on "the whole," is what ultimately unites an ethos and a worldview.[22] Part of the reli-

---

of God as love is suggestive of God as relational relative to creation. There is an attraction to the modern, panentheistic view of a God who suffers with humanity. Process theology also suffers, however, from the weakness of potentially injecting an overly rosy progress, rather than process, view of history (Tracy, "Evil, Suffering, Hope," 24–25). Further, Tracy notes that this sense of God is not limited to the process approach and can be found in potentially more effective theological alternatives (Tracy, "The Hermeneutics of Naming God," 257). By his Gifford Lecture–era work and after, the process approach to God disappears entirely and is not even connected to the "God is Love" name to which it was originally related.

[20] AI 7; Geertz defines culture as "an historically transmitted pattern of meanings embodied in symbols, a system of inherited conceptions expressed in symbolic forms by means of which men communicate, perpetuate, and develop their knowledge about and attitudes toward life" (Clifford Geertz, "Religion as a Cultural System," in *The Interpretation of Cultures* [New York: Basic Books, 1973], 89).

[21] AI 7.

[22] AI 164. Here, Tracy is relying on Geertz's definition of religion: "a system of symbols which acts to establish powerful, pervasive, and long-lasting moods and motivations in men [ethos] by formulating conceptions of a general order of existence [worldview] and clothing these conceptions with such an aura of factuality that the

gious perspective is that the way people ought to live and the reality in which they do live are not incompatible or antagonistic but are instead profoundly interrelated.[23]

The connection to culture also highlights Tracy's discussion of the classic, particularly the religious classic. Recall that Tracy describes the religious classic as "a genuine manifestation of the whole from the reality of that whole itself."[24] The encounter with the religious classic discloses something true, excessive, and permanent about "the whole," the fundamental mystery at the heart of reality, but that disclosure also *comes from* "the whole." It is experienced as "event-gift-manifestation of and from the whole."[25] The religious classic thus has an impact on the person or the community, reshaping and re-orienting their understanding of the life they live and the world in which they live it.

The importance of culture and the classic in Tracy's use of the term "the whole" are suggestive that he treats it as a way of naming God. He describes "the objectively awe-some reality of the otherness of the whole as radical mystery."[26] Moreover, the response that one has to the truth revealed by the classic is that of basic trust or loyalty; when that is the response to the object of faith revealed by the whole, Tracy calls that relationship faith.[27] Yet for Tracy it is significant to recognize the potential challenge of idolatry in such a claim, and he affirms that God alone is the only "ultimate object of loyalty and trust."[28] This further supports the claim that, in *The Analogical Imagination*, "the whole" stands in as a somewhat more general, even more vague, way of naming God than the specifically Christian naming of God as God or as triune.

As a closing example of how these are interconnected for Tracy, consider his description of Christ in the context of the theological portrait of the church. He writes that "Christianity, when true to its

---

moods and motivations seem uniquely realistic" (Geertz, "Religion as a Cultural System," 90).

[23] AI 163.

[24] AI 172.

[25] AI 165. Here, Tracy explicitly connects "the whole" to the "limit-of" term used previously in BRO.

[26] AI 169.

[27] AI 47.

[28] AI 51.

heritage, cannot but recognize that its fundamental faith, its most radical trust and loyalty, is to the all-pervasive reality of the God of love and power disclosed in Jesus Christ."[29] He emphasizes here the fundamental response of trust or faith to God, which is key to his discussion of the whole. He names Christ here as the religious classic (which he elsewhere calls the religious classic *par excellence*), who is therefore a revelation of the power *of the whole* and *by the whole* (i.e., *of God* and *by God*). It is through Christ, then, that the Christian comes to find the unity of ethos (one seeks to live a life in accord with the life of Christ) and worldview (the gracious gift of God makes such a life possible and meaningful). Christian language about God and Christ is thus a specified, more systematic way of engaging Tracy's more general claim about "the whole" and "the religious classic."

Naming God as Ultimate Reality *in* Plurality and Ambiguity

In his next book, *Plurality and Ambiguity*, Tracy again shifts the terminology for the divine, talking now about "Ultimate Reality." The outlines of his argument should now seem familiar: religious believers have a sense of fundamental trust or faith in this Ultimate Reality, which is revealed to them through their religious classics.[30] The encounter with Ultimate Reality is an experience of power and grace that unveils the possibility of liberation, including liberation from sin, from ego, and from control.[31] Tracy is quite explicit in describing Ultimate Reality as a stand-in for the term "God," noting that religions are broadly based on "fundamental beliefs in Ultimate Reality"[32] and the hope that this "Ultimate Reality is grace-ful."[33] Even more clearly than the "limit-of" or "the whole," "Ultimate Reality" is expressly drawn on as a way of connecting the essential similarities of the diverse world religions in terms of the ground and object of belief and of hope.

Tracy is not particularly forthcoming about the motivation for this shift in terminology, but it seems likely that it stems from his increas-

---

[29] AI 51.
[30] PA 112.
[31] PA 89–90, 107.
[32] PA 84.
[33] PA 113.

ing participation in interreligious dialogue. He was most active in Buddhist-Christian dialogue, and he elsewhere describes the Buddhist conception of *sunyata* as a "profound vision of ultimate reality as emptiness."[34] A second likely contributor to this shift is the influence of theologian John Hick. In the Gifford Lectures Hick gave at the University of Edinburgh between 1986 and 1987, he argued for "the Real" as the blanket term for the transcendent reality religions point to.[35] Tracy was clearly familiar with Hick's preceding work: not only does he cite him favorably in *Plurality and Ambiguity*, but Tracy was directing Chester Gillis's dissertation on Hick's theology at this time.[36]

One further important development in his generic terminology for God is a subtle move on this idea of trust. While he had previously described "trust" as the basic attitude or disposition of a person toward the "limit-of" or "the whole," the interruptions of plurality and ambiguity show that such a sense of trust "is not immune to either criticism or suspicion."[37] That critical posture is directed not necessarily at the Ultimate Reality itself but rather at the historically mediated interpretations of Ultimate Reality by particular religious traditions. These traditions are not simply innocent; it is the fundamental trust in Ultimate Reality that empowers and sustains a tradition's self-critique and its work toward human liberation. That encounter with Ultimate Reality is thus what can transform the person and the community "from self-centeredness to Reality-centeredness."[38]

Can One Hope in These Names of God?

In reviewing these three ways of naming God, the common features become evident. Most notably, Tracy has a clear focus on God as the ground of existence, and on the human person having some

---

[34] DWO 5.

[35] John Hick, *An Interpretation of Religion: Human Responses to the Transcendent* (New Haven, CT: Yale University Press, 1989), 11. The original lectures themselves were contemporaneous with Tracy's writing *Plurality and Ambiguity*.

[36] Gillis's dissertation was completed in 1986 and was later published as Chester Gillis, *A Question of Final Belief: John Hick's Pluralistic Theory of Salvation* (New York: St. Martin's Press, 1989). Tracy cites the unpublished dissertation in PA 137n23.

[37] PA 112.

[38] PA 89.

form of trust or faith in that ground. Moreover, each name utilizes language that emphasizes mystery, ultimacy, and relationship. Taken together, these two features suggest that Tracy is seeking to name God in ways that are fully compatible with traditionally Christian approaches to speaking about God but that are not explicitly anchored within the Christian tradition. Rather, each of these names is kept sufficiently distinct from explicitly Christian language so as to be broadly, perhaps even universally, accessible.[39] The "limit-of," "the whole," and "Ultimate Reality" are open to other faith traditions (e.g., Buddhism, Islam) and to other academic fields (e.g., philosophy, anthropology). Such a move provides Tracy a significant opportunity for interreligious and interdisciplinary dialogue that can more fully realize the public character of his theology.

Nevertheless, the generic quality of these terms may also require some significant trade-offs. As much as Tracy closes *Plurality and Ambiguity* with an expression of hope in Ultimate Reality, and specifically in the Christian understanding of that Ultimate Reality, some have challenged him on what that hope really means. In his review of *Plurality and Ambiguity*, Richard J. Bernstein notes that while Tracy emphasizes religions as sources of resistance and hope, he also fully recognizes that the "non-believer can exercise resistance to the status quo and the hope we can find in the radical openness of conversation itself."[40] In other words, it's not clear what is distinctive about *religion* with respect to hope. Bernstein thinks Tracy risks subsuming the religious to the mundane and eliding the radically particular contributions of religious traditions. As such, it is not clear where hope comes from, or more precisely what makes Ultimate Reality a meaningful source of hope. Similarly, Gerard Loughlin argues that "Tracy is too enamoured of the concept of plurality to take difference seriously," thus abstracting what should be a concrete hope.[41] The generic quality of "Ultimate Reality" undermines Tracy's claims to any particular hope.

---

[39] PA 75.

[40] Richard J. Bernstein, "Radical Plurality, Fearful Ambiguity, and Engaged Hope," *The Journal of Religion* 69, no. 1 (January 1989): 90–91.

[41] Gerard Loughlin, "Review of *Plurality and Ambiguity: Hermeneutics, Religion, Hope*," *Modern Theology* 7, no. 5 (October 1991): 485.

While Tracy explicitly noted in *Plurality and Ambiguity* that he was not seeking to argue for the more narrow, specifically Christian notion hope, he does describe himself as chastened by such reviews of his text. In his interview with David Gibson, Tracy referenced these reviews as shaping his turn in the study of God:

> Eventually Tracy himself saw the limitations of this methodological focus. During one of our conversations in Chicago, the theologian cited a review of *Plurality and Ambiguity* as his Damascus moment. The reviewer, he recalled, wrote that after reading Tracy's book, he understood what its author meant by such terms as "plurality," "ambiguity," "hermeneutics," and "religion." Tracy can still recite the rest: " 'But I don't know why he has hope,' wrote the reviewer. 'All he says is one line near the end: "I hope because I believe in God." But what does that mean?' " Tracy was chastened. "The reviewer was right," he told me. "I had to articulate what that means and why I have hope, because of that belief in God, through Christ, and in Christ through Jesus."
>
> That has been his fixation ever since. "I am God-obsessed," Tracy says. Why have hope, and what does it mean? It is the question his unfinished book attempts to answer.[42]

This response to his more generic names for God, to the "limit-of," the "whole," and "Ultimate Reality," is essential to Tracy's deeper turn into the question of naming God and his greater focus on specifically Christian traditions within that.

Gathering the Fragmented Names of God (1990–present)

Following this Damascus moment, Tracy comes to explicitly frame his theological work on God as "naming and thinking God" through reflection on "forms," particularly "fragmenting forms." Here, it will be valuable to recall both the role of fragments that developed from

---

[42] Gibson, "God-Obsessed," 14. In my own discussion with Tracy about this, he specifically referenced the Bernstein review of PA, but that text does not include the quotation he references to Gibson. I have been unable to find that quotation in any of the reviews of PA, but it does comport with the feedback of Bernstein and Loughlin.

his notion of the classic[43] and the discussion of forms in his approach to Christology.[44] "Forms" for Tracy refer to that through which the real presents itself, typically in an ordered and intelligible way.[45] Fragments, meanwhile, are the "saturated and auratic bearers of infinity and sacred hope, fragmentary of genuine hope in some redemption, however undefined."[46] Again, key to his approach to fragments, and thus to fragmenting forms, is that they resist totalizing, reductive language.

According to Tracy, his interest in this discussion on fragmenting forms is about moving away from the "modern" version of naming God, which focuses on the great -isms: atheism, pantheism, deism, theism, panentheism, and so forth. Tracy argues that the postmodern shift is driven by "the question of God's identity" rather than "the question of the existence and nature of God."[47] These fragmenting forms, then, are ways of naming and thinking God that recognize both the excess of a God who cannot be definitively named and the pluralism of traditions that have nonetheless expressed their own particular vision of that name. Attention to fragmenting forms of naming God allows for God to break through, to manifest to potential recipients of revelation.

This work has led Tracy to several central, paradigmatic names for God. This section will focus especially on the three that he has published the most about—the Hidden, the Incomprehensible, and the Infinite God—before turning to those that have been less explicitly developed.

---

[43] See chapter 3, pp. 89–96.

[44] See chapter 5, pp. 134–46.

[45] David Tracy, "Fragments and Forms: Universality and Particularity Today," in *The Church in Fragments: Towards What Kind of Unity*, ed. Giuseppe Ruggieri and Miklos Tomka (London: SCM Press, 1997), 126–27; David Tracy, "Trinitarian Speculation and the Forms of Divine Disclosure," in *The Trinity: An Interdisciplinary Symposium on the Trinity*, ed. Stephen Davis, Daniel Kendall, and Gerald O'Collins (New York: Oxford University Press, 1999), 275.

[46] David Tracy, "Fragments: The Spiritual Situation of Our Times," in *God, the Gift, and Postmodernism*, ed. John D. Caputo and Michael J. Scanlon (Bloomington: Indiana University Press, 1999), 173.

[47] David Tracy, "Literary Theory and Return of the Forms for Naming and Thinking God in Theology," *Journal of Religion* 74, no. 3 (July 1994): 309.

The Hidden God

Tracy's discussion of the Hidden God is shaped by the critical correlation of the Christian tradition and by his appropriation of postmodern discourse around the "other." It is arguably the latter point, demarcated by what he calls the contemporary "turn to the other" (in contrast to the modern "turn to the subject"), that motivates the former point.[48] The experience of the other is often most obvious in the encounter with someone significantly different from the self—a person from another culture, another language, another race, another religious tradition—but it should be discerned in any experience of the neighbor.[49] Even more fundamentally, Tracy notes the Otherness of God, the encounter with whom radically alters one's understanding of reality and the self. One essential mode of that encounter with divine Otherness is the form of the Hidden God.[50]

Tracy argues that the Hidden God is particularly evident in experiences of absence and of suffering and thus most paradigmatically in the theology of the cross. The reality of suffering, especially the "massive global suffering" that is so often the focus of the various liberation theologies, serves as a reminder that God is not merely a consoler but also one who seeks the liberation of the suffering.[51] He claims that "God reveals Godself in hiddenness: in cross and negativity, above all in those others whom the grand narrative of modernity has too often set aside as non-peoples, non-events, non-memories, in a word, non-history."[52] The Hidden God, in a real sense, is in solidarity with those who have been the hidden others throughout human history.

To explore this Hidden God, Tracy reaches back into two central strands of the Christian tradition: the prophetic and the apocalyptic. The prophetic tradition is rooted in the claim that the prophet who speaks does so at the command of the divine and for the benefit of

---

[48] David Tracy, "The Hidden God: The Divine Other of Liberation," *Cross Currents* 46, no. 1 (Spring 1996): 5–6.

[49] Tracy, "The Hidden God," 6.

[50] Tracy, "The Hidden God," 6.

[51] Tracy, "The Hidden God," 7–8.

[52] Tracy, "The Hidden God," 8.

the other, especially the suffering other.[53] The hidden divine breaks through via the prophet, commanding the prophet's audience to turn away from the self and toward the divine. According to Tracy, that turn fundamentally requires the turn to the other, as revealed in the twofold love command of the gospels.[54] As previously mentioned, he sees the contemporary mode of prophetic discourse as being most evident in "liberation, political, African-American and feminist-womanist-mujerista theologies."[55] He further links such a turn to the other with the postmodern ethics of Emmanuel Levinas and his claim that the face of the other makes an ethical, nonviolent demand of "do not kill me" on the self.[56] The ethical component, both in the immediate interpersonal sense and in the larger social liberationist sense, is intimately tied to Tracy's prophetic understanding of the Hidden God.

Tracy also connects the Hidden God to the Christian tradition of apocalypticism, claiming that "when prophecy fails, apocalyptic takes over."[57] He claims that the apocalyptic form fragments our understanding of history, revealing its ruptures and highlighting the God that is "not merely humbled but humiliated" in the life and death of Christ.[58] Moreover, he notes that essential to the New Testament and to Christian theology more broadly is the christological symbol of the second coming. The New Testament ends not only with the *maranatha* invocation and the hope for Jesus to come again but also with the notion that such hope means that all of Christian history is

[53] David Tracy, "Theology and the Many Faces of Postmodernity," *Theology Today* 51, no. 1 (April 1994): 112.

[54] The importance of the prophetic tradition is longstanding for Tracy: in DWO he writes at length about the relationship between the "mystical" and the "prophetic." He adapts this duality from the *Concilium* issue *The Mystical and Political Dimension of the Christian Faith*, substituting instead the word "prophetic" for "political" (see Claude Geffré and Gustavo Gutierrez, *The Mystical and Political Dimension of the Christian Faith*, *Concilium* 96 [New York: Herder and Herder, 1974]).

Moreover, there is a significant overlap between how Tracy describes the forms of manifestation and proclamation in AI with how he understands mystical and prophetic discourses in DWO onward.

[55] David Tracy, "The Post-Modern Re-Naming of God as Incomprehensible and Hidden," *Cross Currents* 50, nos. 1–2 (Spring/Summer 2000): 245.

[56] Tracy, "Theology and the Many Faces of Postmodernity," 112.

[57] Tracy, "Forms of Divine Disclosure," 56.

[58] Tracy, "Form and Fragment: The Recovery of the Hidden and Incomprehensible God," 110.

infused with this already/not yet waiting for that return. Put another way, the entire history of Christianity has been infused with the hiddenness of a God whose return will herald the end of that history.[59] This apocalyptic dimension in the larger Christian tradition is best represented for Tracy in Martin Luther, especially his theology of the cross. Tracy notes, however, the importance of apocalyptic throughout the tradition, including in the Gospel of Mark, the letters of Paul, and the theologies of Blaise Pascal and Simone Weil.[60]

The Incomprehensible God

The Hidden God is often paired with the Incomprehensible God. By naming God as Incomprehensible, Tracy emphasizes both the fundamental inability of human language and concepts to adequately grasp what one means when talking about the divine and the "positive" incomprehensibility of God as an inherent part of the divine nature. As with his prior discussions of analogical language, he does not wish to deny the possibility of saying anything at all about God but rather seeks to highlight those traditions within Christian thought that direct attention toward the poverty and limitation of human understanding. To do so, Tracy connects the Incomprehensible God to the mystical, and especially apophatic-mystical, fragmenting forms.

Like the prophetic, the mystical has been a recurring point of reference throughout Tracy's career. He connects the mystical (sometimes called "meditative") approach to reflections on the limit-experiences of the human person, such as death, joy, and hope.[61] He claims that mystics begin by stripping reality down grammatically "to its most basic elements (God, world, soul)" in order to understand the relations among them.[62] This leads to a branching out within mysticism, where Tracy emphasizes two key approaches: love-mysticism and apophatic-mysticism.[63] For the love-mystics, the focus

---

[59] Tracy, "Form and Fragment," 109.

[60] Tracy, "Form and Fragment," 105–6.

[61] Tracy, "Theology and the Many Faces of Postmodernity," 113.

[62] DWO 24.

[63] Curiously, Tracy claims there are "four principal forms of mystical theologies," but only names or focuses on these two (Tracy, "The Post-Modern Renaming of God," 242).

is on "the self's freedom-in-love and God-as-love-manifesting-Godself in *the sign* Jesus Christ."[64] The key here is how love organizes the relations among God, self, and world and how the mystic enters more fully into participation in that love through union with the divine.

More so than love-mysticism, Tracy focuses on apophatic-mysticism in order to engage the Incomprehensible as a name of God. Apophatic theology is rooted in negation or saying no. For Tracy, the central insight here is that, through apophasis, one is able to break any overly rigid system of thought or understanding, as such a system would inherently limit one's understanding of God. Thus what makes apophasis a "fragmenting form" is that it shatters *conceptual* totality systems.[65] Human efforts to create clear, thoughtful delineations of what God is can assuredly be insightful, but they can never be complete. In fact, Tracy notes that the incomprehensibility of God is not only a negative characteristic of the finite human mind but also a "positive affirmation of God's very reality."[66]

His chief example of the apophatic form is the fifth- to sixth-century theologian Pseudo-Dionysius.[67] Tracy works through Pseudo-Dionysius's naming of God as "the Good," which begins with this positive, kataphatic assertion before making the apophatic move. Tracy writes that Pseudo-Dionysius offers a first negation, whereby the reader recognizes that the positive name, "the Good," requires one to then recognize that this name is inadequate both because of the limits of human understanding and the limitlessness of the reality that is named.[68] This first negation is then followed by a second: these prior efforts to describe and negate are still driven by "the language of predication," of discourse, but to truly enter into knowledge of God requires the language "of praise and prayer."[69] Pseudo-Dionysius invites the reader to go beyond conceptual understanding of the

---

[64] David Tracy, "Freedom, the Self, and the Other," in *On Freedom*, ed. Leroy S. Rouner (Notre Dame, IN: University of Notre Dame Press, 1989), 52.

[65] Tracy, "Form and Fragment," 112.

[66] Tracy, "Literary Theory and Return of the Forms for Naming and Thinking God in Theology," 315–16.

[67] Tracy, "Form and Fragment," 98.

[68] Tracy, "Form and Fragment," 113.

[69] Tracy, "Form and Fragment," 113.

Incomprehensible and instead to seek "mystical union with God."[70] Indeed, here one can see how the apophatic approach leads back to Tracy's understanding of love-mysticism.

While Pseudo-Dionysius is the major figure through whom Tracy works out the Incomprehensible God, he also makes significant reference to the Gospel of John[71] and Gregory of Nyssa.[72] Moreover, he often connects these apophatic and mystical approaches to postmodern approaches to God, seeing many substantive parallels between them and certain approaches to deconstruction.[73]

The Infinite God

Initially, shortly after the turn in his theology of naming God, Tracy seemed suspicious of the category of infinity for talking about God. Its first appearance for him is within a litany of *modern* concepts about God (including also the "Absolute," the "Absolute Subject," and the "Ideal").[74] As he was seeking to move away from the generalized, abstract names he had used previously, turning to the explicitly abstract modern names did not seem like a viable move. The category of the infinite became more compelling to him, however, as he engaged in his study of the fragments and fragmenting forms. Drawing on the philosopher Emmanuel Levinas, he takes seriously the distinction between a closed totality and an open infinity.[75] Fragments challenge, even shatter, such totalities, but they simultaneously can be

[70] Tracy, "Form and Fragment, 113.

[71] Tracy, "Literary Theory and Return of the Forms for Naming and Thinking God in Theology," 312.

[72] David Tracy, "God, the Infinite, the Incomprehensible and Hidden" (The Impossibility of God: International Conference with David Tracy, King's University College, London, Ontario, March 18, 2016).

[73] Tracy, "The Post-Modern Re-Naming of God as Incomprehensible and Hidden," 242–45.

[74] Tracy, "Literary Theory and Return of the Forms," 306.

[75] David Tracy, "African American Thought: The Discovery of Fragments," in *Black Faith and Public Talk: Critical Essays on James H. Cone's* Black Theology and Black Power, ed. Dwight N. Hopkins (Maryknoll, NY: Orbis Books, 1999), 31, 35. Tracy further connects the Infinite to Levinas through reflection on the ethics of the infinite. He argues that Levinas makes two key moves: taking religion to be more or less simply an ethics and taking the infinite other person as the focus of that religion/ethics rather than an infinite other God. See David Tracy, "God as Infinite: Ethical Implications,"

revelatory of the infinite. Given the connection argued for between classics and fragments, one can begin to see here the parallel between the "whole" of *The Analogical Imagination* with the "infinite" pointed to by fragments.

Through this insight, Tracy comes to have a far higher regard for the infinite as a way of naming God. Among a host of theologians who emphasize the image of the infinite God (e.g., Nicholas of Cusa, Pseudo-Dionysius, Thomas Aquinas, William of St. Thierry, Friedrich Schleiermacher, and Karl Rahner),[76] Tracy focuses most fully on the neo-Platonic philosopher Plotinus and patristic theologian Gregory of Nyssa. In Plotinus, Tracy finds the first philosophical argument for the infinite as a positive, actual (not potential) reality. This stands in contrast to both Plato, who saw the infinite as formless and therefore "chaotic, *un*intelligible, and . . . imperfect,"[77] and Aristotle, who thought the unmoved mover could be "potentially infinite in its effects . . . not intrinsically an actual infinite in itself."[78] Plotinus argued that the One Good was the ultimate reality from which all finite reality has emanated. He further describes this oneness as infinite, and thus formless, beyond intelligence, and unbounded.[79] Tracy goes on to note that for Plotinus, the infinity of the One is a positive affirmation, not merely a reference to human finitude. Nonetheless, even as a positive affirmation, it is a relatively adequate name for the One, which can only be uttered apophatically; indeed the word "infinite" is itself apophatic, naming what is *not* finite.[80]

Plotinus's Infinite One is not identical to the Christian claim of the infinite God, however. Tracy notes that what Plotinus describes is impersonal, unconscious, and uncaring, in contrast to the merciful,

---

in *God and the Moral Life,* ed. Myriam Renaud and Joshua Daniel (New York: Routledge, 2018), 141–44.

[76] Tracy, "Form and Fragment," 111; David Tracy, "Trinitarian Theology and Spirituality: Retrieving William of St Thierry for Contemporary Theology," in *Rethinking Trinitarian Theology: Disputed Questions and Contemporary Issues in Trinitarian Theology,* ed. Giulio Maspero and Robert J. Wozniak (London: T&T Clark, 2012), 407; Tracy, "God as Infinite," 135.

[77] Tracy, "God as Infinite," 136.

[78] David Tracy, "The Ultimate Invisible: The Infinite," *Social Research* 83, no. 4 (Winter 2016): 894.

[79] Tracy, "God as Infinite," 137–38.

[80] Tracy, "God as Infinite," 137; Tracy, "The Ultimate Invisible," 898.

just, and loving God of Scripture and the Christian tradition.[81] This leads Tracy to engage also a more theological vision of the infinite in Gregory of Nyssa. Perhaps most striking in this vision for Tracy is that Gregory links the "infinite" as a characteristic of divine nature with the human person's infinite desire for God. Gregory names this *epektasis*, a "stretching out" that moves "out of oneself (*ecstasis*) toward (*epi*) ever greater loving desire for God and love of neighbor."[82] Tracy describes Gregory's view of desire as erotic and unfulfilled, precisely because as each desire for the divine is fulfilled, it simply begets further and deeper desire for the divine. Like Augustine's famous prayer from *The Confessions* ("Our hearts are restless until they rest in you"), Gregory claims that human desire for the infinite God can never be fully satisfied; that desire is itself infinite.[83] Tracy ties this to the love of neighbor, which simply "overflows in love" from this primordial desire for and love of God. Ultimately, Gregory will argue that naming God as infinite recognizes this excessive, boundless, loving quality of God and that God is therefore incomprehensible precisely because God is infinite.[84]

Further Fragmented Names for God

While the Hidden, Incomprehensible, and Infinite God are the primary names Tracy's work has focused on, he has mentioned several other forms for naming God. These tend to get drawn into discussion with the other names for God, but they have not received the same degree of emphasis or analysis. These forms for naming God are the Impossible, Being, Love, and Trinity. Discussion of these must be followed by a return to the christomorphic theocentrism that he sees at the heart of all authentic Christian theologies.

Like the other fragmenting forms, *the Impossible* means for Tracy a way of resisting "the totality system of modernity."[85] It does so in contrast to modernity's effort to delineate what is "possible" according to a fairly narrow understanding of reason. Because religion was

---

[81] Tracy, "God as Infinite," 137.
[82] Tracy, "God as Infinite," 141.
[83] Tracy, "God as Infinite," 147.
[84] Tracy, "God as Infinite," 139–40.
[85] Tracy, "Form and Fragment," 102.

outside the boundaries of this "possible," modernity sought to marginalize and undermine the role of religion in both public and private life. Even the "bizarre parade of isms" for describing religion (monotheism, polytheism, deism, pantheism, panentheism, etc.) serve as efforts to make religion palatable within the narrow, largely instrumental form of reason.[86] In contrast to this, Tracy turns to Søren Kierkegaard, whom he credits with introducing the term "the Impossible" as a referent for God. Tracy sees in Kierkegaard's work, with all its pseudonyms and divergent genres, the effort to know something true about God without wrestling the faith into a system.[87] Kierkegaard rejected the systematizing of Christianity into Christendom, seeing in this a capitulation to Enlightenment principles rather than a commitment to the Christian encounter with the divine. That image of God the Impossible serves as the tool to crack the truncated vision of God and of the faith co-opted by modern rationality.[88]

God as Being is perhaps a more traditional way of naming God than the Impossible. The characteristic figure for Tracy on this name is St. Thomas Aquinas. He describes the Thomistic way of talking about God in terms of Being less as a noun (as in "the Supreme Being") and more as the verb form, "Esse."[89] Interestingly, Tracy's main references are in the context of comparing Thomas to Pseudo-Dionysius. Whereas Pseudo-Dionysius offered the kataphatic name—"the Good"—for God, Thomas emphasized God as "Being." This took the most fundamental characteristic of God to be God's existence, more specifically, God as necessary (in contrast to contingent) being with "no distinction between essence and existence."[90] Tracy considers this shift to be groundbreaking, a tremendous "metaphysical insight," but also one that reshapes the entire Western theological tradition. It is arguably the form for naming God that is most easily tied to his

---

[86] Tracy, "Form and Fragment," 102.

[87] Tracy, "Form and Fragment," 104.

[88] Kierkegaard is Tracy's main example of this fragmenting form, but he also draws connections to the work of Nietzsche in this regard as well. He further connects it to more postmodern thinkers like Jean-Luc Marion, Jacques Derrida, and John Caputo, although these latter connections are more assertions than developed arguments. See Tracy, "Form and Fragment," 104–5, 114.

[89] Tracy compares this emphasis to Aristotle's "Act" and Martin Heidegger's "Sein" (Tracy, "The Ultimate Invisible," 892).

[90] Tracy, "Form and Fragment," 113.

early names for God (the "limit-of" and others), as he focuses so much on how those are connected to the ground or horizon of existence. In his later efforts, however, it is one of the names that has afforded limited critical attention.

Somewhat similar in this regard is the name of *God as Love*. This name, taken from 1 John 4:16, is repeatedly referenced by Tracy in his discussion of the fragmenting forms. Tracy notes two key insights that this name offers about the divine. First, the metaphor of love reveals "the intrinsically relational character of the Divine reality as indeed of all reality."[91] Second, "God is love" is the essential insight underlying the active and self-sacrificial love expressed in the life, death, resurrection, and second coming of Christ.[92] He describes this name of God as both the "central Christian metaphor" and the "highest cataphatic name for God."[93] In each case, the passage from the first letter of John is his focal point, but he does not really move on to other figures from within the tradition to expand on it. Love as a fragmenting form for naming God is obviously important for the tradition and for Tracy, but it similarly suffers from limited development.

Love as the name of God does, however, lead Tracy into the *trinitarian name of God*. Referring to the Trinity as the classical form within the Christian tradition, Tracy sees the Trinity largely as the culmination of his other work in describing the various fragmenting forms.[94] More than any other name for God, Tracy sees in the Trinity the deepest, most explicit expression of the self-giving kenosis that is at the heart of the Christian tradition. The Trinity is central to understanding the incarnation of God the Son in the person of Jesus Christ and the gift of the Spirit that guides the church, its teachings, and its liturgy to the present.[95] Moreover, the Trinity is part of pulling together the various names that went before, including the Hiddenness of God (most perfectly expressed in the Father, who is only revealed through the Son and the Spirit), God as Love (the eternal relations of

---

[91] Tracy, "Literary Theory and the Return of the Forms," 308.

[92] Tracy, "Trinitarian Speculation and the Forms of Divine Disclosure," 285.

[93] Tracy, "Literary Theory and the Return of Forms," 308; Tracy, "Trinitarian Theology and Spirituality," 407.

[94] Tracy, "Form and Fragment," 98.

[95] Tracy, "Trinitarian Speculation," 286.

the persons to one another and the kenotic outpouring for creation), and the Infinite (the transcendent Trinity that is beyond all human limitations). Because of its kataphatic assertions, the trinitarian name is in tension with the apophatic tendencies of the Hidden God.[96] Nonetheless, Tracy sees the deep commitment to trinitarian thought throughout the tradition, serving as one of the most important and most comprehensive analogies for the human understanding of God. He thus draws on a host of figures on the Trinity (including Augustine, Thomas Aquinas, Bernard Lonergan,[97] Karl Barth, Hans Urs von Balthasar,[98] Jürgen Moltmann, and Catherine Mowry LaCugna[99]), although it is worth recognizing that many of these are referenced in passing.

In what is perhaps the most thorough of his recent engagements with the trinitarian name of God, Tracy draws out the trinitarian theology of William of St. Thierry.[100] There, Tracy sees a deep interrelationship for William between theology and spirituality on the Trinity and what that means for one's encounter with the divine.[101] Advocating for the priority of love over intellect (without separating the two), Tracy argues that William's theology leads the human person to more deeply recognize the image of God, specifically the *imago Trinitatis*, in the person him- or herself. This approach to trinitarian theology ultimately leads to a deeper self-awareness motivated by and rooted in love of God. For Tracy, the significance of this move is to help heal modernity's separation between theology and spirituality and between love and knowledge.[102]

Ultimately, this trinitarian form for naming God returns Tracy to the "form of forms," Christ. As was discussed in the previous chapter, what is consistently and ubiquitously distinct about Christian theology is that it is "Christo-morphic theo-centrism."[103] These names

---

[96] Tracy, "Form and Fragment," 99.

[97] Tracy, "Trinitarian Speculation and the Forms of Divine Disclosure," 287.

[98] Tracy, "Literary Theory and Return of the Forms," 312.

[99] Tracy, "Trinitarian Speculation and the Forms of Divine Disclosure," 278.

[100] Tracy, "Trinitarian Theology and Spirituality," 387–420.

[101] Tracy, "Trinitarian Theology and Spirituality," 391.

[102] Tracy, "Trinitarian Theology and Spirituality," 420.

[103] He also offers the slightly more unwieldy "Christo-morphic Trinitarian theo-centrism" to describe Christianity (Tracy, "Trinitarian Speculation and the Forms of Divine Disclosure," 280).

for God are truly the center of the faith, but the Christian can only ever make sense of them in the context of the Christian faith by recognizing how those names are revealed through Christ. There is a tremendously wide range of scriptural sources to draw from for these various names, and they are anchored throughout the tradition (as the breadth of Tracy's references, both developed and in passing, testify to).[104] Yet, ultimately, these names cannot simply be juxtaposed against one another but must be gathered together in the plural, complex set of Christian traditions.[105] The heart of this, the classic *par excellence*, the form of forms in the Christian tradition, must always be the event and person of Jesus Christ.

The Significance of Theological Method for Naming God

While Tracy's shift from his vague, generic ways of naming God to his fragmenting forms for naming God was catalyzed by critical reviews of *Plurality and Ambiguity*, the significance of this shift really lies in the question of theological method. The earlier efforts were exemplary of the work of fundamental theology, with its focus on disciplinary status, norms, and methods of theology. Because fundamental theology proposes a mode of argument that is open to any intelligent, reasonable, responsible person, it does not focus on the specific religious commitments of any given interlocutor.[106] It therefore makes sense that fundamental theology often engages with disciplines other than theology (especially, though not exclusively, philosophy) in its efforts to demonstrate the reasonableness of a particular religious tradition's claims. Such engagements are critical to fundamental theology's success, thus it is the subdiscipline that primarily deals with concepts that are significant for (but not limited to) the task of theology.

The generic ways of naming God—"limit-of," the "whole," and "Ultimate Reality"—are examples of such broadly accessible concepts. None is specific to a particular religious tradition, even as the ideas underlying them can be discerned in a variety of traditions.

---

[104] Tracy, "Theology and the Many Faces of Postmodernity," 111–12.

[105] Tracy, "Form and Fragment," 107–8.

[106] Note here Tracy's continued indebtedness to the transcendental precepts of Lonergan.

Moreover, they draw heavily on other academic disciplines (the "limit-of," with its connection to the philosophy of Karl Jaspers, is perhaps most obvious on this) in their efforts to make sense of the divine. These ways of naming God do not really originate in the Christian tradition per se, but they are not incompatible with that tradition either.

By contrast, Tracy's more recent fragmentary namings are more in line with systematic theology. This subdiscipline focuses on the central claims of a particular faith tradition and seek to interpret it in light of both its historical development and its contemporary context. It is also a type of public theology, but the public it has in mind is the church, the community of believers who hold to the same texts, teachings, practices, and rituals. These names for God are clearly anchored in specific Christian figures and traditions of thought. The Hidden God who inspires prophetic and apocalyptic responses to marginalization, the Incomprehensible God who directs believers to liturgy, the christomorphic God who enters into creation and redeems it—these names tell who the God of the Christian tradition is. They wrestle with God's identity. Moreover, they demonstrate the profound plurality within the Christian tradition, as these various names are held in tension with one another.

What drives this shift from fundamental to systematic approaches to naming God is precisely the question of hope. Tracy recognizes that "limit-of" and other namings were not sufficient to ground or explain the hope that he himself expressed at the end of *Plurality and Ambiguity*.[107] Even as they rightly indicate the human experience of something transcendent, they fall short of grounding and motivating any meaningfully Christian response to that transcendence. Their abstraction is useful at the level of making religious claims reasonable and accessible to diverse audiences, but they also tend to express a lowest-common-denominator understanding of God. To refer back to Tracy's own criteria, the generic ways of naming God fall short of both adequacy to human experience and appropriateness to the tradition.

---

[107] One could potentially extend this to question whether such names inspire faith or charity either.

It must be noted, though, that this does not mean there is no value in fundamental theology on the question of God. There is value in establishing the reasonableness of God and making that case to other disciplines and other religious traditions. When Tracy writes that "the objective referent of all such language . . . is that reality which religious human beings mean when they say 'God,'" one cannot help but hear the concluding lines of St. Thomas Aquinas's five ways for proving the existence of God.[108] Nonetheless, this approach is limited and does not get to the practices, virtues, and dispositions that animate living the Christian faith. Indeed, focusing solely on the fundamental theological approach risks upholding what Tracy calls one of the "fatal separations" of modern thought, that between spirituality and theology.[109] The reintegration of spirituality with theology, of lived practice with creedal claims, and of narrative, doctrine, and liturgy with one another depends profoundly on returning again and again to the fragments of the particular tradition. In gathering these fragments, Tracy intends to name more specifically the God that is the source of hope.

---

[108] BRO 109; ST I, Q. 2, Art. 3, co.: "and this we call God."
[109] Tracy, "Form and Fragment," 100.

Epilogue

The Tracy-Lindbeck Debate

It is precisely this concern for the truth claims of each particular religious tradition that led Tracy to his understanding of the public character of all theological claims. Radical pluralism need not lead to radical relativism or narrow sectarianism.

—T. Howland Sanks[1]

A few years after Tracy published *The Analogical Imagination*, Lutheran theologian George Lindbeck published *The Nature of Doctrine*.[2] Lindbeck had long been interested in ecumenical concerns like intra-Christian doctrinal differences and the visible unity of the church, and the book began as a prolegomenon to that sort of work.[3] He did not expect the expansive response to the text that followed, but he was pleased with the conversation it generated. One notable conversation partner that came from it was David Tracy.

There are three good reasons for concluding this book by looking at the Tracy-Lindbeck debate.[4] First, this book's argument is that

---

[1] T. Howland Sanks, "David Tracy's Theological Project: An Overview and Some Implications," *Theological Studies* 54, no. 4 (December 1993): 725.

[2] George Lindbeck, *The Nature of Doctrine: Religion and Theology in a Postliberal Age*, 25th ann. ed., intro. by Bruce D. Marshall (Louisville, KY: Westminster John Knox Press, 2009).

[3] ND xxix.

[4] It is at first glance somewhat odd that this "debate" exists at all. While Lindbeck does reference Tracy as an example of the experiential-expressive model that he critiques, Tracy is actually not a central counterpoint in *The Nature of Doctrine*. Rather, Lindbeck far more has his sights set on Tracy's mentor, Bernard Lonergan (ND 17). Lonergan died in 1984, however, the same year Lindbeck's text was published, and was thus unable to respond himself. It seems that Tracy essentially took up the flag for the model that included them both. Moreover, the debate between the two of them

conversation is central to understanding both what Tracy thinks theology is and how Tracy's theology has developed. Throughout, we have looked at the influence on his thought of his conversations with Lonergan, Tillich, Marion, Ricoeur, Benjamin, and others. Yet his engagement with George Lindbeck remains perhaps one of the best known. It is surely the best example of Tracy engaging seriously with a figure and an argument that he finds entirely unpersuasive and yet worth considering.

Second, the Tracy-Lindbeck debate remains a theological point of interest to the present day. Scholarly publications regularly return to these two figures and their contrasting claims.[5] A 2016 conference on Tracy's theology featured a panel discussion on "revisiting the Tracy-Lindbeck debate thirty years later."[6] The demarcations between the public "hermeneutical-political" and the postliberal "cultural-linguistic" approaches are provocative and illuminating, thus leading to their utility decades after first being drawn.[7]

---

is largely limited to Lindbeck's book itself and Tracy's review of it: David Tracy, "Lindbeck's New Program for Theology: A Reflection," *The Thomist* 49, no. 3 (July 1985): 460–72. The debate clearly continued, but mostly through the analytical work of other theologians.

[5] E.g., Kristin E. Heyer, "How Does Theology Go Public? Rethinking the Debate Between David Tracy and George Lindbeck," *Political Theology* 5, no. 3 (July 2004); Boyd Blundell, *Paul Ricoeur between Theology and Philosophy: Detour and Return* (Bloomington: Indiana University Press, 2010).

[6] The panel was part of the "Impossibility of God: International Conference with David Tracy" held at King's University College in London, Ontario, March 18–19, 2016. The panelists were John Berkman, Shaun Brown, Gill Goulding, Murray Johnston, and Joseph Mangina.

[7] A note on terminology: the different sides of the Tracy-Lindbeck debate have been subjected to a wide range of descriptors: Chicago vs. Yale (Scott Holland, "How Do Stories Save Us? Two Contemporary Theological Responses," *The Conrad Grebel Review* 12, no. 2 [Spring 1994]: 131); revisionist vs. postliberal (Charles W. Allen, "Between Revisionists and Postliberals: A Review Article," *Encounter* 51, no. 4 [Autumn 1990]: 389); progressive liberal vs. postliberal (Dwight N. Hopkins, *Being Human: Race, Culture, and Religion* [Princeton, NJ: Fortress Press, 2005], 16–29); impurist vs. purist (Gary L. Comstock, "Two Types of Narrative Theology," *Journal of the American Academy of Religion* 55, no. 4 [Winter 1987]: 688); and experiential-expressivist vs. cultural-linguistic (ND 2–4). Except when referring to the specific arguments of any of these scholars, I will describe Tracy's theology as public and Lindbeck's as postliberal, as these are the terms they most clearly use to describe themselves.

Third, and related, these different approaches find purchase in a diverse set of theological concerns. As this conclusion will show, each of the six themes explored in this book have been drawn into the Tracy-Lindbeck debate as a way of understanding the differences between these theologians' understandings of theology. By looking to that debate here, it helps to illustrate the deep interconnections of these themes within Tracy's thought while illuminating Tracy's core concerns.

This conclusion thus proceeds in three parts. First, it looks at "round 1" of the Tracy-Lindbeck debate by focusing on the main claims staked out by Lindbeck and Tracy. Lindbeck offers three models for religion and experience and then critiques the experiential-expressive model in which he locates Tracy. In response, Tracy rejects the experiential-expressive label and in turn challenges Lindbeck on the truth-status of theological claims. "Round 2" focuses on the subsequent life of the Tracy-Lindbeck debate and how, through the work of other scholars, it has borne fruit in a range of theological areas. In particular, the emphasis here is on how the six themes from this book are intertwined with the issues raised in the Tracy-Lindbeck debate. Finally, the conclusion will look at the significance of this ongoing conversation for Tracy's theology.

The Debate, Round 1—Tracy and Lindbeck

Lindbeck's Models for Theology

Lindbeck's *The Nature of Doctrine* opens by looking at the ecumenical context and offering a way forward for thinking about the different models of religion and doctrine present among the various traditions.[8] The first, the cognitivist-propositionalist model, focuses on "the ways in which church doctrines function as informative propositions or truth claims about objective realities."[9] Doctrines are simply universal truth claims, always and everywhere true, which

---

[8] Lindbeck does not assign these models to particular denominations; theologians within the same tradition may advocate for different models, while theologians of different traditions might advocate for the same (e.g., a cultural-linguistic model can be found among Roman Catholic and Protestant theologians alike).

[9] ND 2.

either correspond to reality (true) or do not (false). Lindbeck connects propositionalism to traditional approaches to orthodoxy, and it is consistent with Tracy's description of the orthodox model.[10]

Lindbeck's second model is the experiential-expressive approach. Here, doctrines are symbolic representations of "feelings, attitudes, or existential orientations."[11] This model particularly emphasizes the common human dimension of religious experiences, suggesting that essentially what happens to a Catholic and to a Buddhist is the same, even though it comes to be expressed differently due to their subsequent and different religious formulations of that experience.[12] Lindbeck situates the experiential-expressive approach within the broader liberal tradition within theology, which would include Tracy's liberal and revisionist models for theology.

Lindbeck's third, and preferred, model is the cultural-linguistic one. Here, religions are like languages, which have interpretive power for how one understands God, the self, and the world.[13] The religion shapes the inner experience (in contrast to the experiential-expressive, whereby the internal shapes the outer). It does so because doctrines in this model are not truth claims requiring belief but are rules to be followed.[14] In a linguistic approach, doctrines are the communally determined grammar that order how one believes and acts. After introducing and comparing these models, Lindbeck goes on to further develop the cultural-linguistic model and to assess it by looking at various common Christian doctrines.

Lindbeck's critique of the experiential-expressive model is the key connecting point to Tracy. In reality, his representative figures for the best version of that model are Karl Rahner and Bernard Lonergan; Tracy is mentioned a few times but is a footnote as often as a main focus. Lindbeck's critique rests on three key pressure points. The first is the assertion of an underlying religious experience common to all persons.[15] Lindbeck notes that Lonergan recognizes this as an assertion that cannot necessarily be proven. Yet Lindbeck pushes further

---

[10] BRO 24–25; see chapter 1, pp. 17–19.
[11] ND 2.
[12] ND 17.
[13] ND 18.
[14] ND 4.
[15] ND 18.

to argue that theories of religion that are built on this claim must reckon with the vast diversity of what is called religious experience, such that any description of what these have in common is ultimately "logically and empirically vacuous."[16] At best, these are a set of family resemblances, which Lindbeck ties together as divergent systems that "shape and produce our most profound sentiments, attitudes, and awarenesses."[17]

This relates to a second pillar, which is made up of competing notions of truth. The experiential-expressive model operates largely on a manifestation and transformation understanding of truth. The symbolic expressions of one's religious experience resonate as true, as is seen in Tracy's description of the classics as disclosing possible modes of being in the world. The cultural-linguistic model understands truth differently, focusing on how it functions within the context of the system.[18] Lindbeck describes theology as second-order reflection, which cannot comment on whether or not God exists (or whether other doctrines are propositionally true) but only on how those claims function within an existing religious system/language.[19]

Finally, Lindbeck claims that his cultural-linguistic model simply has better explanatory power for what is observed and described as religion. It allows for the same relationship of religion and experience, but with a shift in emphasis (whereby religion orders experience more than experience gives rise to religion).[20] It allows for the power of symbol and ritual essential to the experiential-expressive model but reframes them as part of how the grammar of a particular religion is learned by religious persons.[21] Lindbeck connects this to the rise of cultural-linguistic models in a range of academic disciplines, even as the experiential-expressive model was growing in influence in theology and religious studies.[22]

---

[16] ND 18.

[17] ND 26. This latter point is somewhat strange as a critique, as Tracy also claims that there is no universal definition of religion and that what is generally considered religious is so on a "family resemblances" model (BRO 92–93).

[18] ND 50–51.

[19] ND 54–55.

[20] ND 20.

[21] ND 22.

[22] ND 11.

Tracy's Critique of Postliberalism

Tracy's response to Lindbeck focuses on two concerns. The first deals with the experiential-expressive label and the meaning Lindbeck gives to it. Tracy notes that Lindbeck describes the liberal theological tradition as deeply indebted to the anthropological turn, the "turn to the self," such that it focuses on an individual, pre-reflective religious experience that is the driving basis for religion. He recognizes that this approach is historically grounded in the larger liberal tradition, but he faults Lindbeck for ignoring significant work in that liberal tradition in the decades preceding *The Nature of Doctrine* that sought to critique that very problem.[23] Tracy highlights two specific oversights on Lindbeck's part. First, the broader liberal tradition had come to focus much more on questions of hermeneutics, which engages with many of the linguistic concerns Lindbeck raises. Indeed, Tracy notes how central this shift was for him in moving from *Blessed Rage for Order* to *The Analogical Imagination*. Second, Tracy notes the work of diverse liberation theologies that encourage a "radical 'deprivatizing'" of the liberal tradition. Based on these, Tracy proposes instead the term "hermeneutical-political" as a better descriptor for his cohort of theologians than "experiential-expressive."[24] While Lindbeck critiques Tracy and others for a "unilateral" approach whereby experience leads to language and religion, Tracy argues that Lindbeck has entirely overlooked the deeply dialectical relationship between experience and language that is the hallmark of contemporary liberal theologies. Put another way, Tracy thinks many liberal theologians are performing a critique of "'expressivist' and 'privativist' tendencies" more effectively and accurately than Lindbeck's cultural-linguistic approach does.[25]

In fact, Tracy goes on to argue that Lindbeck's concern is not about the methodological relationship of language and experience but the substantive desire for theology to simply be confessional, not public.[26] Because the religion is like a linguistic system and the doctrine is the grammar, there is no sense in which anything external to the religious

---

[23] Tracy, "Lindbeck's New Program for Theology," 462–63.
[24] Tracy, "Lindbeck's New Program for Theology," 463.
[25] Tracy, "Lindbeck's New Program for Theology," 465.
[26] Tracy, "Lindbeck's New Program for Theology," 465–66.

tradition can make judgments about the tradition. This is consistent with the postliberal approach to truth, which downplays both propositionalist and symbolic visions and subsumes them into the intra-systematic perspective. Doctrinal claims are second-order reflections on the tradition itself, not specifically claims about objective reality. Thus there is no position apart from a tradition that could be critical of the tradition; one must instead enter into it and into its grammar in order to make judgments about whether or not a particular claim is consistent with the established system. This sense of truth privileges a confessional approach to theology and religion.

Moreover, the confessionalism is evident in Lindbeck's understanding of the relationship between language and experience. Because he advocates for the outer linguistic system always shaping the inner experience, the postliberal approach is unilateral in a comparable way to the projected experiential-expressivist alternative. Yet, as noted, what Tracy and his cohort are doing is bilateral, evident already in the correlation approach to theology. The claim that it is a mutually critical correlation emphasizes the *mutuality* of that.[27] While some postliberal (and other) critics of Tracy's correlation think that it ultimately sells out to secular reason or is unable to offer anything theologically distinctive, this is a misreading both of Tracy's intent and of his practice. Lindbeck's inclusion of Paul Ricoeur in the experiential-expressivist camp, rightly critiqued by Tracy as bizarre, is indicative of his neglect of the hermeneutical and mutually critical approaches that the public, hermeneutical-political relies on.

Tracy's second main critique of Lindbeck picks up on the implications of the confessional approach. While the cultural-linguistic model can give an effective description of how a religion functions and how its claims shape the lives of its adherents, it offers little in terms of theology's larger concern with truth claims.[28] While Lindbeck is concerned with avoiding the challenges of relativism (where there is no sense of objective truth) and fideism (where faith and reason are not only separate but opposed, with faith being the better half), Tracy argues that he never really gets away from it. The grammatical approach has no real way to make judgments about the truth

---

[27] Tracy, "Lindbeck's New Program for Theology," 470.
[28] Tracy, "Lindbeck's New Program for Theology," 468–69.

or veracity of particular doctrines, or to compare them meaningfully across cultural-linguistic systems.[29]

The Debate, Round 2—Ripples Outward

For all the attention that the Tracy-Lindbeck debate has generated, it is striking that it is really limited to two core texts: Lindbeck's book and Tracy's review of the same. The conversation does not really become a central or recurring theme for either figure, at least not directly. Yet conversations, particularly theological ones, often expand beyond their initial interlocutors. The parameters of the discussion between Tracy's public hermeneutical-political model and Lindbeck's postliberal cultural-linguistic model become a useful heuristic guide for thinking through many essential questions of theology. Subsequent readers of Tracy have often used the debate as a means for engaging other questions in his thought. Indeed, a review of their publications reveal that the six core themes presented in this book have each wound their way into the Tracy-Lindbeck debate.

First, the idea that theology might be construed as a public discipline is deeply contested in this debate. While Tracy's demand for publicness in theology in all its subdisciplines is core to his thought, this is largely rejected within postliberal circles. As Gary Comstock argues, the postliberal approach is "purist" in the sense that theology should really only be concerned with the history and self-understanding of religious community. These parameters are determined and judged by the long biblical narrative, and thus there need be no appeal to public arguments that allow for those outside the tradition to critique and challenge. To do so is seen as "overstepping" the regulative bounds of the tradition.[30] Put another way, Christian theology will explain Christian beliefs and practices on inner Christian terms, or it will not explain it at all.[31] T. Howland Sanks similarly argues that for Lindbeck, and by extension for other postliberals, Christian

---

[29] Richard Lints notes this issue of truth claims as a key issue between Tracy and Lindbeck and their respective models. See Richard Lints, "The Postpositivist Choice: Tracy or Lindbeck?," *Journal of the American Academy of Religion* 61, no. 4 (Winter 1993): 668–69.

[30] Comstock, "Two Types of Narrative Theology," 695–96.

[31] Comstock, "Two Types of Narrative Theology," 699.

doctrine and tradition can be understood only by those already shaped by that doctrine and tradition. To appeal to any arguments that are not already within the tradition is nonsensical.[32]

Intriguingly, Kristin Heyer argues that there are places of complementarity between Tracy and Lindbeck on the question of public theology. She claims that Lindbeck is a "better descriptor of Christianity" with his cultural-linguistic model, as he highlights the distinctiveness and particularity of the Christian community. By contrast, the conversational approach of Tracy is better adapted to "communicating the Christian message beyond its 'borders.'"[33] A complementary public approach would highlight both aspects and could in turn promote better scriptural and theological literacy, a greater evangelical outreach to the world, and more sustained engagement with ethical issues in the world. The church must both live and communicate what it teaches. Heyer ultimately considers Tracy's approach to be more effective, given the widespread reality of pluralism and the utility of conversation and classics for engaging with it.[34]

Given the connection between public-ness and method for Tracy, it is to be expected that this too is a point of contention in the Tracy-Lindbeck debate. Charles Allen argues that postliberal theologians tend to view the "revisionists" as "preoccupied with translating Christian convictions into supposedly generic terms in order to assess their adequacy."[35] In effect, Allen argues that postliberal theologians entirely misconstrue what happens in mutually critical correlation, as all they are able to see is one of the internal trajectories of that method. Sanks connects this to a generalized postliberal fear that theologians like Tracy commit so fully to rationalist, Enlightenment standards of critical thought that they will undermine, ignore, or even eviscerate what is distinctive about the Christian tradition.[36] As such, postliberals reject theological methods that are rooted in

---

[32] Sanks, "Tracy's Theological Project," 723–24.

[33] Heyer, "How Does Theology Go Public," 325.

[34] Heyer, "How Does Theology Go Public," 326.

[35] Allen, "Between Revisionists and Postliberals," 395. In this essay, Allen is mostly focused on postliberal theologian William Placher, whom he sees as being more sympathetic to revisionist-theology than Lindbeck.

[36] Sanks, "Tracy's Theological Project," 725.

critical conversation between the sources of the tradition and their cultural context.[37]

The concern about the distinctiveness of Christianity is manifested particularly strongly with regard to Tracy's approach to fundamental theology. In Tracy's formulation, this subdiscipline is not anchored in the explicit faith commitments of those doing the work; they must instead rely on open, rational criteria, typically derived from the field of philosophy. Boyd Blundell focuses his critique of Tracy on this weakness, arguing that it surrenders the distinctiveness of Christianity while gaining nothing in return.[38] Yet this argument tends to overlook two points Tracy makes regarding fundamental theology. First, the intention to make the case for theological principles on nonfaith grounds has a longstanding warrant within the tradition itself (Tracy cites a range of figures in this respect, including Justin Martyr, Origen of Alexandria, and Thomas Aquinas).[39] Thus even though the terms of the argument in fundamental theology are not distinctive to the faith, the impetus behind engaging that argument is founded in the tradition. Second, Tracy does not see fundamental theology as separable from systematic and practical theologies. It is not a different discipline but a subdiscipline of the larger theological project.

Within this debate, the classic becomes an interesting place of reflection. On one hand, Tracy's classics and fragments are highly distinctive, as they arise from within particular traditions. They are among the texts, images, symbols, and so on that would help form the cultural-linguistic system of a particular faith. Their rootedness within the tradition is essential to their potential to be revelatory to those who are not part of the tradition. This move from within the system to outside seems to fall afoul of Lindbeck's claim that one must be within the tradition to understand it, but it also undermines

---

[37] Lints, "The Postpositivist Choice," 668.

[38] Blundell, *Paul Ricoeur between Philosophy and Theology*, 27. Blundell is building on Stanley Hauerwas's argument that engaging a pluralistic culture requires deeper commitment to one's particularity, not abandonment thereof. One can also see Gener's argument about Tracy on public-ness in the same vein (Timoteo D. Gener, "With/Beyond Tracy: Re-Visioning Public Theology," *Evangelical Review of Theology* 33, no. 2 [April 2009]: 130–33).

[39] AI 63–64.

those critiques of Tracy that suggest he is not committed to the distinctiveness of the Christian tradition. In fact, when Stanley Hauerwas argues that one must be deeply committed to a particular Christian tradition in order to productively engage pluralism, this seems less a critique of Tracy and more a reinforcement of Tracy's own argument. It in fact affirms Tracy's approach to public theology, theological method, and the value of the classics.[40] Scott Holland upholds this essential role of the classics, which support theology's ability to speak beyond the confines of a particular tradition.[41]

This leads to the question of pluralism. While Tracy encourages active engagement with the pluralism within and among cultures, traditions, languages, and Christianity itself, the postliberal model seems to have fewer resources for or interest in such engagement. Holland argues that, while intratextuality is deeply important within this system, there is little understanding of intertextuality and its possibilities.[42] Patrick Keifert rightly notes that Lindbeck has in fact, throughout his career, been deeply invested in ecumenical and interfaith conversations, and so he is not unaware of or uninterested in wrestling with pluralism. Keifert describes the ideal postliberal version of such engagement as "the painstaking task of learning one another's cultural-linguistic systems. Most likely this would be a lifetime task, since most of the system is an unconscious performance."[43] The postliberal approach can, however, also tend toward sectarianism, abandoning the universality that Keifert argues "critical pluralism" reaches for through consideration of the particular.[44] Tracy emphasizes the power of that particularity to find places of common understanding, not to eliminate difference or distinctiveness altogether. Allen rightly describes the analogical imagination as asserting that people "have enough in common to enable and demand working for practically viable, if tension-fraught, varieties of solidarity in both our understanding and our common life."[45]

---

[40] Stanley Hauerwas, *Against the Nations: War and Survival in a Liberal Society* (Minneapolis: Winston Press, 1985), 44.

[41] Holland, "How Do Stories Save Us," 149–50.

[42] Holland, "How Do Stories Save Us," 143.

[43] Patrick R. Keifert, "Labor Room or Morgue: The Power and Limits of Pluralism and Christology," *Word & World* 5, no. 1 (Winter 1985): 86.

[44] Keifert, "Labor Room or Morgue," 81.

[45] Allen, "Between Revisionists and Postliberals," 396.

The tension between public and postliberal theologies becomes evident in their approaches to Christology. Both Tracy and Lindbeck take Christ as the essential claim of the Christian tradition by which other doctrines are judged. For Lindbeck, within theology Christ functions as the core narrative, the heart of the intratextual world, and the center of intrasystematic truth. According to Stephen Stell, Lindbeck's approach does not then consider seriously "the norm . . . of the living Christ," focusing instead on how Christ as part of Christian grammar shapes a Christian worldview.[46] This links back with the critique of the postliberal approach to truth: it largely prescinds from that ontological question of whether or not it really is the case that Christ is God incarnate. By contrast, Tracy's Christology highlights how this particular expression of the "whole," of God, given in the incarnation, crucifixion, and resurrection, discloses the "graciousness of all reality."[47]

Finally, Tracy's own approach to naming God has often emphasized the nondistinctive in ways consistent with some of his postliberal critics. While he never sought to fully separate the limit-of, the whole, or Ultimate Reality from the Christian tradition, it is true that they do not have the deep roots in that tradition that might allow them to inspire a specifically Christian hope. Of course, Tracy has turned more and more to particular Christian efforts to name God, and he's always tied them back to Christ as the focal expression of the reality of God. Heyer notes that Tracy's emphasis on the universality of God and of grace supports the Christian call to go out into the world and be open as a community.[48] With regard to Lindbeck, though, she argues that the cultural-linguistic approach's emphasis on doctrines as grammar risks limiting God to "the God of the narrative rather than God identified in the narrative."[49] Put another way, Lindbeck may undermine a core aspect of the Christian understanding of God precisely by "underestimat[ing] the dynamic reality to which the privileged narratives only point."[50] Again, understanding

---

[46] Stephen L. Stell, "Hermeneutics in Theology and the Theology of Hermeneutics: Beyond Lindbeck and Tracy," *Journal of the American Academy of Religion* 61, no. 4 (Winter 1993): 693.

[47] Stell, "Hermeneutics in Theology," 689–90.

[48] Heyer, "How Does Theology Go Public," 321.

[49] Heyer, "How Does Theology Go Public," 321.

[50] Heyer, "How Does Theology Go Public," 321.

doctrines as rules limits the assertion of truth claims about what those rules point to.

The preceding does not represent the final word about Tracy's core themes. Rather, it is an indication of how this debate, one of his best-known engagements with a fellow theologian, touches on his most significant concerns. Some of that is evident in Tracy's and Lindbeck's own writings, and some of it only comes out in the responses of others. Yet even that fact—that the conversation between Tracy and Lindbeck might spiral out into other scholars and other concerns—is indicative of the extent and attraction of theological conversation.

Theology as Conversation, Conversation about Theology

This concluding, all-too-cursory turn to the Tracy-Lindbeck debate helpfully highlights the core thesis of this text. The perception of theology as an ongoing conversation among diverse interlocutors, including other persons, traditions, and the wider, even nonreligious, world in which we live has guided Tracy's thought throughout his career. Conversation with others can be risky, challenging one to conversion, as evident in the shift in naming God after *Plurality and Ambiguity* or in the turn from the "classic" to the "fragment." Conversation with others can also help to clarify differences and lead one into a more complete understanding of the self, as evident in Tracy's respectful but forceful disagreement with Lindbeck's theological models.[51]

In his own way, Tracy has sought to be the theologian as host, bringing together a range of arguments and ideas, seeking what is convincing in each while charitably setting aside what is not. That table of conversation has at times been overcrowded and boisterous and at other times has needed to be expanded, refinished, or rebuilt entirely. Yet that desire to speak with others, to share of oneself and genuinely encounter the other, has endured.

[51] An example of Tracy's charitableness is that a few years after his review of *The Nature of Doctrine*, he contributed an essay to a Lindbeck festschrift. He notes at the beginning of his essay that despite his strong criticism of that earlier text, he would spend the current essay "articulating what [Lindbeck and his Yale colleagues have] taught me." David Tracy, "On Reading the Scriptures Theologically," in *Theology and Dialogue: Essays in Conversation with George Lindbeck*, ed. Bruce D. Marshall (Notre Dame, IN: University of Notre Dame Press, 1990), 35–68.

The many figures who took up the terms of the Tracy-Lindbeck debate are representative of how to pick up on a conversation within theology about theology and take it further. Tracy hopes that such conversation will go on and will always be open to engaging the church, the academy, and the wider society. The task that comes to each new generation of theologians is to continue the conversation, to deepen its insights, and to expand its vision. Hopefully, we will do so with the same rigor, passion, and charity that Tracy has.

Appendix A

The David Tracy Bibliography[1]

Doctoral Dissertation

Tracy, David. "The Development of the Notion of Theological Methodology in the Works of Bernard J. Lonergan." STD diss., Pontificia Universitas Gregoriana, Facultas Theologica, 1969.[2]

Books

Tracy, David. *The Achievement of Bernard Lonergan*. New York: Herder and Herder, 1970.

———. *Blessed Rage for Order: The New Pluralism in Theology*. New York: Seabury Press, 1975.[3]

———. *The Analogical Imagination: Christian Theology and the Culture of Pluralism*. New York: Crossroad, 1981.

McCready, William C., David Tracy, John Shea, Mary G. Durkin, and Andrew M. Greeley. *Parish, Priest and People: New Leadership for the Local Church*. Chicago: Thomas More, 1981.[4]

---

[1] Two significant bibliographies of Tracy's work have been previously published: Stephen H. Webb, "Bibliography of David Tracy," in *Radical Pluralism & Truth: David Tracy and the Hermeneutics of Religion*, ed. Werner G Jeanrond and Jennifer L Rike (New York: Crossroad, 1991), 286–93; and Andreas S. Telser, *Theologie als öffentlicher Diskurs: Zur Relevanz der Systematischen Theologie David Tracys* (Innsbruck: Tyrolia, 2016), 377–92. This bibliography is deeply indebted to both of these efforts. It also corrects some oversights present in both.

[2] This text was the basis for Tracy's first published book, *The Achievement of Bernard Lonergan*.

[3] A new edition with a new preface by Tracy was released by University of Chicago Press in 1996.

[4] Although this text was collaboratively produced by all five authors, Tracy's contributions were primarily in chapters 4, 8, and 11, which are listed below under his articles and essays from 1981.

Cobb, John B., and David Tracy. *Talking about God: Doing Theology in the Context of Modern Pluralism*. New York: Seabury Press, 1983.[5]

Grant, Robert M., and David Tracy. *A Short History of the Interpretation of the Bible*. Philadelphia: Augsburg Fortress, 1984.

Happel, Stephen, and David Tracy. *A Catholic Vision*. Philadelphia: Fortress Press, 1984.

Tracy, David. *Plurality and Ambiguity: Hermeneutics, Religion, Hope*. San Francisco: Harper & Row, 1987.[6]

———. *Dialogue with the Other: The Inter-Religious Dialogue*. Grand Rapids, MI: Eerdmans, 1990.

———. *On Naming the Present: Reflections on God, Hermeneutics, and Church*. Maryknoll, NY : London: Orbis Books, 1994.

Edited Volumes

Tracy, David, ed. *Celebrating the Medieval Heritage: A Colloquy on the Thought of Aquinas and Bonaventure*. Chicago: University of Chicago Press, 1978.

Tracy, David, Hans Küng, and Johannes Baptist Metz, eds. *Toward Vatican III: The Work That Needs to Be Done*. New York: Seabury Press, 1978.

Gerrish, Brian A., David Tracy, and Anthony C. Yu, eds. "Norman Perrin, 1920–1976." *Journal of Religion* 64, no. 4 (October 1984): 407–512, 548–58.

Küng, Hans, and David Tracy, eds. *Paradigm Change in Theology: A Symposium for the Future*. Translated by Margaret Köhl. New York: Crossroad, 1989.[7]

Reynolds, Frank, and David Tracy, eds. *Myth and Philosophy*. Albany: SUNY Press, 1990.

———. *Discourse and Practice*. Albany: SUNY Press, 1992.

———. *Religion and Practical Reason: New Essays in the Comparative Philosophy of Religions*. Albany: SUNY Press, 1994.

[5] The first three chapters in this book are by Tracy; the latter three chapters are by Cobb.

[6] This text was reprinted by University of Chicago Press in 1994.

[7] This was originally published as two separate German volumes: Hans Küng and David Tracy, eds., *Theologie, wohin? Auf dem Weg zu einem neuen Paradigma* (Zürich: Benziger, 1984) and Hans Küng and David Tracy, eds., *Das neue Paradigma von Theologie: Strukturen und Dimensionen* (Zürich: Benziger, 1986).

Concilium Issues Edited by Tracy

Eliade, Mircea, and David Tracy, eds. *What Is Religion? An Inquiry for Christian Theology*. *Concilium* 136. New York: Seabury Press, 1980.

Kepnes, Steven, and David Tracy, eds. *The Challenge of Psychology to Faith*. *Concilium* 156. New York: Seabury Press, 1982.

Tracy, David, and Nicholas Lash, eds. *Cosmology and Theology*. *Concilium* 166. New York: Seabury Press, 1983.

Schüssler Fiorenza, Elisabeth, and David Tracy, eds. *The Holocaust as Interruption*. *Concilium* 175. Edinburgh: T&T Clark, 1984.

Tracy, David, and Hermann Häring, eds. *The Fascination of Evil*. *Concilium* 1998/1. Maryknoll, NY: Orbis, 1998.

Interviews with, Profiles of, and Tributes to David Tracy

Woodward, Kenneth L. "David Tracy, Theologian." *Newsweek* (August 24, 1981): 73.

Cully, Kendig B. "Interview with David W. Tracy." *Review of Books and Religion* 10, no. 4 (January 1982): 6.

Lamb, Matthew L. "David Tracy." In *A Handbook of Christian Theologians*, edited by Dean G. Peerman and Martin E. Marty, 677–90. Nashville: Abingdon Press, 1984.

Kennedy, Eugene. "A Dissenting Voice: Catholic Theologian David Tracy." *New York Times Magazine* 136 (November 9, 1986): 20–28.

Breyfogle, Todd, and Thomas Levergood. "Conversation with David Tracy." *Cross Currents* 44, no. 3 (Fall 1994): 293–315.

Burrows, William R. "Reasons to Hope for Reform: An Interview with David Tracy." *America* 173, no. 11 (October 14, 1995): 12–18.

McCarthy, John P. "David Tracy." In *A New Handbook of Christian Theologians*, edited by Donald W. Musser and Joseph L. Price, 468–78. Nashville: Abingdon Press, 1996.

Holland, Scott. "This Side of God: A Conversation with David Tracy." *Cross Currents* 52, no. 1 (Spring 2002): 54–59.

Malcolm, Lois. "The Impossible God: An Interview with David Tracy." *Christian Century* 119, no. 4 (February 13, 2002): 24–30.

Shepard, Christian. "An Interview with David Tracy." *Philosophy and Social Criticism* 30, no. 7 (2004): 867–80.

Doniger, Wendy, Franklin I. Gamwell, and Bernard McGinn. "Tributes to David Tracy." *Criterion* 46, no. 1 (Winter 2008): 2–9.

Gibson, David. "God-Obsessed: David Tracy's Theological Quest." *Commonweal* 137, no. 2 (January 29, 2010): 10–17.

Articles, Essays, and Book Chapters

1968

Tracy, David. "Horizon Analysis and Eschatology." *Continuum* 6 (Summer 1968): 166–79.

———. "New Catechism: Catholic Faith for Adults." *Theology Today* 25, no. 3 (October 1968): 402–3.

———. "The Holy Spirit as Philosophical Problem." *Commonweal* 89 (November 8, 1968): 205–13.

1969

Tracy, David. "Lonergan's Interpretation of St. Thomas Aquinas: The Intellectualist Nature of Speculative Theology. *Excerpta Ex Dissertatione . . .*" Rome: Pontificia Universitas Gregoriana, Facultas Theologica, 1969.

———. "Prolegomena to a Foundational Theology." *Criterion* 9 (Autumn 1969): 12–14.

———. "Review: Jesus, God and Man, and Revelation as History by Wolfhart Pannenberg." *Catholic Biblical Quarterly* 31, no. 2 (April 1969): 285–88.

1970

Tracy, David. "Method as Foundation for Theology: Bernard Lonergan's Option." *The Journal of Religion* 50, no. 3 (July 1970): 292–318.

———. "Why Orthodoxy in a Personalist Age." *Proceedings of the Catholic Theological Society of America* 25 (1970): 78–110.

1971

Tracy, David. "Hans Küng: Loving Critic of His Church." *Christian Century* 88, no. 20 (May 19, 1971): 631–33.

———. "Lonergan's Foundational Theology: An Interpretation and a Critique." In *Foundations of Theology: Papers from the International Lonergan Conference, 1970*, edited by Philip McShane, 197–222. Dublin: Gill & MacMillan, 1971.

————. "Reviews of *Spirit, Faith, and Church* by Wolfhart Pannenberg, Avery Dulles, and Carl E. Braaten, *Basic Questions in Theology, v 1.* by Wolfhart Pannenberg, and *What Is Man: Contemporary Anthropology in Theological Perspective*, by Wolfhart Pannenberg." *Journal of the American Academy of Religion* 39, no. 4 (December 1971): 543–48.

1972

Tracy, David. "Foundational Theology as Contemporary Possibility." *The Dunwoodie Review* 12 (1972): 3–20.

————. "God's Reality: The Most Important Issue." *National Catholic Reporter* 8 (June 23, 1972): 10–11.[8]

————. "Catholic Presence in the Divinity School." *Criterion* 11 (Winter 1972): 29–31.

————. "The Dialectical Nature of Religion (Review of Louis Dupré, *The Other Dimension: A Search for the Meaning of Religious Attitudes*)." *The Christian Century* 89, no. 44 (December 6, 1972): 1252–53.

1973

Tracy, David. "The Religious Dimension of Science." In *The Persistence of Religion*, edited by Andrew M. Greeley and Gregory Baum. *Concilium* 81:128–35. New York: Herder and Herder, 1973.

1974

Tracy, David. "Bernard Lonergan as Interpreter of St. Thomas Aquinas." *Listening* 9 (Winter/Spring 1974): 173–77.

————. "Religious Language as Limit Language." *Theology Digest* 22 (Winter 1974): 291–307.

————. "St. Thomas and the Religious Dimension of Experience: The Doctrine of Sin." *Proceedings of the American Catholic Philosophical Association* 48 (1974): 166–76.

————. "Task of Fundamental Theology." *The Journal of Religion* 54, no. 1 (January 1974): 13–34.

————. "Two Cheers for Thomas Aquinas." *The Christian Century* 91, no. 9 (March 6, 1974): 260–62.

---

[8] This was republished the following year as David Tracy, "God's Reality: The Most Important Issue," *Anglican Theological Review* 55, no. 2 (April 1973): 218–24.

1975

Tracy, David. "A Response and Commentary on Heidegger and Theology." *Listening* 10 (Winter 1975): 73–77.

———. "Editors' Bookshelf: Contemporary Theology and Philosophy of Religion." *The Journal of Religion* 55, no. 4 (October 1975): 489–92.

———. "Eschatological Perspectives on Aging." *Pastoral Psychology* 24 (Winter 1975): 119–34.

———. "Method in Theology." *Journal of the American Academy of Religion* 43, no. 2 (June 1975): 380–81.

———. "Response to Professor Connelly." *Proceedings of the Catholic Theological Society of America* 29 (1974): 67–75.

———. "Theology as Public Discourse." *The Christian Century* 92, no. 10 (March 19, 1975): 280–84.

———. "Tradition and Innovation: The Medieval Religious Heritage Lectures." *Criterion* 14 (Winter 1975): 20–22.

———. "Whatever Happened to Theology? (Symposium)." *Christianity and Crisis* 35 (May 12, 1975): 119–20.

1976

Tracy, David. "A Theological Brief." *American Academy of Religion, Philosophy of Religion and Theology Proceedings* (1976): 197–200.

———. "An Analogical Vision: Some Reflections on the American Roman Catholic Bicentennial Social Justice Program." *Criterion* 15 (Autumn 1976): 10–16.

———. "Review of *The Great Mysteries: An Essential Catechism*, by Andrew Greeley." *New Review of Books and Religion* 1, no. 1 (September 1976): 6.

1977

Tracy, David. "Ethnic Pluralism and Systematic Theology: Reflections." In *Ethnicity*, edited by Andrew M. Greeley and Gregory Baum. *Concilium* 101:91–99. New York: Seabury Press, 1977.

———. "John Cobb's Theological Method: Interpretation and Reflections." In *John Cobb's Theology in Process*, edited by David Ray Griffin and Thomas J. J. Altizer, 25–38. Philadelphia: Westminster, 1977.

———. "Modes of Theological Argument." *Theology Today* 33, no. 4 (January 1977): 387–95.

———. "A Christocentric Vision of Reality (review of Hans Küng, *On Being a Christian*)." *The Christian Century* 94, no. 7 (March 2, 1977): 202–4.

———. "On Galatians 3:28." *Criterion* 16 (Autumn 1977): 10–12.

———. "Reflections on the Challenge of Marxism." *New Catholic World* 220 (May 1977): 116–17.

———. "Revisionist Practical Theology and the Meaning of Public Discourse." *Pastoral Psychology* 26, no. 2 (Winter 1977): 83–94.

———. "Sin Against God, Man: Moral Choices in Contemporary Society." *National Catholic Reporter* 13 (May 6, 1977): 14.

———. "The Catholic Analogical Imagination." *Proceedings of the Catholic Theological Society of America* 32 (1977): 234–44.

———. "Theological Classics in Contemporary Theology." *Theology Digest* 25 (Winter 1977): 347–55.

———. "We Still Have Some Unresolved Theological Differences: Symposium with Martin Marty, David Burrell, and Avery Dulles." *National Catholic Reporter* 14 (November 4, 1977): 9–10.

1978

Gilkey, Langdon, Schubert Miles Ogden, and David Tracy. "Responses to Peter Berger." *Theological Studies* 39, no. 3 (September 1978): 486–507.

Tracy, David. "A Catholic Answer." In *Why Did God Make Me?*, edited by Hans Küng and Jürgen Moltmann. *Concilium* 108:37–42. New York: Seabury Press, 1978.

———. "Christian Faith and Radical Equality." *Theology Today* 34, no. 4 (January 1978): 370–77.

———. "Introduction." In *Celebrating the Medieval Heritage*, edited by David Tracy, v–ix. Chicago: University of Chicago Press, 1978.

———. "Introductory Address." In *Toward Vatican III: The Work That Needs to Be Done*, edited by David Tracy, Hans Küng, and Johann Baptist Metz, 11–13. New York: Seabury Press, 1978.

———. "Metaphor and Religion: The Test Case of Christian Texts." *Critical Inquiry* 5, no. 1 (1978): 91–106.[9]

---

[9] Translated and republished as David Tracy, "Metapher und Religion am Beispiel Christlicher Texte," in *Erinnern: Um Neues zu Sagen*, ed. Jean Pierre van Noppen (Frankfurt-am-Main: Athenäum, 1988), 218–40.

———. "The Particularity and Universality of Christian Revelation." In *Revelation and Experience*, edited by Edward Schillebeeckx and Bas van Iersel. *Concilium* 113:106–16. New York: Seabury Press, 1978.[10]

———. "Preface." In *Toward Vatican III: The Work That Needs to Be Done*, edited by David Tracy, Hans Küng, and Johann Baptist Metz, ix–xi. New York: Seabury Press, 1978.

———. "The Public Character of Systematic Theology." *Theology Digest* 26 (Winter 1978): 400–411.

———. "Theological Response to 'Kingdom and Community.'" *Zygon* 13, no. 2 (June 1978): 131–35.

1979

Tracy, David. "Metaphor and Religion." In *On Metaphor*, edited by Sheldon Sacks, 89–104. Chicago: University of Chicago Press, 1979.[11]

———. "The Catholic Model of Caritas: Self-Transcendence and Transformation." In *Family in Crisis or in Transition: A Sociological and Theological Perspective*, edited by Andrew M. Greeley. *Concilium* 121:100–110. New York: Seabury Press, 1979.[12]

———. "Theological Pluralism and Analogy." *Thought* 54 (1979): 24–37.

1980

Tracy, David. "A Response to Fr. Metz." In *Theology and Discovery: Essays in Honor of Karl Rahner, SJ*, edited by William J. Kelly, 184–87. Milwaukee: Marquette University Press, 1980.

———. "Books: Critics' Christmas Choices." *Commonweal* 107 (December 5, 1980): 703.

———. "Does God Exist? An Answer for Today." *New Republic* 183, no. 19 (November 8, 1980): 27–30.

———. "Editorial." In *What Is Religion? An Inquiry for Theology*, edited by David Tracy and Mircea Eliade. *Concilium* 136:vii–ix. New York: Seabury Press, 1980.

———. "Grace and the Search for the Human: The Sense of the Uncanny." *Proceedings of the Catholic Theological Society of America* 34 (1980): 64–77.

---

[10] Reprinted as chapter 10 of *On Naming the Present*.
[11] This republishes the article of the same name from 1978.
[12] Reprinted as chapter 9 of *On Naming the Present*.

———. "Narrative and Symbol: Key to New Testament Spiritualities." In *Scripture Today: Handling the Word Rightly*, edited by Durstan R. McDonald, 71–87. Wilton, CT: Morehouse-Barlow, 1980.

———. "Particular Questions within General Consensus." *Journal of Ecumenical Studies* 17, no. 1 (Winter 1980): 33–39.

———. "Reflections on John Dominic Crossan's *Cliffs of Fall: Paradox and Polyvalence in the Parables of Jesus*." In *Society of Biblical Literature 1980 Seminar Papers*, edited by P. J. Achtemeier, 69–74. Chico, CA: Scholars Press, 1980.

1981

Tracy, David. "Author's Response (Review Symposium of David Tracy's *The Analogical Imagination*)." *Horizons* 8, no. 2 (Fall 1981): 329–39.

———. "Defending the Public Character of Theology: How My Mind Has Changed." *The Christian Century* 98, no. 11 (April 1, 1981): 350–56.

———. "Foreword." In *The Tremendum*, by Arthur A. Cohen, vii–xiii. New York: Crossroad, 1981.

———. "Introduction." In *The Challenge of Liberation Theology: A First World Response*, edited by Brian Mahan and L. Dale Richesin, 1–3. Maryknoll, NY: Orbis Books, 1981.

———. "Local Religious Leadership and Social Justice." In *Parish, Priest and People: New Leadership for the Local Church*, by Andrew Greeley, Mary Durkin, John Shea, David Tracy, and William McCready, 187–200. Chicago: Thomas More, 1981.

———. "Systematic Theology of the Local Community." In *Parish, Priest and People: New Leadership for the Local Church*, by Andrew Greeley, Mary Durkin, John Shea, David Tracy, and William McCready, 86–99. Chicago: Thomas More, 1981.

———. "The Question of Pluralism in Contemporary Theology." *The Chicago Theological Seminary Register* 71 (Spring 1981): 29–38.

———. "Theological Models: An Exercise in Dialectics." In *Lonergan Workshop*, edited by Frederick Lawrence, 2:83–109. Chico, CA: Scholars Press, 1981.

———. "Theological Reflection on Local Religious Leadership." In *Parish, Priest and People: New Leadership for the Local Church*, by Andrew Greeley, Mary Durkin, John Shea, David Tracy, and William McCready, 147–58. Chicago: Thomas More, 1981.

————. "Theologies of Praxis." In *Creativity and Method: Essays in Honor of Bernard Lonergan, SJ*, edited by Matthew Lamb, 35–51. Milwaukee: Marquette University Press, 1981.

————. "Theoria and Praxis: A Partial Response." *Theological Education* 17, no. 2 (Spring 1981): 167–74.

1982

Kepnes, Steven, and David Tracy. "Editorial." In *The Challenge of Psychology to Faith*, edited by Steven Kepnes and David Tracy. *Concilium* 156:vii–viii. New York: Seabury Press, 1982.

Tracy, David. "Religious Values after the Holocaust: A Catholic View." In *Jews and Christians After the Holocaust*, edited by Abraham J. Peck, 87–107. Philadelphia: Fortress Press, 1982.[13]

————. "Some Reflections on Christianity in China." *Criterion* 21 (Spring 1982): 19–20.

————. "The Enigma of Pope John Paul II." *The Christian Century* 99, no. 3 (January 27, 1982): 96–101.

————. "The Necessity and Insufficiency of Fundamental Theology." In *Problems and Perspectives of Fundamental Theology*, edited by René Latourelle and Gerald O'Collins, 23–36. New York: Paulist Press, 1982.

————. "Theological Method." In *Christian Theology: An Introduction to Its Traditions and Tasks*, edited by Peter C. Hodgson, 35–60. Philadelphia: Fortress Press, 1982.

1983

Tracy, David. "Editorial." In *Cosmology and Theology*, edited by David Tracy and Nicholas Lash. *Concilium* 166:vii–viii. New York: Seabury Press, 1983.

————. "Editorial Reflections." In *Cosmology and Theology*, edited by David Tracy and Nicholas Lash. *Concilium* 166:87–92. New York: Seabury Press, 1983.[14]

---

[13] Republished as David Tracy, "Religious Values after the Holocaust: A Catholic View," in *A Holocaust Reader: Responses to the Nazi Extermination*, ed. Michael L. Morgan (New York: Oxford University Press, 2001), 223–37.

[14] The section of this that was written by David Tracy was reprinted as chapter 7 of *On Naming the Present*.

―――. "Foreword." In *Edward Schillebeeckx: In Search of the Kingdom of God*, by John S. Bowden, vii–ix. New York: Crossroad, 1983.

―――. "On Thinking with the Classics." *Criterion* 22 (1983): 9–10.

―――. "'Project X': Retrospect and Prospect." In *Twenty Years of Concilium*, edited by Paul Brand, Edward Schillebeeckx, and Anton Weiler, 30–36. New York: Seabury Press, 1983.

―――. "Religion and Human Rights in the Public Realm." *Daedalus* 112 (1983): 237–54.

―――. "Schubert M. Ogden: Doctor of Humane Letters." *Criterion* 22 (Autumn 1983): 3–4.

―――. "The Foundations of Practical Theology." In *Practical Theology: The Emerging Field in Theology, Church and World*, edited by Don S. Browning, 61–82. San Francisco: Harper and Row, 1983.

―――. "The Questions of Pluralism: The Context of the United States." *Mid-Stream: An Ecumenical Journal* 22, no. 3–4 (October 1983): 273–85.

1984

Schüssler Fiorenza, Elisabeth, and David Tracy. "Editorial." In *The Holocaust as Interruption*, edited by Elisabeth Schüssler Fiorenza and David Tracy. *Concilium* 175:xi. Edinburgh: T&T Clark, 1984.

―――. "The Holocaust as Interruption and the Christian Return to History." In *The Holocaust as Interruption*, edited by Elisabeth Schüssler Fiorenza and David Tracy. *Concilium* 175:83–86. Edinburgh: T&T Clark, 1984.[15]

Tracy, David. "A Thoughtful Life (Review of Arthur A. Cohen's *An Admirable Woman*)." *Commonweal* 111 (February 10, 1984): 92–93.

―――. "Creativity in the Interpretation of Religion: The Question of Radical Pluralism." *New Literary History* 15, no. 2 (Winter 1984): 289–309.

―――. "Existential Trust." *Commonweal* 111 (August 10, 1984): 429.

―――. "Hermeneutische Überlegungen im neuen Paradigma." In *Theologie—Wohin? Auf Dem Weg zu einem neuen Paradigma*, edited by Hans Küng and David Tracy, 76–102. Zürich: Benziger, 1984.

―――. "Is a Hermeneutics of Religion Possible?" In *Religious Pluralism*, edited by Leroy S. Rouner, 116–29. Notre Dame, IN: University of Notre Dame Press, 1984.

―――. "Karl Rahner, SJ: All Is Grace." *Commonweal* 111 (April 20, 1984): 230.

---

[15] The section of this that was written by David Tracy was reprinted as chapter 5 of *On Naming the Present*.

———. "Levels of Liberal Consensus." *Commonweal* 111 (August 10, 1984): 426–31.

———. "The Religious Classic and the Classic of Art." In *Art, Creativity, and the Sacred: An Anthology in Religion and Art*, edited by Diane Apostolos-Cappadona, 236–49. New York: Crossroad, 1984.

———. "The Role of Theology in Public Life: Some Reflections." *Word & World: Theology for Christian Ministry* 4, no. 3 (Summer 1984): 230–39.

———. "To Trust or Suspect." *Commonweal* 111 (October 5, 1984): 532–34.

1985

Tracy, David. "Analogy, Metaphor and God-Language: Charles Hartshorne." *Modern Schoolman* 62 (May 1985): 249–64.

———. "Correlation between Theology and Catholic Charities." *Social Thought* 11 (Winter 1985): 24–31.

———. "Lindbeck's New Program for Theology: A Reflection." *The Thomist* 49, no. 3 (July 1985): 460–72.

———. "Notwendigkeit Und Ungenügen Der Fundamentaltheologie." In *Probleme Und Aspekte Der Fundamentaltheologie*, edited by René Latourelle and Gerald O'Collins, 38–56. Innsbruck-Wien: Tyrolia-Verlag, 1985.

———. "Tillich and Contemporary Theology." In *The Thought of Paul Tillich*, edited by James Luther Adams, Wilhelm Pauck, and Roger Lincoln Shinn, 260–77. San Francisco: Harper and Row, 1985.

1986

Tracy, David. "Abschliessende Gedanken zur Konferenz: Einigkeit mitten in Verschiedenheit und Konflikt." In *Das Neue Paradigma von Theologie: Strukturen und Dimensionen*, edited by Hans Küng and David Tracy, 233–42. Zürich: Benziger Verlag, 1986.

———. "Hermeneutics as Discourse Analysis: Sociality, History, Religion." *Archivio Di Filosofia* 54 (1986): 261–84.

———. "Particular Classics, Public Religion, and the American Tradition." In *Religion and American Public Life: Interpretations and Explorations*, edited by Robin Lovin, 115–31. New York: Paulist Press, 1986.

———. "Religious Studies and Its Community of Inquiry." *Criterion* 25 (Autumn 1986): 21–24.

———. "The Dialogue of Jews and Christians: A Necessary Hope." *Chicago Theological Seminary Register* 76, no. 1 (Winter 1986): 20–28.

1987

Tracy, David. "Can Virtue Be Taught? Education, Character and the Soul."
In *Theology and the University*, edited by John V. Apczynski, 131–48.
The Annual Publication of the College Theology Society 33. Lanham,
MD: University Press of America, 1987.[16]

———. "Christianity in the Wider Context: Demands and Transformations."
In *Worldviews and Warrants: Plurality and Authority in Theology*, edited
by William Schweiker and Per M. Anderson, 1–15. Lanham, MD: University Press of America, 1987.[17]

———. "Comparative Theology." In *The Encyclopedia of Religion*, edited by
Mircea Eliade, 14:446–55. New York: MacMillan, 1987.

———. "Exodus: Theological Reflection." In *Exodus: A Lasting Paradigm*,
edited by Bas van Iersel and Anton Weiler. *Concilium* 189:118–24. Edinburgh: T&T Clark, 1987.[18]

———. "On Hope as a Theological Virtue in American Catholic Theology."
In *The Church in Anguish: Has the Vatican Betrayed Vatican II?*, edited by
Hans Küng and Leonard Swidler, 268–72. San Francisco: Harper and
Row, 1987.

———. "Practical Theology in the Situation of Global Pluralism." In *Formation and Reflection: The Promise of Practical Theology*, edited by Lewis S.
Mudge and James N. Poling, 139–54. Philadelphia: Fortress Press, 1987.

———. "The Christian Understanding of Salvation-Liberation." *Buddhist-Christian Studies* 7 (1987): 129–38.[19]

1988

Tracy, David. "Für eine Kirche des Dialogs: John Courtney Murrays Kampf
um die Kultur des theologischen Konflikts." In *Gegenentwürfe: 24
Lebensläufe für eine andere Theologie*, edited by Hermann Häring and
Karl-Josef Kuschel, 311–23. München: Piper, 1988.

———. "Models of God: Three Observations (Reply to Sallie McFague)."
Religion and Intellectual Life 5, no. 3 (Spring 1988): 24–28.

---

[16] Republished as David Tracy, "Can Virtue Be Taught? Education, Character and
the Soul," *Theological Education* 24, Supplement 1 (1988): 33–52.

[17] Republished as David Tracy, "Christianity in the Wider Context: Demands and
Transformations," *Religion and Intellectual Life* 4 (Summer 1987): 7–20.

[18] Reprinted as chapter 6 of *On Naming the Present*.

[19] Reprinted as David Tracy, "The Christian Understanding of Salvation-Liberation,"
Face to Face: An Interreligious Bulletin 19 (1988): 35–40.

———. "Mystics, Prophets, Rhetorics: Religion and Psychoanalysis." In *The Trial(s) of Psychoanalysis*, edited by Francoise Meltzer, 259–72. Chicago: University of Chicago Press, 1988.

———. "Review Symposium on *Plurality and Ambiguity*: Author's Response." *Theology Today* 44, no. 4 (January 1988): 513–19.

———. "The Problem of Comparative Religion." In *Metaphysik Nach Kant?*, edited by Dieter Henrich and Rolf-Peter Horstmann. Stuttgart: Klett-Cotta, 1988.

———. "The Question of Criteria for Inter-Religious Dialogue: A Tribute to Langdon Gilkey." In *The Whirlwind in Culture*, edited by Donald W. Musser and Joseph L. Price, 246–62. Bloomington, IN: Meyer-Stone, 1988.

———. "Theology and the Hermeneutical Turn." *Proceedings of the American Catholic Philosophical Association* 62 (1988): 46–57.

———. "Theology and the Symbolic Imagination: A Tribute to Andrew Greeley." In *The Incarnate Imagination: Essays in Honor of Andrew Greeley*, edited by Ingrid H. Shafer, 235–47. Bowling Green, OH: Bowling Green State University Popular Press, 1988.

1989

Tracy, David. "Afterword: Theology, Public Discourse, and the American Tradition." In *Religion and Twentieth-Century American Intellectual Life*, edited by Michael Lacey, 193–203. Cambridge: Cambridge University Press, 1989.

———. "Argument, Dialogue and the Soul in Plato." In *Witness and Existence: Essays in Honor of Schubert M. Ogden*, edited by Philip E. Devenish and George L. Goodwin, 91–105. Chicago: University of Chicago Press, 1989.

———. "Freedom, the Self, and the Other." In *On Freedom*, edited by Leroy S. Rouner, 46–58. Notre Dame, IN: University of Notre Dame Press, 1989.

———. "Interpretation (Hermeneutics)." *International Encyclopedia of Communication*, edited by Erik Barnouw, 343–49. New York: Oxford University Press, 1989.

———. "Recent Catholic Spirituality: Unity and Diversity." In *Christian Spirituality: Post-Reformation and Modern*, edited by Louis Dupré and Donald E. Saliers, 143–73. World Spirituality 18. New York: Crossroad, 1989.

———. "The Uneasy Alliance Reconceived: Catholic Theological Method, Modernity, and Postmodernity." *Theological Studies* 50, no. 3 (September 1989): 548–70.[20]

———. "World Church or World Catechism: The Problem of Eurocentrism." In *World Catechism or Inculturation?*, edited by Johann Baptist Metz and Edward Schillebeeckx. *Concilium* 204:28–37. Edinburgh: T&T Clark, 1989.

1990

Tracy, David. "Charity, Obscurity, Clarity: Augustine's Search for True Rhetoric." In *Morphologies of Faith: Essays in Religion and Culture in Honor of Nathan A. Scott, Jr.*, edited by Mary Gerhart and Anthony C. Yu, 123–43. Atlanta: Scholars Press, 1990.[21]

———. "Contemporary Trends in Catholic Thought." *Sacred Heart University Review* 10, no. 2 (1990): 34–48.

———. "Foreword." In *The Divine Good: Modern Moral Theory and the Necessity of God*, by Franklin I. Gamwell, ix–x. San Francisco: HarperCollins, 1990.

———. "Freedom, Responsibility, Authority." In *Empowering Authority: The Charisms of Episcopacy and Primacy in the Church Today*, edited by Gary Chamberlain and Patrick Howell, 34–47. Kansas City, MO: Sheed & Ward, 1990.

———. "God, Dialogue, and Solidarity: A Theologian's Refrain." *Christian Century* 107, no. 28 (October 10, 1990): 900–904.

———. "Kenosis, Sunyata, and Trinity: A Dialogue with Masao Abe." In *Emptying God: A Buddhist-Jewish-Christian Conversation*, edited by John Cobb and Christopher Ives, 135–54. Maryknoll, NY: Orbis Books, 1990.

---

[20] Republished as David Tracy, "The Uneasy Alliance Reconceived: Catholic Theological Method, Modernity and Postmodernity," in *Theology after Liberalism: A Reader*, ed. John Webster and George P. Schner (Malden, MA: Blackwell Publishers, 2000), 335–57.

[21] This was republished as David Tracy, "Charity, Obscurity, Clarity: Augustine's Search for Rhetoric and Hermeneutics," in *Rhetoric and Hermeneutics in Our Time: A Reader*, ed. Walter Jost and Michael J. Hyde (New Haven, CT: Yale University Press, 1997), 254–74; and again as David Tracy, "Charity, Obscurity, Clarity: Augustine's Search for a True Rhetoric (1990)," in *The Rhetoric of Saint Augustine of Hippo: De Doctrina Christiana and the Search for a Distinctly Christian Rhetoric*, ed. Richard Enos and Roger Thompson (Waco, TX: Baylor University Press, 2008), 267–88.

————. "On Naming the Present." In *On the Threshold of the Third Millennium*, edited by Philip Hillyer. *Concilium* 1990/1:66–85. Philadelphia: Trinity Press International, 1990.[22]

————. "On Reading the Scriptures Theologically." In *Theology and Dialogue: Essays in Conversation with George Lindbeck*, edited by Bruce D. Marshall, 35–68. Notre Dame, IN: University of Notre Dame Press, 1990.

————. "On the Origins of Philosophy of Religion: The Need for a New Narrative of Its Founding." In *Myth and Philosophy*, edited by Frank E. Reynolds and David Tracy, 11–36. Albany: SUNY Press, 1990.

————. "Response to Robert Sokolowski." In *God and Creation: An Ecumenical Symposium*, edited by David Burrell and Bernard McGinn, 193–96. Notre Dame, IN: University of Notre Dame Press, 1990.

1991

Tracy, David. "A Plurality of Readers and a Possibility of a Shared Vision." In *The Bible and Its Readers*, edited by Wim Beuken, Sean Freyne, and Anton Weiler. *Concilium* 1991/1:115–24. Philadelphia: Trinity, 1991.[23]

————. "Approaching the Christian Understanding of God." In *Systematic Theology: Roman Catholic Perspectives*, edited by Francis Schüssler Fiorenza and John Galvin, 1:133–48. Minneapolis: Fortress Press, 1991.[24]

————. "Foreword." In *God without Being: Hors-Texte*, by Jean-Luc Marion, ix–xv. Translated by Thomas A. Carlson. Chicago: University of Chicago Press, 1995.

————. "Hermeneutical Reflections in the New Paradigm." In *Paradigm Change in Theology*, edited by Hans Küng and David Tracy. New York: Crossroad, 1991.[25]

————. "New Wisdom, New Magic (Review of Ari L. Goldman, *The Search for God at Harvard*)." *New York Times Book Review* 96 (June 2, 1991): 14.

————. "Reply to 'The Influence of Feminist Theory on My Theological Work,' by FS Fiorenza." *Journal of Feminist Studies in Religion* 7, no. 1 (Spring 1991): 122–25.

---

[22] Reprinted as chapter 1 of *On Naming the Present*.

[23] Reprinted as chapter 11 of *On Naming the Present*.

[24] This essay was revised for the 2011, single volume edition of *Systematic Theology*; see the entry below.

[25] This is the English text of David Tracy, "Hermeneutische Überlegungen im neuen Paradigma," in *Theologie—Wohin? Auf Dem Weg zu einem neuen Paradigma*, ed. Hans Küng and David Tracy (Zürich: Benziger, 1984), 76–102.

————. "Some Concluding Reflections on the Conference: Unity amidst Diversity and Conflict?" In *Paradigm Change in Theology*, edited by Hans Küng and David Tracy, 461–71. New York: Crossroad, 1991.[26]

————. "The Hermeneutics of Naming God." *Irish Theological Quarterly* 57, no. 4 (December 1991): 253–64.

1992

Tracy, David. "Beyond Foundationalism and Relativism: Hermeneutics and the New Ecumenism." In *New Europe—A Challenge for Christians*, edited by Norbert Greinacher and Norbert Mette. *Concilium* 1992/2:103–11. London: SCM, 1992.[27]

————. "God Is Love: The Central Christian Metaphor." *Living Pulpit* 1, no. 3 (September 1992): 10–11.

————. "L'hermenetique de La Designation de Dieu, Hommage à Claude Geffré." In *Interpréter: Mélanges Offerts à Claude Geffré*, edited by Jean-Pierre Jossua and Nicolas-Jean Séd, translated by M. Falandry, 49–67. Paris: Cerf, 1992.[28]

————. "The Word and Written Texts in the Hermeneutics of Christian Revelation." *Archivio Di Filosofia* 60 (1992): 265–80.

————. "Theology, Critical Social Theory, and the Public Realm." In *Habermas, Modernity, and Public Theology*, edited by Don Browning and Elisabeth Schüssler Fiorenza, 19–42. New York: Crossroad, 1992.

1993

Tracy, David. "God of History, God of Psychology." In *Reincarnation or Resurrection*, edited by Hermann Häring. *Concilium* 1993/5:101–11. Maryknoll, NY: Orbis Books, 1993.[29]

————. "Some Aspects of the Buddhist-Christian Dialogue." In *The Christian Understanding of God Today*, edited by James M. Byrne, 145–53. Dublin: Columba Press, 1993.

---

[26] This is the English translation of David Tracy, "Abschliessende Gedanken zur Konferenz: Einigkeit mitten in Verschiedenheit und Konflikt," in *Das Neue Paradigma von Theologie: Strukturen und Dimensionen*, ed. Hans Küng and David Tracy (Zürich: Benziger Verlag, 1986), 233–42.

[27] Reprinted as chapter 12 of *On Naming the Present*.

[28] With minor revisions, this is the French translation of David Tracy, "The Hermeneutics of Naming God," *Irish Theological Quarterly* 57, no. 4 (December 1991): 253–64.

[29] Reprinted as chapter 4 of *On Naming the Present*.

————. "Truthfulness in Catholic Theology." In *Hans Küng: New Horizons for Faith and Thought*, edited by Karl-Josef Kuschel and Hermann Häring, 81–92. New York: Continuum, 1993.

1994

Meltzer, Françoise, and David Tracy. "Editor's Introduction." *Critical Inquiry* 20, no. 4 (1994): 569–71.

Tracy, David. "Bernard Lonergan and the Return of Ancient Practice." In *Lonergan Workshop*, edited by Frederick Lawrence, 10:319–31. Missoula, MT: Scholars Press, 1994.

————. "Catholic Classics in American Liberal Culture." In *Catholicism and Liberalism: Contributions to American Public Philosophy*, edited by Bruce Douglass and David Hollenbach, 196–213. Cambridge: Cambridge University Press, 1994.

————. "Christian Witness and the Shoah." In *Holocaust Remembrance: The Shapes of Memory*, edited by Geoffrey H. Hartman, 81–89. Cambridge, MA: Oxford University Press, 1994.

————. "Foreword." In *Nietzsche, God, and the Jews*, by Weaver Santaniello, xi–xii. Albany: SUNY Press, 1994.

————. "Literary Theory and Return of the Forms for Naming and Thinking God in Theology." *Journal of Religion* 74, no. 3 (July 1994): 302–19.

————. "Martin & Malcolm & America: Theology in the Public Realm." *Union Seminary Quarterly Review* 48, no. 1–2 (1994): 27–29.

————. "Revelation, Hermeneutics, Criteria." *Archivio Di Filosofia* 62 (1994): 603–15.

————. "Roman Catholic Identity amid the Ecumenical Dialogues." In *Catholic Identity*, edited by James Provost and Knut Walf. *Concilium* 1994/5:109–17. Maryknoll, NY: Orbis Books, 1994.[30]

————. "The Return of God in Contemporary Theology." In *Why Theology?*, edited by Claude Geffré. *Concilium* 1994/6:37–46. Maryknoll, NY: Orbis Books, 1994.[31]

————. "Theology and the Many Faces of Postmodernity." *Theology Today* 51, no. 1 (April 1994): 104–14.

---

[30] Reprinted as chapter 8 of *On Naming the Present*.
[31] Reprinted as chapter 3 of *On Naming the Present*.

1995

Tracy, David. "Evil, Suffering, Hope: The Search for New Forms of Contemporary Theodicy." *Proceedings of the Catholic Theological Society of America* 50 (1995): 15–36.

———. "Interpretation as Conversation: The Challenge to the Modern University." In *Ideas for the University: Proceedings of Marquette University's Mission Seminar and Conference*, edited by Edwin Block, 127–42. Milwaukee: Marquette University Press, 1995.

———. "Introduction." In *Preaching Biblical Texts: Expositions by Jewish and Christian Scholars*, edited by Fredrick C. Holmgren and Herman E. Schaalman, xvi–xvii. Grand Rapids, MI: Eerdmans, 1995.

———. "Modernity, Antimodernity, and Postmodernity in the American Setting." In *Knowledge and Belief in America*, edited by William M. Shea and Peter A. Huff, 328–34. Washington, DC: Woodrow Wilson Center Press, 1995.

———. "Response to Adriaan Peperzak on Transcendence." In *Ethics as First Philosophy: The Significance of Emmanuel Levinas for Philosophy, Literature and Religion*, edited by Adrian T. Peperzak, 193–98. New York: Routledge, 1995.

———. "Review Essay: Ricoeur's Philosophical Journey: Its Import for Religion." Edited by Richard Kearney. *Philosophy and Social Criticism* 21, no. 5/6 (1995): 201–3.[32]

———. "The Paradox of the Many Faces of God in Monotheism." In *The Many Faces of the Divine*, edited by Hermann Häring and Johann Baptist Metz. *Concilium* 1995/2:30–38. Maryknoll, NY: Orbis Books, 1995.[33]

1996

Tracy, David. "Ascoltare Le Voci Di Liberazione : Omaggio a Rosino Gibellini." In *Cammino E Visione: Universalità E Regionalità Della Teologia Nel 20° Secolo: Scritti in Onore Di Rosino Gibellini*, edited by Dietmar Mieth, 87–95. Brescia: Queriniana, 1996.

---

[32] This special journal issue was subsequently republished (with the same pagination) as Richard Kearney, ed., *Paul Ricoeur: The Hermeneutics of Action* (London: SAGE Publications, 1996).

[33] This essay was actually published as chapter 2 of *On Naming the Present* before the issue of *Concilium* came out.

―――. "Iris Murdoch and the Many Faces of Platonism." In *Iris Murdoch and the Search for Human Goodness*, edited by William Schweiker and Maria Antonaccio, 54–75. Chicago: University of Chicago Press, 1996.

―――. "Tendresse et Violence de Dieu: Le Retour Du Dieu Caché Dans La Théologie Contemporaine." *Lumière & Vie* 226 (1996): 63–74.

―――. "The Hidden God: The Divine Other of Liberation." *Cross Currents* 46, no. 1 (Spring 1996): 5–16.

Tracy, David, Marciano Vidal, Norbert Mette, Julia Ching, and William R. Burrows. "Concilium Round Table: The Impact of Feminist Theologies on Roman Catholic Theology." In *Feminist Theology in Different Contexts*, edited by Elisabeth Schüssler Fiorenza and M. Shawn Copeland. *Concilium* 1996/1:90–97. Maryknoll, NY: Orbis Books, 1996.

1997

Tracy, David. "A Theological View of Philosophy: Revelation and Reason." In *That Others May Know and Love: Essays in Honor of Zachary Hayes, OFM—Franciscan, Educator, Scholar*, edited by Michael F. Cusato, 193–209. St. Bonaventure, NY: Franciscan Institute Publications, 1997.[34]

―――. "Forms and Sacred Space in the Duomo: A Contemporary Reflection." *Vivens Homo* 8, no. 2 (1997): 389–99.

―――. "Fragments and Forms: Universality and Particularity Today." In *The Church in Fragments: Towards What Kind of Unity*, edited by Giuseppe Ruggieri and Miklos Tomka. *Concilium* 1997/3:122–29. London: SCM Press, 1997.

―――. "God as Other: A Contemporary Call to Luther's Great Challenge." *Living Pulpit* 6, no. 1 (March 1997): 6–7.

1998

Tracy, David. "Catholic Theology at Its Best." *Harvard Divinity Bulletin* 27, no. 2–3 (1998): 13–14.

---

[34] This was republished as David Tracy, "A Theological View of Philosophy: Revelation and Reason," in *Question of Christian Philosophy Today*, ed. Francis J. Ambrosio (New York: Fordham University Press, 1999), 142–62. It was republished a second time, with minor changes, as David Tracy, "A Catholic View of Philosophy: Revelation and Reason," in *Mormonism in Dialogue with Contemporary Christian Theologies*, ed. David L. Paulsen and Donald W. Musser (Macon, GA: Mercer University Press, 2007), 449–46.

———. "Fragments of Synthesis: The Hopeful Paradox of Dupré's Modernity." In *Christian Spirituality and the Culture of Modernity: The Thought of Louis Dupré*, edited by Peter J. Casarella and George P. Schner, 9–24. Grand Rapids, MI: Eerdmans, 1998.

———. "Human Cloning and the Public Realm: A Defense of Intuitions of the Good." In *Clones and Clones: Facts and Fantasies about Human Cloning*, edited by Martha C. Nussbaum and Cass R. Sunstein, 190–203. New York: W.W. Norton, 1998.

———. "Is There Hope for the Public Realm? Conversation as Interpretation." *Social Research* 65, no. 3 (Fall 1998): 597–609.

———. "The Gospels as Revelation and Transformation: A Tribute to Sebastian Moore." In *Jesus Crucified and Risen: Essays in Spirituality and Theology in Honor of Dom Sebastian Moore*, edited by William P. Loewe and Vernon J. Gregson, 195–210. Collegeville, MN: Liturgical Press, 1998.

———. "Traditions of Spiritual Practice and the Practice of Theology." *Theology Today* 55, no. 2 (July 1998): 235–41.

———. "Writing." In *Critical Terms for Religious Studies*, edited by Mark C. Taylor, 383–93. Chicago: University of Chicago Press, 1998.

Tracy, David, and Hermann Häring. "Introduction." In *The Fascination of Evil*, edited by David Tracy and Hermann Häring. *Concilium* 1998/1:1–8. Maryknoll, NY: Orbis Books, 1998.

———. "Saving from Evil: Salvation and Evil Today." In *The Fascination of Evil*, edited by David Tracy and Hermann Häring. *Concilium* 1998/1:107–16. Maryknoll, NY: Orbis Books, 1998.

1999

Tracy, David. "African American Thought: The Discovery of Fragments." In *Black Faith and Public Talk: Critical Essays on James H. Cone's* Black Theology and Black Power, edited by Dwight N. Hopkins, 29–38. Maryknoll, NY: Orbis Books, 1999.

———. "Fragments: The Spiritual Situation of Our Times." In *God, the Gift, and Postmodernism*, edited by John D. Caputo and Michael J. Scanlon, 170–84. Bloomington: Indiana University Press, 1999.

———. "Trinitarian Speculation and the Forms of Divine Disclosure." In *The Trinity: An Interdisciplinary Symposium on the Trinity*, edited by Stephen Davis, Daniel Kendall, and Gerald O'Collins, 273–93. New York: Oxford University Press, 1999.

———. "T.S. Eliot as Religious Thinker: *Four Quartets.*" In *Literary Imagination, Ancient and Modern: Essays in Honor of David Green*, edited by Todd Breyfogle, 269–84. Chicago: University of Chicago Press, 1999.

2000

Tracy, David. "God as Trinitarian: A Christian Response to Peter Ochs." In *Christianity in Jewish Terms*, edited by Tikva Frymer-Kensky, David Novak, Peter Ochs, David Fox Sandmel, and Michael A. Signer, 77–84. Boulder, CO: Westview Press, 2000.

———. "Inculturazione Della Fede Negli USA." In *Il Concilio Vaticano II: Recezione E Attualità Alla Luce Del Giubileo*, edited by Rino Fisicella, 593–97. Cinisello Balsamo: San Paolo Edizioni, 2000.

———. "Prophetic Rhetoric and Mystical Rhetoric." In *Rhetorical Invention and Religious Inquiry: New Perspectives*, edited by Walter Jost and Wendy Olmsted, 182–95. New Haven, CT: Yale University Press, 2000.

———. "Public Theology, Hope, and the Mass Media: Can the Muses Still Inspire?" In *God and Globalization: Religion and the Powers of the Common Life*, edited by Max Stackhouse and Peter Paris, 1:231–54. Harrisburg, PA: Trinity Press International, 2000.

———. "The Post-Modern Re-Naming of God as Incomprehensible and Hidden." *Cross Currents* 50, no. 1–2 (Spring/Summer 2000): 240–47.[35]

2001

Tracy, David. "Foreword." In *Confronting the Mystery of God: Political, Liberation, and Public Theologies*, by Gaspar Martinez, vii–ix. New York: Continuum, 2001.

2002

Tracy, David. "Hope in Christianity: An Interpretation." In *Interpretations of Hope in Chinese Religions and Christianity*, edited by Daniel L. Overmyer and Chi-tim Lai, 181–91. Hong Kong: Christian Study Centre on Chinese Religion and Culture, 2002.

---

[35] This essay was translated into Italian and republished as David Tracy, "La Ri-Nominazione Post-Moderna Di Dio Come Incomprensibile E Nascosto," *Studia Patavina* 48 (2001): 7–18.

————. "On Theological Education: A Reflection." In *Theological Literacy for the Twenty-First Century*, edited by Rodney L. Petersen and Nancy M. Rourke, 13–22. Grand Rapids, MI: Eerdmans, 2002.

————. "Theology in the University: A Reflection." In *Relevance of Theology: Nathan Söderblom and the Development of an Academic Discipline*, edited by Carl Reinhold Bråkenhielm and Gunhild Winqvist Hollman, 159–67. Uppsala, Sweden: Uppsala University Press, 2002.

2003

Fishbane, Michael, Kevin Madigan, and David Tracy. "Tributes to Bernard McGinn." *Criterion* 42, no. 3 (Autumn 2003): 36–42.

Marty, Martin E., and David Tracy. "Tributes to Anne Carr." *Criterion* 42, no. 3 (Autumn 2003): 30–35.

Tracy, David. "Afterword: A Reflection on *Mystics—Presence and Aporia*." In *Mystics—Presence and Aporia*, edited by Michael Kessler and Christian Sheppard, 239–43. Chicago: University of Chicago Press, 2003.

————. "Forma E Frammento: Il Recupero Del Dio Nascosto E Incomprensibile." In *Prospettive Teologiche per Il XXI Secolo*, edited by Rosino Gibellini, 251–73. Brescia: Queriniana, 2003.

2004

Tracy, David. "God's Realist (Review of Elizabeth Sifton's *The Serenity Prayer: Faith and Politics in Times of Peace and War*)." *The New Republic* (April 26, 2004): 33–37.

————. "Simone Weil and the Impossible: A Radical View of Religion and Culture." In *Critical Spirit: Theology at the Crossroads of Faith and Culture*, edited by Andrew Pierce and Geraldine Smyth, 208–22. Dublin: Columba Press, 2004.[36]

————. "Statement for the Critical Inquiry Board Symposium." *Critical Inquiry* 30, no. 2 (2004): 440–41.

2005

Tracy, David. "Foreword." In *How Christian Is Our Present-Day Theology?*, by Franz Overbeck, xii–xiv. New York: Bloomsbury T&T Clark, 2005.

---

[36] Republished as David Tracy, "Simone Weil: The Impossible," in *The Christian Platonism of Simone Weil*, ed. Jane E. Doering and Eric O. Springsted (Notre Dame, IN: University of Notre Dame Press, 2004), 229–41.

———. "Form and Fragment: The Recovery of the Hidden and Incomprehensible God." In *The Concept of God in Global Dialogue*, edited by Werner Jeanrond and Aasulv Lande, 98–114. Maryknoll, NY: Orbis Books, 2005.

———. "Forms of Divine Disclosure." In *Believing Scholars: Ten Catholic Intellectuals*, edited by James L. Heft, 47–57. New York: Fordham University Press, 2005.

———. "The Divided Consciousness of Augustine on Eros." In *Erotikon—Essays on Eros, Ancient and Modern*, edited by Shadi Bartsch and Thomas Bartscherer, 91–106. Chicago: University of Chicago Press, 2005.

———. "The Roots of Diversity in Christianity." In *A Longing for Peace: The Challenge of a Multicultural, Multireligious World*, edited by Edmund Chia and James W. Heisig, 21–29. Bilbao: Asociación Haretxa, 2005.

———. "Verbondenheid En Afstand. Een Pleidooi Voor Het Bijeenhouden van Religieuze Polariteiten." In *Ons Rakelings Nabij. Gedaanteveranderingen van God En Geloof. Ter Ere van Edward Schillebeeckx*, edited by Manuela Kalsky, André Lascaris, Leo Oosterveen, and Inez van der Spek, 110–24. Nijmegen: Boekencentrum, 2005.

2006

Tracy, David. "God: The Possible/Impossible (Interview with Christian Sheppard)." In *After God: Richard Kearney and the Religious Turn in Continental Philosophy*, edited by John Panteleimon Manoussakis, 340–54. New York: Fordham University Press, 2006.[37]

2007

Tracy, David. "A Catholic View of Philosophy: Revelation and Reason." In *Mormonism in Dialogue with Contemporary Christian Theologies*, edited by David L. Paulsen and Donald W. Musser, 449–62. Macon, GA: Mercer University Press, 2007.

———. "Jean-Luc Marion: Phenomenology, Hermeneutics, Theology." In *Counter-Experiences: Reading Jean-Luc Marion*, edited by Kevin Hart, 57–65. Notre Dame, IN: University of Notre Dame Press, 2007.

———. "Limit-Situations in the World of the Everyday." In *The Christianity Reader*, edited by Mary Gerhart and Fabian Udoh, 709–12. Chicago: University of Chicago Press, 2007.

---

[37] This reprints the Christian Sheppard interview listed above from 2004.

————. "On Tragic Wisdom." In *Wrestling with God and with Evil: Philosophical Reflections*, edited by Hendrik M. Vroom. *Currents of Encounter* 31:13–24. Amsterdam: Rodopi, 2007.

————. "The Christian Option for the Poor." In *Option for the Poor in Christian Theology*, edited by Daniel G. Groody, 119–31. Notre Dame, IN: University of Notre Dame Press, 2007.

2008

Tracy, David. "Augustine's Christomorphic Theocentrism." In *Orthodox Readings of Augustine*, edited by George E. Demacopoulos and Aristotle Papanikolaou, 263–89. Crestwood, NY: St. Vladimir's Seminary Press, 2008.

————. "Foreword." In *The Quest for Plausible Christian Discourse in a World of Pluralities: The Evolution of David Tracy's Understanding of "Public Theology,"* edited by Younhee Kim, 7–9. Religions and Discourse 35. Oxford: Peter Lang, 2008.

————. "On Longing: The Void, the Open, God." In *Longing in a Culture of Cynicism*, edited by Stephan van Erp and Lea Verstricht, 15–32. Zürich: Lit Verlag, 2008.

2009

Tracy, David. "Foi et Raison: Union, Contemplation, Critique." Translated by Georges Chevallier. *Transversalités* 110 (June 2009): 53–74.

————. "Foreword." In *The Trinity: Life of God, Hope for Humanity; Towards a Theology of Communion*, by Thomas J. Norris, 11–12. Hyde Park, NY: New City Press, 2008.[38]

2010

Tracy, David. "God as Infinite Love: A Roman Catholic Perspective." In *Divine Love: Perspectives from the World's Religious Traditions*, edited by Jeff Levin and Stephen G. Post, 131–62. West Conshohocken, PA: Templeton Press, 2010.

————. "Quão Dialogais São Os Diálogos Inter Religiosos?" *Tempo Brasileiro* 183 (2010): 137–45.

[38] This text erroneously names him as "David C. Tracy," despite his middle name being William.

———. "Review of *Theology for Pilgrims*, by Nicholas Lash." *Modern Theology* 26, no. 2 (April 2010): 287–89.

———. "Western Hermeneutics and Interreligious Dialogue." In *Interreligious Hermeneutics*, edited by Catherine Cornille and Christopher Conway, 1–43. Eugene, OR: Cascade Books, 2010.

2011

Tracy, David. "A Correlational Model of Practical Theology Revisited." In *Religion, Diversity, and Conflict*, edited by Edward Foley, 49–61. International Practical Theology 15. Zürich: Lit Verlag, 2011.

———. "Approaching the Christian Understanding of God." In *Systematic Theology: Roman Catholic Perspectives*, edited by Francis Schüssler Fiorenza and John Galvin, 109–29. Minneapolis, MN: Fortress Press, 2011.

———. "L'etica Cattolica: L'amore Che Trasforma Il Desiderio E La Ragione." In *Amore E Verità. Sintesi Prospettica Di Teologia Fondamentale*, edited by Gianluigi Pasquale and Carmelo Dotolo, 833–73. Vatican City: Lateran University Press, 2011.

———. "On Naming Saints." In *Saints: Faith without Borders*, edited by Françoise Meltzer and Jaś Elsner, 97–126. Chicago: University of Chicago Press, 2011.

———. "The Necessity and Character of Fundamental Theology." Loyola University of Chicago, April 8, 2011. Accessed April 20, 2018. https://media.luc.edu/media/The+Public+Character+of+TheologyA+Prospects+for+the+21st+Century+Part+1/1_4rtapi8y/21880401 (Part 1) and https://media.luc.edu/media/The+Public+Character+of+Theology A+Prospects+for+the+21st+Century+Part+2/1_6fldnvrr (Part 2).

2012

Tracy, David. "Incarnation and Suffering: On Rereading Augustine." In *Godhead Here in Hiding: Incarnation and the History of Human Suffering*, edited by Terrence Merrigan and Frederik Glorieux, 75–92. Bibliotheca Ephemeridum Theologicarum Lovaniensium 234. Leuven: Peeters, 2012.

———. "Trinitarian Theology and Spirituality: Retrieving William of St. Thierry for Contemporary Theology." In *Rethinking Trinitarian Theology: Disputed Questions and Contemporary Issues in Trinitarian Theology*, edited by Giulio Maspero and Robert J. Wozniak, 387–420. London: T&T Clark, 2012.

2013

Tracy, David. "Religion Im Öffentlichen Bereich: Öffentliche Theologie." In *Dialog: Systematische Theologie Und Religionssoziologie*, edited by Franz Gruber and Ansgar Kreutzer, translated by Andreas S. Telser, 189–207. Quaestiones Disputatae 258. Freiburg: Herder-Verlag, 2013.

2014

Tracy, David. "A Hermeneutics of Orthodoxy." In *Christian Orthodoxy*, edited by Felix Wilfred and Daniel Franklin Pilario. *Concilium* 2014/2:71–81. London: SCM Press, 2014.

———. "Horrors and Horror: The Response of Tragedy." *Social Research* 81, no. 4 (Winter 2014): 739–67.

———. "Religion in the Public Realm: Three Forms of Publicness." In *At the Limits of the Secular: Reflections on Faith and Public Life*, edited by William A. Barbieri Jr., 29–50. Grand Rapids, MI: Eerdmans, 2014.

———. "Simone Weil: Le Masque et La Personne." In *Simone Weil*, edited by Emmanuel Gabellieri and François L'Yvonnet, 301–6. Paris: Les Cahiers de l'Herne, 2014.

———. "Three Kinds of Publicness in Public Theology." *International Journal of Public Theology* 8, no. 3 (2014): 330–34.

2015

Tracy, David. "Die Theologie Und Die Dialogische Wende Im Zeitgenössischen Denken. Theologie Als Potentiell Unendliche Hermeneutik Eines Aktual Unendlichen Gottes." In *Verstehen Und Verdacht: Hermeneutische Und Kritische Theologie Im Gespräch*, edited by Franz Gruber, Ansgar Kreutzer, and Andreas S. Telser, 41–69. Ostfildern: Matthias Grünewald Verlag, 2015.

———. "Martin Luther's Deus Theologicus." In *Luther Refracted: The Reformer's Ecumenical Legacy*, edited by Petyr Malysz and Derek Nelson, 105–39. Minneapolis: Fortress Press, 2015.

———. "Paul Ricoeur: Hermeneutic and the Dialectics of Forms." In *Hermeneutics and the Philosophy of Religion: The Legacy of Paul Ricoeur*, edited by Ingolf U. Dalferth and Marlene A Block, 11–34. Tübingen: Mohr Siebeck, 2015.

———. "Remembering Robert Grant." *Criterion* 51, no. 1 (Spring 2015): 4.

———. "The Other of Dialectic and Dialogue." In *Dynamics of Difference: Christianity and Alterity: A Festschrift for Werner G. Jeanrond*, edited by Ulrich Schmiedel and James M. Matarazzo Jr., 105–13. New York: T&T Clark, 2015.

———. "Troisième Leçon—D'une Métaphysique de L'infini À Une Théologie Trinitaire Infinie." In *Métaphysique et Christianisme*, 69–95. Paris: Presses universitaires de France, 2015.

2016

Tracy, David. "Foreword." In *Exercises in Religious Understanding*, by David Burrell. Eugene, OR: Wipf and Stock, 2016.

———. "Foreword." In *Theologie als öffentlicher Diskurs: Zur Relevanz der Systematischen Theologie David Tracys*, by Andreas Tesler, 13–14. Innsbruck: Tyrolia, 2016.

———. "Foreword." In *Transfiguring Luther: The Planetary Promise of Luther's Theology*, by Vitor Westhelle, ix–x. Eugene, OR: Cascade Books, 2016.

———. "On Suffering: The Event of Many Forms." In *Suffering and God*, edited by Luiz Carlos Susin, Solange Lefebvre, Daniel Franklin Pilario, and Diego Irarrazaval. *Concilium* 2016/3:24–31. London: SCM Press, 2016.

———. "The Ultimate Invisible: The Infinite." *Social Research* 83, no. 4 (Winter 2016): 879–904.

2017

Tracy, David. "Foreword." In *The Rigor of Things: Conversations with Dan Arbib*, by Jean-Luc Marion and Dan Arbib, translated by Christina M. Gschwandtner, ix–x. New York: Fordham University Press, 2017.

Tracy, David, Paul R Mendes-Flohr, Wendy Doniger, and Richard B Miller. "Honoring Dean Margaret M. Mitchell." *Criterion* 52, no. 1 (2017): 20–25.

2018

Tracy, David. "Augustine Our Contemporary: Two Ways, Two Selfs in Augustine." In *Augustine Our Contemporary: Examining the Self in Past and Present*, edited by Susan Schreiner and Willemien Otten, 27–74. Notre Dame, IN: University of Notre Dame Press, 2018.

———. "Foreword." In *A Theology of Conversation: An Introduction to David Tracy*, by Stephen Okey, ix–xi. Collegeville, MN: Liturgical Press, 2018.

————. "God as Infinite: Ethical Implications." In *God and the Moral Life*, edited by Myriam Renaud and Joshua Daniel, 135–56. New York: Routledge, 2018.

————. "Heavenly Bodies, from Michelangelo to Dolce & Gabbana." *America* 281, no. 11 (May 14, 2018): 45–48.

Appendix B

Bibliography of Non-Tracy Works

"About Concilium." *Concilium*. Accessed April 21, 2018. http://www.concilium .in/about.

Allen, Charles W. "Between Revisionists and Postliberals: A Review Article." *Encounter* 51, no. 4 (Autumn 1990): 389–401.

Anselm. *Anselm of Canterbury: The Major Works*. Edited by Brian Davies and G. R. Evans. New York: Oxford University Press, 2008.

Benjamin, Walter. "The Work of Art in the Age of Mechanical Reproduction." In *Illuminations: Essays and Reflections*. Translated by Harry Zohn. New York: Schocken Books, 1986.

Bernstein, Richard J. "Radical Plurality, Fearful Ambiguity, and Engaged Hope." *The Journal of Religion* 69, no. 1 (January 1989): 85–91.

Blundell, Boyd. *Paul Ricoeur Between Theology and Philosophy: Detour and Return*. Bloomington: Indiana University Press, 2010.

Boeve, Lieven. *God Interrupts History: Theology in a Time of Upheaval*. New York: Continuum, 2007.

Breyfogle, Todd, and Thomas Levergood. "Conversation with David Tracy." *Cross Currents* 44, no. 3 (Fall 1994): 293–315.

Buckley, William F., Jr. *Nearer, My God: An Autobiography of Faith*. New York: Doubleday, 1997.

Bultmann, Rudolf. "New Testament and Mythology: The Problem of Demythologizing New Testament Proclamation." In *New Testament & Mythology and Other Basic Writings*, edited by Schubert Ogden, 1–43. Philadelphia: Fortress Press, 1984.

Casanova, José. *Public Religions in the Modern World*. Chicago: University of Chicago Press, 1994.

Clairmont, David A. *Moral Struggle and Religious Ethics: On the Person as Classic in Comparative Theological Contexts*. Malden, MA: Wiley-Blackwell, 2011.

———. "Persons as Religious Classics: Comparative Ethics and the Theology of Bridge Concepts." *Journal of the American Academy of Religion* 78, no. 3 (September 2010): 687–720. https://doi.org/10.1093/jaarel/lfq052.

Collura, Nicholas. "Some Reflections on the Eucharist as Fragment." *Worship* 88, no. 2 (March 2014): 151–70.

Comstock, Gary L. "Two Types of Narrative Theology." *Journal of the American Academy of Religion* 55, no. 4 (Winter 1987): 687–717.

Cone, James H. *God of the Oppressed*. Maryknoll, NY: Orbis Books, 1997.

Crawford, Nathan. "Theology as Improvisation: Seeking the Unstructured Form of Theology with David Tracy." *Irish Theological Quarterly* 75, no. 3 (August 2010): 300–312.

Cumming, Ryan P. "Contrasts and Fragments: An Exploration of James Cone's Theological Methodology." *Anglican Theological Review* 91, no. 3 (Summer 2009): 395–416.

Doniger, Wendy, Franklin I. Gamwell, and Bernard McGinn. "Tributes to David Tracy." *Criterion* 46, no. 1 (Winter 2008): 2–9.

Dulles, Avery. *Models of the Church*. New York: Image, 1991.

Elizondo, Virgilio P. *Galilean Journey: The Mexican-American Promise*. Translated by Eva Fleischner. Rev. and exp. ed. Maryknoll, NY: Orbis Books, 2005.

Eveleth, Rose. "The *Star Wars* George Lucas Doesn't Want You To See." *The Atlantic*, August 27, 2014. Accessed February 20, 2017. https://www.theatlantic.com/technology/archive/2014/08/the-star-wars-george-lucas-doesnt-want-you-to-see/379184/.

Forsyth, Andrew C. "The Implications for Christology of David Tracy's Theological Epistemology." *Scottish Journal of Theology* 63, no. 3 (2010): 302–17.

Gadamer, Hans-Georg. *Truth and Method*. 2nd rev. ed. Bloomsbury Academic, 2004.

Geertz, Clifford. "Religion as a Cultural System." In *The Interpretation of Cultures*, 87–125. New York: Basic Books, 1973.

———. *The Interpretation Of Cultures*. New York: Basic Books, 2000.

Geffré, Claude, and Gustavo Gutierrez. *The Mystical and Political Dimension of the Christian Faith. Concilium* 96. New York: Herder and Herder, 1974.

Gener, Timoteo D. "The Catholic Imagination and Popular Religion in Lowland Philippines: Missiological Significance of David Tracy's Theory of Religious Imaginations." *Mission Studies* 22, no. 1 (2005): 25–57.

———. "With/Beyond Tracy: Re-Visioning Public Theology." *Evangelical Review of Theology* 33, no. 2 (April 2009): 118–38.

Gibson, David. "God-Obsessed: David Tracy's Theological Quest." *Commonweal* 137, no. 2 (January 29, 2010): 10–17.

Gillis, Chester. *A Question of Final Belief: John Hick's Pluralistic Theory of Salvation*. New York: St. Martin's Press, 1989.

Gutierrez, Gustavo. *A Theology of Liberation: History, Politics, and Salvation*. Translated by Caridad Inda and John Eagleson. Rev. ed. Maryknoll, NY: Orbis Books, 1988.

Habermas, Jürgen. "Transcendence from within, Transcendence within This World." In *Habermas, Modernity, and Public Theology*, edited by Don Browning and Francis Schüssler Fiorenza. New York: Crossroad, 1992.

Hauerwas, Stanley. *Against the Nations: War and Survival in a Liberal Society*. Minneapolis: Winston Press, 1985.

Hawks, James. "Juan Luis Segundo's Critique of David Tracy." *Heythrop Journal* 31 (July 1990): 277–94.

Heyer, Kristin E. "How Does Theology Go Public? Rethinking the Debate between David Tracy and George Lindbeck." *Political Theology* 5, no. 3 (July 2004): 307–27.

Hick, John. *An Interpretation of Religion: Human Responses to the Transcendent*. New Haven, CT: Yale University Press, 1989.

Holland, Scott. "How Do Stories Save Us? Two Contemporary Theological Responses." *The Conrad Grebel Review* 12, no. 2 (Spring 1994): 131–53.

Hopkins, Dwight N. *Being Human: Race, Culture, and Religion*. Princeton, NJ: Fortress Press, 2005.

Hoyt, Robert G., ed. *The Birth Control Debate*. Kansas City, MO: National Catholic Reporter, 1968.

Jaspers, Karl. *Philosophy*. Vol. 2. Translated by E. B. Ashton. Chicago: University of Chicago Press, 1970.

Jones, Tamsin. *A Genealogy of Marion's Philosophy of Religion: Apparent Darkness*. Bloomington: Indiana University Press, 2011.

Keifert, Patrick R. "Labor Room or Morgue: The Power and Limits of Pluralism and Christology." *Word & World* 5, no. 1 (Winter 1985): 78–88.

Kelly, Anthony J. "Refreshing Experience: The Christ-Event as Fact, Classic, and Phenomenon." *Irish Theological Quarterly* 77, no. 4 (2012): 335–48.

Kennedy, Eugene C. "A Dissenting Voice: Catholic Theologian David Tracy." *New York Times Magazine* 136 (November 9, 1986): 20–28.

Kierkegaard, Søren. *The Concept of Anxiety: A Simple Psychologically Orienting Deliberation on the Dogmatic Issue of Hereditary Sin.* Edited and translated by Reidar Thomte. Princeton, NJ: Princeton University Press, 1980.

Lamb, Matthew L. "David Tracy." In *A Handbook of Christian Theologians*, 677–90. Nashville: Abingdon Press, 1984.

L'Engle, Madeleine. *And It Was Good: Reflections on Beginnings.* New York: Convergent Books, 2017.

Lints, Richard. "The Postpositivist Choice: Tracy or Lindbeck?" *Journal of the American Academy of Religion* 61, no. 4 (Winter 1993): 655–77.

Lonergan, Bernard. *Method in Theology.* 2nd ed. Toronto: University of Toronto Press, 1990.

Loughlin, Gerard. "Review of *Plurality and Ambiguity: Hermeneutics, Religion, Hope.*" *Modern Theology* 7, no. 5 (October 1991): 483–87.

Malcolm, Lois. "The Impossible God: An Interview with David Tracy." *Christian Century* 119, no. 4 (February 13, 2002): 24–30.

Marion, Jean-Luc. *Being Given: Toward a Phenomenology of Givenness.* Translated by Jeffrey L. Kosky. Stanford, CA: Stanford University Press, 2002.

———. *God without Being: Hors-Texte.* Translated by Thomas A. Carlson. Chicago: University Of Chicago Press, 1995.

———. *In Excess: Studies of Saturated Phenomena.* Translated by Robyn Horner and Vincent Berraud. New York: Fordham University Press, 2004.

Martinez, Gaspar. *Confronting the Mystery of God: Political, Liberation, and Public Theologies.* New York: Continuum, 2001.

McCarthy, John P. "David Tracy." In *A New Handbook of Christian Theologians*, edited by Donald W. Musser and Joseph L. Price, 468–78. Nashville: Abingdon Press, 1996.

Miller, Mark T. *The Quest for God and the Good Life: Lonergan's Theological Anthropology.* Washington, DC: The Catholic University of America Press, 2013.

Miller, Vincent J. *Consuming Religion: Christian Faith and Practice in a Consumer Culture.* New York: Continuum, 2003.

Myatt, William. "Public Theology and 'the Fragment': Duncan Forrester, David Tracy, and Walter Benjamin." *International Journal of Public Theology* 8, no. 1 (2014): 85–106. https://doi.org/10.1163/15697320 -12341331.

Niebuhr, H. Richard. *Christ and Culture.* New York: Harper Collins, 2001.

"Obituary of John C. Tracy." *The Herald Statesman*. January 18, 1952.

Ogden, Schubert. *The Point of Christology*. San Francisco: Harper & Row, 1982.

Pope Francis. *Laudato Sì*. Vatican Website, May 24, 2015. http://w2.vatican
.va/content/francesco/en/encyclicals/documents/papa-francesco
_20150524_enciclica-laudato-si.html.

Rahner, Karl. *Foundations of Christian Faith: An Introduction to the Idea of Christianity*. Translated by William V. Dych. Rev. ed. New York: Crossroad, 1982.

————. "Membership of the Church According to the Teaching of Pius XII's Encyclical 'Mystici Corporis Christi.'" In *Theological Investigations*, 2:191–257. Baltimore: Helicon Press, 1963.

————. "Reflections on Methodology in Theology." In *Theological Investigations*, 11:68–114. New York: Seabury Press, 1974.

————. "The Church and the Sacraments." In *Inquiries*, 191–257. New York: Herder and Herder, 1964.

Ricoeur, Paul. *Interpretation Theory: Discourse and the Surplus of Meaning*. Fort Worth: Texas Christian University Press, 1976.

————. "The Hermeneutic Function of Distanciation." In *Hermeneutics and the Human Sciences*, 131–44. New York: Cambridge University Press, 1981.

Sanks, T. Howland. "David Tracy's Theological Project: An Overview and Some Implications." *Theological Studies* 54, no. 4 (December 1993): 698–727.

Schillebeeckx, Edward. *Christ: The Experience of Jesus as Lord*. New York: Crossroad, 1980.

————. *Christ the Sacrament of the Encounter with God*. New York: Sheed & Ward, 1963.

————. *Jesus: An Experiment in Christology*. New York: Vintage Books, 1981.

Shea, William M., David B. Burrell, Bernard J. Cooke, and William J. O'Brien. "Review Symposium." *Horizons* 8, no. 2 (Fall 1981): 313–39.

Shelley, Thomas J. *Dunwoodie: The History of St. Joseph's Seminary, Yonkers, New York*. Westminster, MD: Christian Classics, 1993.

Sobrino, Jon. *Christology at the Crossroads: A Latin American Approach*. Maryknoll, NY: Orbis Books, 1978.

Stell, Stephen L. "Hermeneutics in Theology and the Theology of Hermeneutics: Beyond Lindbeck and Tracy." *Journal of the American Academy of Religion* 61, no. 4 (Winter 1993): 679–702.

Taylor, Charles. *A Secular Age*. Cambridge, MA: Belknap Press of Harvard University Press, 2007.

Telser, Andreas S. *Theologie als öffentlicher Diskurs: Zur Relevanz der Systematischen Theologie David Tracys*. Innsbruck: Tyrolia, 2016.

Thomas, Owen C. "Public Theology and Counter-Public Spheres." *Harvard Theological Review* 85, no. 4 (October 1992): 453–66.

Tillich, Paul. *Systematic Theology*. Vol. 1. Chicago: University of Chicago Press, 1951.

Toulmin, Stephen E. *Human Understanding*. Vol. 1: *The Collective Use and Evolution of Concepts*. Princeton, NJ: Princeton University Press, 1972.

Vissers, John A. "Interpreting the Classic: The Hermeneutical Character of David Tracy's Theology in *The Analogical Imagination*." *Calvin Theological Journal* 25, no. 2 (November 1990): 194–206.

Wilfred, Felix. *Asian Public Theology: Critical Concerns in Challenging Times*. Delhi: ISPCK, 2010.

Wilson, Charles A. "Christology and the Pluralist Consciousness." *Word & World* 5, no. 1 (Winter 1985): 68–77.

Wimberly, Edward P. "Unnoticed and Unloved: The Indigenous Storyteller and Public Theology in a Postcolonial Age." *Verbum et Ecclesia* 32, no. 2 (2011).

Yoder, John Howard. *The Politics of Jesus*. Grand Rapids, MI: Eerdmans, 1994.

Index